OpenCV 2 Computer Vision Application Programming Cookbook

Over 50 recipes to master this library of programming functions for real-time computer vision

Robert Laganière

[PACKT] open source ✳
PUBLISHING   community experience distilled

BIRMINGHAM - MUMBAI

OpenCV 2 Computer Vision Application Programming Cookbook

First published: May 2011

Production Reference: 1180511

Published by Packt Publishing Ltd.
32 Lincoln Road
Olton
Birmingham, B27 6PA, UK.

ISBN 978-1-849513-24-1

www.packtpub.com

Cover Image by Asher Wishkerman (a.wishkerman@mpic.de)

Credits

Author
Robert Laganière

Reviewers
Wajihullah Biaq
Luis Gomez
Vladislav Gubarev
Haikel Guemar
Xiangjun Shi

Acquisition Editor
Usha Iyer

Development Editor
Roger D'souza

Technical Editor
Kavita Iyer

Copy Editor
Neha Shetty

Project Coordinator
Srimoyee Ghoshal

Proofreader
Joel Johnson

Indexer
Tejal Daruwale

Graphics
Nilesh Mohite

Production Coordinator
Kruthika Bangera

Cover Work
Kruthika Bangera

About the Author

Robert Laganière is a professor at the University of Ottawa, Canada. He received his Ph.D. degree from INRS-Telecommunications in Montreal in 1996. Dr. Laganière is a researcher in computer vision with an interest in video analysis, intelligent visual surveillance, and image-based modeling. He is a co-founding member of the VIVA research lab. He is also a Chief Scientist at iWatchLife.com, a company offering a cloud-based solution for remote monitoring. Dr. Laganière is the co-author of *Object-oriented Software Engineering* published by McGraw Hill in 2001.

Visit the author's website at http://www.laganiere.name.

I wish to thank all my students at the VIVA lab. I learn so much from them. I am also grateful to my beloved Marie-Claude, Camille, and Emma for their continuous support.

About the Reviewers

Wajih Ullah Baig holds a Honors. Degree in Computer Science from Hamdard University, Karachi. He works mostly with with desktop applications and has good experience working with large-scale distributed systems. He has interest in DSP, image processing, pattern recognition, and network programming. He has worked on a large-scale content-based video retrieval project which is one of its kind. Currently, he is working with the Center for Advanced Research in Engineering, Islamabad, Pakistan where he holds a position as a design engineer.

As a freelancer, he contributes work for open source projects and posts codes of his own.

I would like to thank all my friends and family for their support whilst reviewing the book. Especially my roommate, Dara Baig!

Lluís Gómez i Bigordà holds a Masters degree in Computer Science from the Universitat Oberta de Catalunya.

I would like to thank all my family and friends for their support while I was reviewing this book, especially to Antonia, my daughter. I owe you one!

Vladislav Gubarev was born in 1987 in Baku, USSR.

He graduated from Southern Federal University (Russia) with honors. He has a Bachelor (2007) and a Specialist (2008) diplomas of applied mathematics and computer science.

He started his career as a researcher and engineer in "Laboratory of Mathematical Methods of Artificial Intelligence". He later became a co-founder of CVisionLab company which provides computer vision solutions.

His areas of research interests are mostly related to image and video processing. In addition to researcher skills, he has wide experience in software development.

Many thanks to my wife Agatha. She is an applied mathematician, software developer, and the person who helped me a lot in reviewing this book. Also, thanks to my colleagues—a team of great researchers and professional developers.

Haïkel Guémar has been a free software enthusiast and a Fedora developer for a few years now. He currently works as a senior software engineer in a startup in Lyon (France): SysFera. Turning coffee into code, QA process, and technical coaching are part of his daily occupation.

SysFera's main product is SysFera-DS, the commercial version of the award-winning open source grid computing middleware DIET. DIET is an innovative grid middleware that offers seamless, robust, and high-performance access to heterogeneous computing resources.

Besides being a code monkey, Haïkel enjoys practicing kendo and watching chambara movies.

Xiangjun Shi received the M.E. degree in Computer Graphics from Zhengjian University, China in 1989, M.S. degree in Statistics, and Ph.D. degree in Computer Science from Utah State University in 2006. From 1989 to 1998, he was an Assistant Professor in Hangzhou University (1989–1995) and Shantou University (1995–1998). From 1998 to 2000, he was an Associate Professor in Shantou University. Since 2007, he has worked on the design and development of Intelligent Video Surveillance System. His research interests include: Data Mining, Data Cleansing, Statistical Inference/Analysis, Digital Video Mining, Computer Vision, Pattern Recognition and Image Processing, Mathematical modeling, and Algorithm Design and Optimization.

www.PacktPub.com

Support files, eBooks, discount offers and more

You might want to visit www.PacktPub.com for support files and downloads related to your book.

Did you know that Packt offers eBook versions of every book published, with PDF and ePub files available? You can upgrade to the eBook version at www.PacktPub.com and as a print book customer, you are entitled to a discount on the eBook copy. Get in touch with us at service@packtpub.com for more details.

At www.PacktPub.com, you can also read a collection of free technical articles, sign up for a range of free newsletters and receive exclusive discounts and offers on Packt books and eBooks.

http://PacktLib.PacktPub.com

Do you need instant solutions to your IT questions? PacktLib is Packt's online digital book library. Here, you can access, read and search across Packt's entire library of books.

Why Subscribe?

- ▶ Fully searchable across every book published by Packt
- ▶ Copy and paste, print and bookmark content
- ▶ On demand and accessible via web browser

Free Access for Packt account holders

If you have an account with Packt at www.PacktPub.com, you can use this to access PacktLib today and view nine entirely free books. Simply use your login credentials for immediate access.

Table of Contents

Preface

In today's digital world, images and videos are everywhere, and with the advent of powerful and affordable computing devices, it has never been easier to create sophisticated imaging applications. Plentiful software tools and libraries manipulating images and videos are offered, but for anyone who wishes to develop his/her own applications, the OpenCV library is the tool to use.

OpenCV (Open Source Computer Vision) is an open source library containing more than 500 optimized algorithms for image and video analysis. Since its introduction in 1999, it has been largely adopted as the primary development tool by the community of researchers and developers in computer vision. OpenCV was originally developed at Intel by a team led by Gary Bradski as an initiative to advance research in vision and promote the development of rich, vision-based CPU-intensive applications. After a series of beta releases, version 1.0 was launched in 2006. A second major release occurred in 2009 with the launch of OpenCV 2 that proposed important changes, especially the new C++ interface which we use in this book. At the time of writing, the latest release is 2.2 (December 2010).

This book covers many of the library's features and shows how to use them to accomplish specific tasks. Our objective is not to provide a complete and detailed coverage of every option offered by the OpenCV functions and classes, but rather to give you the elements you need to build your applications from the ground up. In this book we also explore fundamental concepts in image analysis and describe some of the important algorithms in computer vision.

This book is an opportunity for you to get introduced to the world of image and video analysis. But this is just the beginning. The good news is that OpenCV continues to evolve and expand. Just consult the OpenCV online documentation to stay updated about what the library can do for you:

`http://opencv.willowgarage.com/wiki/`

What this book covers

Chapter 1, Playing with Images, introduces the OpenCV library and shows you how to run simple applications using the MS Visual C++ and Qt development environments.

Chapter 2, Manipulating the Pixels, explains how an image can be read. It describes different methods for scanning an image in order to perform an operation on each of its pixels. You will also learn how to define region of interest inside an image.

Chapter 3, Processing Images with Classes, consists of recipes which present various object-oriented design patterns that can help you to build better computer vision applications.

Chapter 4, Counting the Pixels with Histograms, shows you how to compute image histograms and how they can be used to modify an image. Different applications based on histograms are presented that achieve image segmentation, object detection, and image retrieval.

Chapter 5, Transforming Images with Morphological Operations, explores the concept of mathematical morphology. It presents different operators and how they can be used to detect edges, corners, and segments in images.

Chapter 6, Filtering the Images, teaches you the principle of frequency analysis and image filtering. It shows how low-pass and high-pass filters can be applied to images. It presents the two image derivative operators: the gradient and the Laplacian.

Chapter 7, Extracting Lines, Contours, and Components, focuses on the detection of geometric image features. It explains how to extract contours, lines, and connected components in an image.

Chapter 8, Detecting and Matching Interest Points, describes various feature point detectors in images. It also explains how descriptors of interest points can be computed and used to match points between images.

Chapter 9, Estimating Projective Relations in Images, analyzes the different relations involved in image formation. It also explores the projective relations that exist between two images of a same scene.

Chapter 10, Processing Video Sequences, provides a framework to read and write a video sequence and to process its frames. It also shows you how it is possible to track feature points from frame to frame, and how to extract the foreground objects moving in front of a camera.

Who this book is for

If you are a novice C++ programer who wants to learn how to use the OpenCV library to build computer vision applications, then this cookbook is appropriate for you. It is also suitable for professional software developers wishing to be introduced to the concepts of computer vision programming. It can be used as a companion book in university-level computer vision courses. It constitutes an excellent reference for graduate students and researchers in image processing and computer vision. The book provides a good combination of basic to advanced recipes. Basic knowledge of C++ is required.

Conventions

In this book, you will find a number of styles of text that distinguish between different kinds of information. Here are some examples of these styles, and an explanation of their meaning.

Code words in text are shown as follows: "We can include other contexts through the use of the `include` directive."

A block of code is set as follows:

```
// get the iterators
cv::Mat_<cv::Vec3b>::const_iterator it=
                         image.begin<cv::Vec3b>();
```

When we wish to draw your attention to a particular part of a code block, the relevant lines or items are set in bold:

```
// Converting to Lab color space
cv::cvtColor(image, converted, CV_BGR2Lab);
// get the iterators of the converted image
cv::Mat_<cv::Vec3b>::iterator it=
```

New terms and **important words** are shown in bold. Words that you see on the screen, in menus or dialog boxes for example, appear in the text like this: "This value is read when the **Process** button is clicked, which also triggers the processing and displays the result".

 Tips and tricks appear like this.

Reader feedback

Feedback from our readers is always welcome. Let us know what you think about this book—what you liked or may have disliked. Reader feedback is important for us to develop titles that you really get the most out of.

To send us general feedback, simply send an e-mail to `feedback@packtpub.com`, and mention the book title via the subject of your message.

If there is a book that you need and would like to see us publish, please send us a note in the **SUGGEST A TITLE** form on `www.packtpub.com` or e-mail `suggest@packtpub.com`.

If there is a topic that you have expertise in and you are interested in either writing or contributing to a book, see our author guide on `www.packtpub.com/authors`.

Customer support

Now that you are the proud owner of a Packt book, we have a number of things to help you to get the most from your purchase.

Downloading the example code

You can download the example code files for all Packt books you have purchased from your account at `http://www.PacktPub.com`. If you purchased this book elsewhere, you can visit `http://www.PacktPub.com/support` and register to have the files e-mailed directly to you.

Errata

Although we have taken every care to ensure the accuracy of our content, mistakes do happen. If you find a mistake in one of our books—maybe a mistake in the text or the code—we would be grateful if you would report this to us. By doing so, you can save other readers from frustration and help us improve subsequent versions of this book. If you find any errata, please report them by visiting `http://www.packtpub.com/support`, selecting your book, clicking on the **errata submission form** link, and entering the details of your errata. Once your errata are verified, your submission will be accepted and the errata will be uploaded on our website, or added to any list of existing errata, under the Errata section of that title. Any existing errata can be viewed by selecting your title from `http://www.packtpub.com/support`.

Piracy

Piracy of copyright material on the Internet is an ongoing problem across all media. At Packt, we take the protection of our copyright and licenses very seriously. If you come across any illegal copies of our works, in any form, on the Internet, please provide us with the location address or website name immediately so that we can pursue a remedy.

Please contact us at `copyright@packtpub.com` with a link to the suspected pirated material.

We appreciate your help in protecting our authors, and our ability to bring you valuable content.

Questions

You can contact us at `questions@packtpub.com` if you are having a problem with any aspect of the book, and we will do our best to address it.

1

Playing with Images

In this chapter, we will cover:

- ▶ Installing the OpenCV Library
- ▶ Creating an OpenCV project with MS Visual C++
- ▶ Creating an OpenCV project with Qt
- ▶ Loading, displaying, and saving images
- ▶ Creating a GUI application using Qt

Introduction

This chapter will teach you the basic elements of OpenCV and will show you how to accomplish the most fundamental tasks: reading, displaying, and saving images. Before you can start with OpenCV, you need to install the library. This is a simple process that is explained in the first recipe of this chapter.

You also need a good development environment (IDE) to run your OpenCV applications. We propose two alternatives here. The first is to use the well-known Microsoft Visual Studio platform. The second option is to use an open source tool for C++ project development called Qt. Two recipes will show you how to set up a project with these two tools, but you can also use other C++ IDEs. In fact, in this cookbook, the tasks will be presented in a way that is independent of any particular environment and operating system, so you are free to use the one of your choice. However, be aware that you need to use the compiled version of the OpenCV library that is appropriate to the compiler and operating system you are using. If you obtain strange behaviors, or if your application crashes without apparent reasons, that could be a symptom of incompatibilities.

Installing the OpenCV library

OpenCV is an open source library for developing computer vision applications. It can be used in both academic and commercial applications under a BSD license that allows you to freely use, distribute, and adapt it. This recipe will show you how to install the library on your machine.

Getting ready

When you visit the OpenCV official website at `http://opencv.willowgarage.com/wiki/`, you will find the latest release of the library, the online documentation, and many other useful resources about OpenCV.

How to do it...

From the OpenCV website, go to the Download page that corresponds to the platform of your choice (Linux/Unix/Mac or Windows). From there you will be able to download the OpenCV package. You will then uncompress it, normally under a directory with a name corresponding to the library version (for example, `OpenCV2.2`). Once this is done, you will find a collection of directories, notably the `doc` directory containing the OpenCV documentation, the `include` directory containing all of the include files, the `modules` directory which contains all of the source files (yes, it is open source), and the `samples` directory containing many small examples to help you to get started.

If you are working under Windows with Visual Studio, you also have the option to download the executable installation package corresponding to your IDE and Windows platform. Executing this setup program will not only install the source library, but also all of the precompiled binaries you will need to build your applications. In that case, you are ready to start using OpenCV. If not, you need to take few additional steps.

In order to use OpenCV under the environment of your choice, you need to generate the library binary files using the appropriate C++ compiler. To build OpenCV, you need to use the CMake tool available at `http://www.cmake.org/`. CMake is another open source software tool designed to control the compilation process of a software system using platform-independent configuration files. You therefore need to download and install CMake. You can then run it using the command line, but it is easier to use CMake with its Graphical User Interface (GUI). In this latter case, all you need to do is to specify the folder containing the OpenCV library and the one that will contain the binaries. You then click on **Configure** in order to select the compiler of your choice (here we chose Visual Studio 2010), and you click on **Configure** again, as seen in the following screenshot:

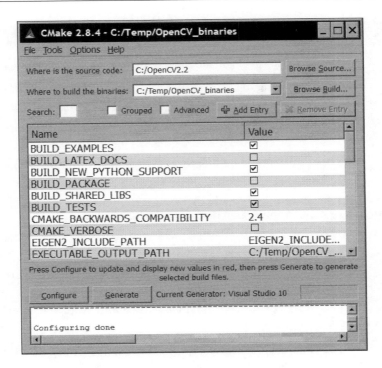

You are now ready to generate your `makefiles` and workspace files by clicking on the **Generate** button. These files will allow you to compile the library. This is the last step of the installation process.

Compiling the library will make it ready to use for your development environment. If you selected an IDE like Visual Studio, then all you need to do is to open the top-level solution file that CMake has created for you. You then issue the **Build Solution** command. In Unix environments, you will use the generated `makefiles` by running your `make utility` command.

If everything went well, you should now have your compiled and ready-to-use OpenCV library in the specified directory. This directory will contain, in addition to the directories we already mentioned, a `bin` directory containing the compiled library. You can move everything to your preferred location (for example, `c:\OpenCV2.2`) and add the `bin` directory to your system path (under Windows, this is done by opening your **Control Panel**. You start the **System** utility and under the **Advanced** tab, you will find the **Environment Variables** button).

How it works...

Since version 2.2, the OpenCV library is divided into several modules. These modules are built in library files located in the `lib` directory. They are:

- The `opencv_core` module that contains the core functionalities of the library, in particular, the basic data structures and arithmetic functions.
- The `opencv_imgproc` module that contains the main image processing functions.
- The `opencv_highgui` module that contains the image and video reading and writing functions, along with other user interface functions.
- The `opencv_features2d` module that contains the feature point detectors and descriptors and the feature point matching framework.
- The `opencv_calib3d` module that contains the camera calibration, two-view geometry estimation, and stereo functions.
- The `opencv_video` module that contains the motion estimation, feature tracking, and foreground extraction functions and classes.
- The `opencv_objdetect` module containing the object detection functions such as the face and people detectors.

The library also includes other utility modules containing machine learning functions (`opencv_ml`), computational geometry algorithms (`opencv_flann`), contributed code (`opencv_contrib`), obsolete code (`opencv_legacy`), and GPU accelerated code (`opencv_gpu`).

All of these modules have a header file associated with them (located in `include` directory). Typical OpenCV C++ code will therefore start by including the required modules. For example (and this is the suggested declaration style):

```
#include <opencv2/core/core.hpp>
#include <opencv2/imgproc/imgproc.hpp>
#include <opencv2/highgui/highgui.hpp>
```

If you see OpenCV code starting with:

```
#include "cv.h"
```

it is because it uses the old style, before the library was restructured into modules.

There's more...

You can also access the latest code being developed from the OpenCV SVN server located at:

`https://code.ros.org/svn/opencv/trunk/opencv/`

You will find that there are a large number of examples that can help you learn how to use the library and give you many development tips.

Creating an OpenCV project with MS Visual C++

Using MS Visual C++, you can easily create OpenCV applications for Windows. You can build simple console application or you can create more sophisticated applications with a nice graphical user interface (GUI). Since it is the easiest option, we will create a simple console application here. We'll use Visual Studio 2010, however, the same principles also apply to any other versions of the Microsoft IDE since the menus and options are very similar in the different versions.

When you run Visual Studio for the first time, you can set it up in a way such that C++ becomes your default development environment. This way, when you will launch the IDE, it will be in Visual C++ mode.

We assume that you have installed OpenCV under the C:\OpenCV2.2 directory as explained in the previous recipe.

Getting ready

When working with Visual Studio, it is important to understand the difference between a solution and a project. Basically, a solution is made of several projects (each project is a distinct software module, for example, a program and a library). This way the projects of your solution can share files and libraries. Usually, you create one master directory for your solution that contains all of your projects directories. But you can also group the solution and a project into one single directory. This is what you will most often do for a one-project solution. As you become more familiar with VC++, and build more complex applications, you should take advantage of the multi-project solution structure.

Also, when you compile and execute your Visual C++ projects, you can do it under two different configurations: Debug and Release. The Debug mode is there to help you create and debug your application. It is a more protected environment, for example, it will tell you if your application contains memory leaks or it will check at runtime if you are using certain functions properly. However, it generates slower executable files. This is why, once your application has been tested and is ready to be used, you build it under the Release mode. This will produce the executable that you will distribute to the users of your application. Note that it may happen that you have code running perfectly well in debug mode but has problems in release mode. You then need to do more testing in order to identify the potential sources of errors. Debug and Release modes are not unique to Visual C++, most IDEs also support these two modes of compilation.

How to do it...

We are now ready to create our first project. This is done by using the **File|New Project | Project...** menu option. You can create different project types here. Let's start with the simplest option which is to select a Win32 Console Application, seen in the following screenshot:

You need to specify where your want to create your project, and what name you want to give to your project. There is also an option for creating or not creating a directory for the solution (the bottom-right checkbox). If you check this option, an additional directory will be created (with the name you specify) that will contain your solution directory. If you simply leave this option unchecked, a solution file (extension .sln) will still be created, but this one will be contained within the same (single) project directory. Click on **OK** and then **Next** to go to the **Application Settings** window of the Win32 Application Wizard. As seen in the following screenshot, a number of options are offered there. We will simply create an empty project.

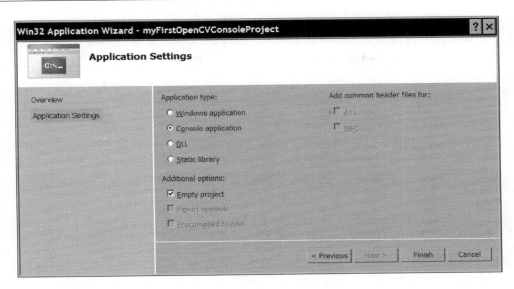

Note that we also have unchecked the **Precompiled header** option which is an MS Visual Studio-specific feature to make the compilation process faster. Since we want to stay within the ANSI C++ standard, we will not use this option. If you click on **Finish**, your project will be created. It is empty for now, but we will add a main file to it soon.

But first, to be able to compile and run your future OpenCV application, you need to tell Visual C++ where to find the OpenCV libraries and include files. Since you will probably create several OpenCV projects in the future, the best option is to create a Property Sheet that you will be able to reuse from project to project. This is done through the **Property Manager**. If it is not already visible in your current IDE, you can access it from the **View** menu.

In Visual C++ 2010, a property sheet is an XML file that describes your project settings. We will now create a new one by right-clicking on the **Debug | Win32** node of the project, and by selecting the **Add New Project Property Sheet** option (as seen in the following screenshot):

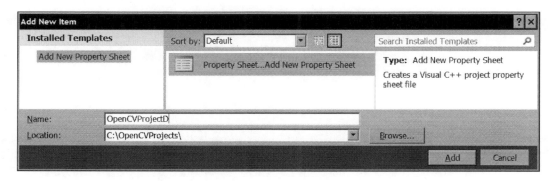

The new property sheet is then added once we click on **Add**. We now need to edit it. Simply double-click on the property sheet's name and select VC++ Directories, as seen here:

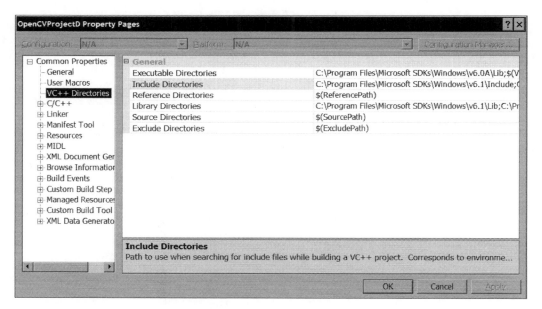

Edit the **Include Directories** textfield and add the path to the include files of your OpenCV library:

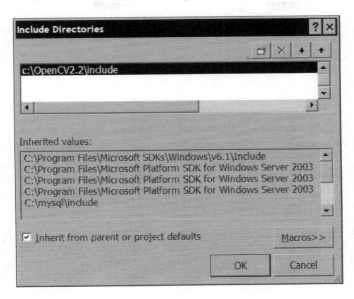

Do the same thing with the **Library Directories**. This time you add the path to your OpenCV library files:

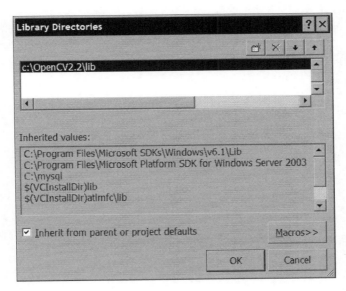

It is important to note that we used the explicit path to the OpenCV library in our property sheet. It is generally a better practice to use an environment variable to designate the library location. This way, if you switch to another version of the library, you simply change the definition of this variable so that it points to the library's new location. Also, in the case of a team project, the different users might have installed the library at different locations. Using an environment variable would avoid needing to edit the property sheet for each user. Consequently, if you define the environment variable OPENCV2_DIR to be c:\OpenCV2.2, then the two OpenCV directories will be specified as $(OPENCV_DIR)\include and $(OPENCV_DIR)\lib in the property sheet.

The next step is to specify the OpenCV library files which need to be linked with your code in order to produce an executable application. Depending on the application, you may need different OpenCV modules. Since we want to reuse this property sheet in all of our projects, we will simply add the library modules we need to run the applications of this book. Go to the **Input** item of the **Linker** node, as seen in the following screenshot:

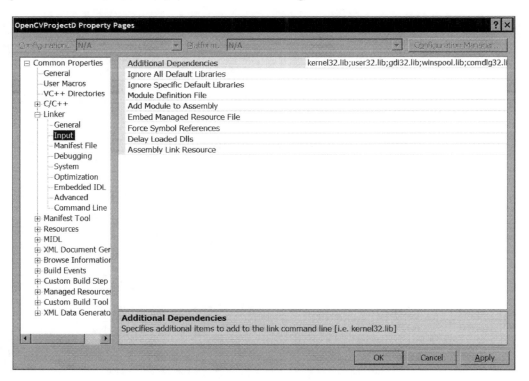

Edit the **Additional Dependencies** textfield and add the following list of library modules:

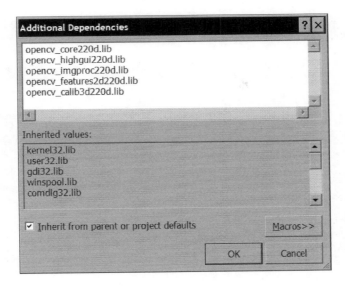

Note that we specified the libraries with names ending with the letter "d". These are the binaries for the Debug mode. You will need to create another (almost identical) property sheet for the Release mode. You follow the same procedure, but you add it under the **Release | Win32** node. This time, the library names are specified without appending a "d" at the end.

We are now ready to create, compile, and run our first application. We add a new source file by using the **Solution Explorer**, and right-clicking the **Source Files** node. You select **Add New Item...** which gives you the opportunity to specify `main.cpp` as the name of this C++ file:

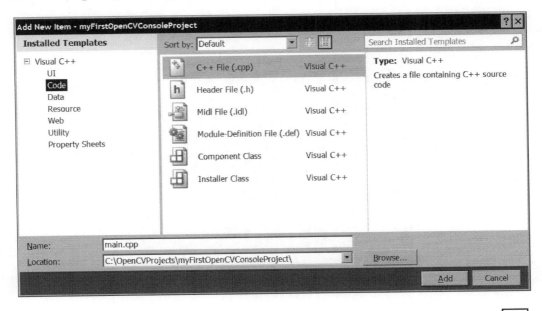

You can also use the **File|New|File...** menu option to do this. Now, let's build a simple application that will display an image named img.jpg located under the default directory.

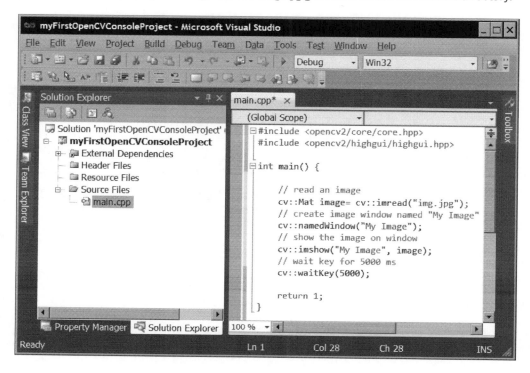

Once you have recopied the code in the preceding figure (it will be explained later), you can compile it and run it using the **Start** green arrow in the Toolbar at the top of your screen. You will see your image displayed for five seconds. An example is seen here:

If it is the case, then you have completed your first successful OpenCV application! If the program fails when executed, it is probably because it cannot find the image file. See the following section to find out how to put it in the correct directory.

How it works...

When you click on the **Start Debugging** button (or push *F5*), your project will be compiled and then executed. You can also just compile the project by selecting **Build Solution** (*F7*) under the **Build** menu. The first time you compile your project, a `Debug` directory will be created. This will contain the executable file (extension `.exe`). Similarly, you can also create the release version by simply selecting the **Release configuration** option using the drop-down menu, to the right of the green arrow button (or using the **Configuration Manager...** option under the **Build** menu). A `Release` directory will then be created.

When you execute a project using the **Start** button of Visual Studio, the default directory will always be the one that contains your solution file. However, if you choose to execute your application outside of your IDE (that is, from Windows Explorer) by double-clicking on your `.exe` file (normally the `Release` directory), then the default directory will become the one that contains the executable file. Therefore, make sure your image file is located in the appropriate directory before you execute this application.

See also

The *Loading, displaying, and saving images* recipe later in this chapter that explains the OpenCV source code we have used in this task.

Creating an OpenCV project with Qt

Qt is a complete Integrated Development Environment (IDE) for C++ application that was originally developed by Trolltech, a Norwegian software company which was acquired in 2008 by Nokia. It is offered under the LPGL open source license as well as under a commercial (and paying) license for the development of proprietary projects. It is composed of two separate elements: a cross-platform IDE, called Qt Creator, and a set of Qt class libraries and development tools. Using the Qt Software Development Kit (SDK) to develop C++ applications has many benefits:

- ▶ It is an open source initiative, developed by the Qt community, that gives you access to the source code of the different Qt components.
- ▶ It is cross-platform, meaning that you can develop applications that can run on different operating systems such as Windows, Linux, Mac OS X, and so on.
- ▶ It includes a complete and cross-platform GUI library that follows an effective object-oriented and event-driven model.

> ▶ Qt also includes several cross-platform libraries to develop multimedia, graphics, database, multithreading, web application, and many other interesting building blocks useful for designing advanced applications.

Getting ready

Qt can be downloaded from `http://qt.nokia.com`. It is free if you select the LPGL license. You should download the complete SDK. However, make sure to select the Qt libraries package that is appropriate for your platform. Obviously, since we are dealing with open source software, it is always possible to re-compile the library under the platform of your choice.

Here, we use Qt Creator version 1.2.1 with Qt version 4.6.3. Note that under the **Projects** tab of Qt Creator, it is possible to manage the different Qt versions that you might have installed. This ensures you can always compile your projects with the appropriate Qt version.

How to do it...

When you start Qt, it will ask you if you wish to create a new project or if you want to open a recent one. You can also create a new project by going under the **File** menu and selecting the **New...** option. To replicate what we did in the previous recipe, we will select the `Qt4 Console Application` as seen in the following screenshot:

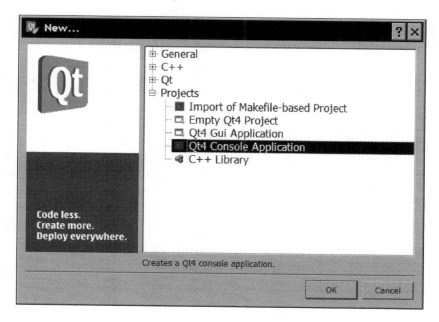

You then specify a name and a project location as seen here:

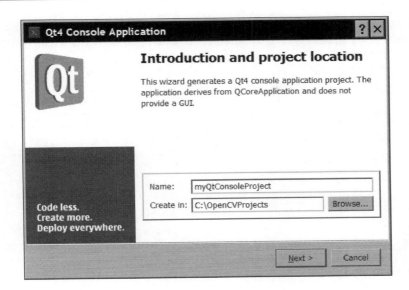

The following screen will ask you to select the modules you want to include in your project. Just keep the one selected by default and click on **Next**, and then **Finish**. An empty console application is then created as seen here:

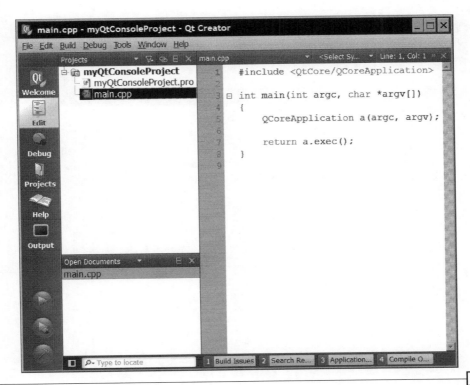

The code generated by Qt creates a `QCoreApplication` object and calls its `exec()` method. This is only required when your application needs an event handler to process the user interactions with a GUI. In our simple open and display image example, this is not needed. We can simply replace the generated code by the one we use in the previous task. The simple open and display image program would then read as follows:

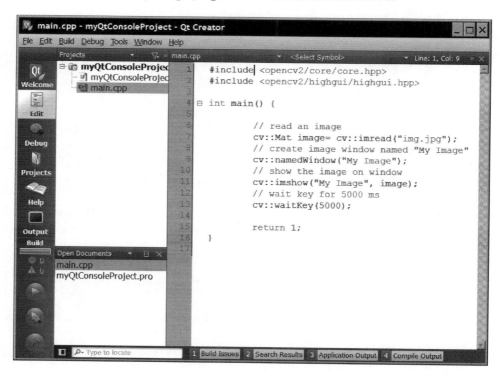

In order to be able to compile this program, the OpenCV library files and header files location need to be specified. With Qt, this information is given in a project file (with extension `.pro`) which is a simple text file describing the project parameters. You can edit this project file in Qt Creator by selecting the corresponding project file as seen in the following screenshot:

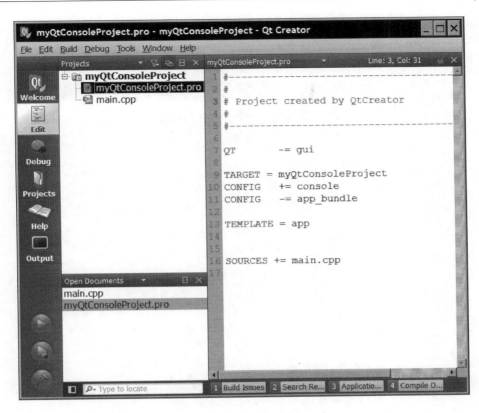

The information required to build an OpenCV application is provided by appending the following lines at the end of the project file:

```
INCLUDEPATH += C:\OpenCV2.2\include\

LIBS += -LC:\OpenCV2.2\lib \
-lopencv_core220 \
-lopencv_highgui220 \
-lopencv_imgproc220 \
-lopencv_features2d220 \
-lopencv_calib3d220
```

Downloading the example code

You can download the example code files for all Packt books you have purchased from your account at http://www.PacktPub.com. If you purchased this book elsewhere, you can visit http://www.PacktPub.com/support and register to have the files e-mailed directly to you.

The program is now ready to be compiled and executed. This is accomplished by clicking the bottom-left green arrow (or by pressing *Ctrl+R*). There is also a **Debug** and a **Release** mode that you set up using the **Build Settings** of the **Projects** tab.

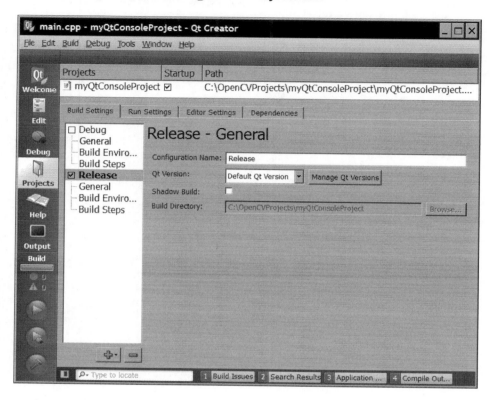

How it works...

A Qt project is described by a project file. This is a text file that declares a list of variables containing the relevant information required to build the project. This file is in fact processed by a software tool called **qmake** which Qt invokes when a compilation is requested. Each variable defined in a project file is associated with a list of values. The main variables that are recognized by qmake in Qt are as follows:

- ▸   TEMPLATE: Defines the type of project (applications, library, and so on).
- ▸   CONFIG : Specifies different options that the compiler should use when building the project.
- ▸   HEADERS : Lists the header files of the project.
- ▸   SOURCES : Lists the source files (.cpp) of the project.

- ▶ QT : Declares the required Qt extension modules and libraries. By default, the core and the GUI modules are included. If you want to exclude one of them, you use the `-=` notation.
- ▶ INCLUDEPATH : Specifies the header file directories that should be searched.
- ▶ LIBS : Contains the list of library files that should be linked with the project. You use the flag `-L` for directory paths and the flag `-l` for library names.

Several other variables are defined but the ones listed here are most commonly used.

There's more...

Many additional features can be used in qmake project files. For example, scopes can be defined to add declarations that apply to a specific platform:

```
win32 {
    # declarations for Windows 32 platforms only
}
unix {
    # declarations for Unix 32 platforms only
}
```

You can also use the `pkg-config` utility package. It is an open source tool that helps to use the correct compiler options and library files. When you install OpenCV with CMake, the `unix-install` contains an `opencv.pc` file that is read by `pkg-config` to determine the compilation parameters. A multi-platform qmake project file could then look as follows:

```
unix {
    CONFIG += link_pkgconfig
    PKGCONFIG += opencv
}

Win32 {

INCLUDEPATH += C:\OpenCV2.2\include\

LIBS += -LC:\OpenCV2.2\lib \
-lopencv_core220 \
    -lopencv_highgui220 \
    -lopencv_imgproc220 \
    -lopencv_features2d220 \
    -lopencv_calib3d220
}
```

See also

The next recipe, *Loading, displaying, and saving images* explains the OpenCV source code we used in this task.

Consult the website `http://qt.nokia.com` for the complete documentation about Qt, Qt Creator, and all of the Qt extension modules.

Loading, displaying, and saving images

The two preceding recipes taught you how to create a simple OpenCV project but we have not explained the OpenCV code that was used. This task will show you how to perform the most fundamental operations needed in the development of an OpenCV application. These include loading an input image from file, displaying an image on a window, and storing an output image on disk.

Getting ready

Using either MS Visual Studio or Qt, create a new console application with a main function ready to be filled. See the first two recipes on how to proceed.

How to do it...

The first thing to do is to declare a variable that will hold the image. Under OpenCV 2, you define an object of class `cv::Mat`.

```
cv::Mat image;
```

This definition creates an image of size 0 by 0. This can be confirmed by calling the `cv::Mat` method `size()` that allows you to read the current size of this image. It returns a structure containing the height and width of the image:

```
std::cout << "size: " << image.size().height << " , "
          << image.size().width << std::endl;
```

Next a simple call to the reading function will read an image from file, decode it, and allocate the memory:

```
image=  cv::imread("img.jpg");
```

You are now ready to use this image. However, you should first check if the image has been correctly read (an error will occur if the file is not found or if the file is corrupted, or is not a recognizable format). The validity of the image is tested by:

```
if (!image.data) {
    // no image has been created...
}
```

The member variable `data` is in fact a pointer to the allocated memory block that will contain the image data. It is simply set to 0 when no image has been read. The first thing you might want to do with this image is to display it. You do it using the `highgui` module provided by OpenCV. You start by declaring the window on which you want to display images, and then you specify the image to be shown on this special window:

```
cv::namedWindow("Original Image"); // define the window
cv::imshow("Original Image", image); // show the image
```

Now, you would normally apply some processing to the image. OpenCV offers a wide selection of processing functions, and several of them are explored in this book. Let's start with a very simple one that will simply flip the image horizontally. Several image transformations in OpenCV can be performed **in-place**, meaning that the transformation is applied directly on the input image (no new image being created). This is the case of the flipping method. However, we can always create another matrix to hold the output result and that is what we will do:

```
cv::Mat result;
cv::flip(image,result,1); // positive for horizontal
                          // 0 for vertical,
                          // negative for both
```

And the result is displayed on another window:

```
cv::namedWindow("Output Image");
cv::imshow("Output Image", result);
```

Since it is a console window that will terminate at the end of the main function, we add an extra `highgui` method to wait for a user key before ending the program:

```
cv::waitKey(0);
```

You can then see both the input and output images displayed on two distinct windows. Finally, you will probably want to save the processed image on your disk. This is done using the following `highgui` function:

```
cv::imwrite("output.bmp", result);
```

The file extension determines which codec will be used to save the image.

How it works...

All classes and functions defined in the C++ API of OpenCV are defined within the name space `cv`. You have two options to access them. First, precede the main function definition by the following declaration:

```
using namespace cv;
```

Alternatively, prefix all OpenCV class and function names by the namespace specification that is `cv::`, as we did in this recipe.

The class `cv::Mat` is the data structure used to hold your images (and obviously other matrix data). By default, they have a zero size but you can also specify an initial size:

```
cv::Mat ima(240,320,CV_8U,cv::Scalar(100));
```

In this case, you also need to specify the type of each matrix element, here `CV_8U` which corresponds to 1-byte pixel images. Letter `U` means unsigned. You can also declare signed numbers by using the letter `S`. For a color image, you would specify three channels (`CV_8UC3`). You can also declare integers (signed or unsigned) of size 16 and 32 (for example, `CV_16SC3`). You also have access to 32-bit and 64-bit floating point numbers (for example, `CV_32F`).

When the `cv::Mat` object goes out of scope, the memory allocated is automatically released. This is very convenient because you avoid having problems with memory leaks. Moreover, the `cv::Mat` class implements reference counting and shallow copy such that when an image is assigned to another one, the image data (that is the pixels) is not copied, and both images will point to the same memory block. This also applies to images passed by value or returned by value. A reference count is kept such that the memory will be released only when all of the references to the image will be destructed. If you wish to create an image that will contain a new copy of the original image, you will use the method `copyTo()`. You can test this behavior by declaring a few extra images in the example of this project, as follows:

```
cv::Mat image2, image3;
image2= result; // the two images refer to the same data
result.copyTo(image3); // a new copy is created
```

Now if you again flip the output image and display the two additional images, you will see that `image2` is also affected by the transformation (because it points to the same image data than result image) while `image3` remains unchanged as it holds a copy of the image. This allocation model for `cv::Mat` objects also means that you can safely write functions (or class methods) that return an image:

```
cv::Mat function() {
   // create image
   cv::Mat ima(240,320,CV_8U,cv::Scalar(100));
   // return it
   return ima;
}
```

If we call this function from our `main` function:

```
// get a gray-level image
cv::Mat gray= function();
```

The gray variable will now hold the image created by the function without extra memory allocation. Indeed, only a shallow copy of the image will be transferred from the returned cv::Mat instance to the gray image. When the ima local variable goes out of scope, this variable is de-allocated, but since the associated reference counter indicates that its internal image data is being referred by another instance (that is the gray variable) its memory block is not released.

However, in the case of classes, you should be careful and not return image class attributes. Here is an example of an error-prone implementation:

```
class Test {
    // image attribute
    cv::Mat ima;
    public:
        // constructor creating a gray-level image
        Test() : ima(240,320,CV_8U,cv::Scalar(100)) {}
        // method return a class attribute, not a good idea...
        cv::Mat method() { return ima; }
};
```

Here, if a function calls the method of this class, it obtains a shallow copy of the image attributes. If later, this copy is modified, the class attribute will also be modified which can affect the subsequent behavior of the class (and vice versa). To avoid these kinds of errors, you should instead return a copy of the attribute.

There's more...

With version 2 of the OpenCV, a new C++ interface has been introduced. Previously, C-like functions and structures were used (and can still be used). In particular, images were manipulated using the IplImage structure. This structure was inherited from the IPL library (that is the Intel Image Processing Library) now integrated with the IPP library (the Intel Integrated Performance Primitive library). If you use code and libraries that were created with the old C interface, you might need to manipulate those IplImage structures. Fortunately, there is a convenient way to convert an IplImage into a cv::Mat object.

```
IplImage* iplImage = cvLoadImage("c:\\img.jpg");
cv::Mat image4(iplImage,false);
```

The function cvLoadImage is the C-interface function to load images. The second parameter in the constructor of the cv::Mat object indicates that the data will not be copied (set it to true if you want a new copy, while false is the default value so it could have been omitted), that is both IplImage and image4 will share the same image data. You need to be careful here to not create dangling pointers. For this reason, it is safer to encapsulate the IplImage pointer into the reference-counting pointer class provided by OpenCV 2:

```
cv::Ptr<IplImage> iplImage = cvLoadImage("c:\\img.jpg");
```

Otherwise, if you need to deallocate the memory pointed by your `IplImage` structure, you need to do it explicitly:

```
cvReleaseImage(&iplImage);
```

Remember, you should avoid using this deprecate data structure. Instead, always use `cv::Mat`.

Creating a GUI application using Qt

Qt offers a rich library to build a sophisticated GUI with a professional look. Using Qt Creator, the process of GUI creation is made easy. This recipe will show you how to build an OpenCV application with Qt that a user can control using a GUI.

Getting ready

Start Qt Creator which we will use to create our GUI application. It is also possible to create a GUI without this tool, but the use of a visual IDE in which the widgets can simply be dragged and dropped is the easiest way to build a nice looking GUI.

How to do it...

Select **Create New Project...** and choose **Qt GUI Application** as seen in the following screenshot:

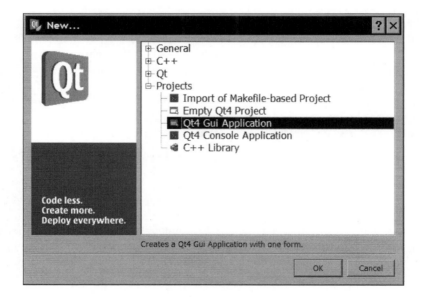

Give a name and a location to your project. If you then click on **Next**, you will see that the **QtGUI Module** is checked. Since we do not need other modules, you can click on **Finish** at this point. This will create your new project. In addition to the usual project file (`.pro`) and the `main.cpp` file, you see two `mainwindow` files defining the class that contains your GUI window. You will also find a file having the extension `.ui`, which is the one that describes the UI layout. In fact, if you double-click on it, you will see the current user interface as seen here:

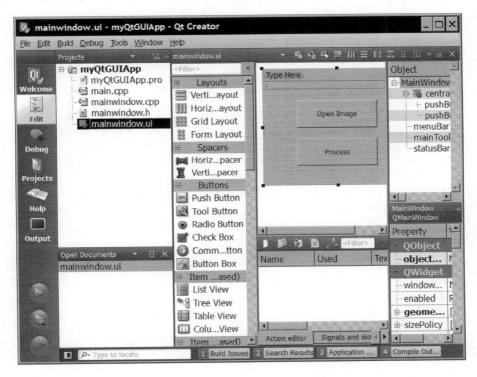

You can drag-and-drop different widgets on it. Drop two **Push Buttons** as we did in the preceding example. You can resize them and resize the window to make it nice. You should also rename the button labels. Just click on the text and insert the name of your choice.

Let's now add a signal method in order to handle the click button event. Right-click on the first button and select **Go to slot...** in the contextual menu. The list of possible signals is then displayed as seen in the following screenshot:

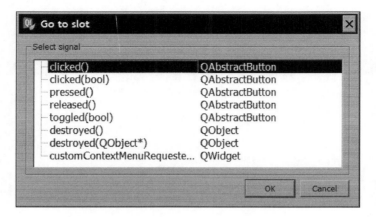

Simply select the `clicked()` signal. This is the one that handles the button pushed events. By doing this, you will be brought to the `mainwindow.cpp` file. You will see that a new method has been added. This is the slot method that is called when the `click()` signal is received:

```cpp
#include "mainwindow.h"
#include "ui_mainwindow.h"
MainWindow::MainWindow(QWidget *parent)
: QMainWindow(parent), ui(new Ui::MainWindow)
{
    ui->setupUi(this);
}
MainWindow::~MainWindow()
{
    delete ui;
}
void MainWindow::on_pushButton_clicked()
{
}
```

In order to be able to display and then process the image, we need to define a `cv::Mat` class member variable. This is done in the header file of the `MainWindow` class. This header now reads as follows:

```cpp
#ifndef MAINWINDOW_H
#define MAINWINDOW_H

#include <QtGui/QMainWindow>
```

```
#include <QFileDialog>
#include <opencv2/core/core.hpp>
#include <opencv2/highgui/highgui.hpp>
namespace Ui
{
    class MainWindow;
}
class MainWindow : public QMainWindow
{
    Q_OBJECT
public:
    MainWindow(QWidget *parent = 0);
    ~MainWindow();
private:
    Ui::MainWindow *ui;
    cv::Mat image; // the image variable
private slots:
    void on_pushButton_clicked();
};
#endif // MAINWINDOW_H
```

Note that we have also included the `core.hpp` and the `highgui.hpp` header files. As we learned in a preceding recipe, we must not forget to edit the project file in order to append the OpenCV library information.

OpenCV code can then be added. The first button opens the source image. This is done by adding the following code to the corresponding slot method:

```
void MainWindow::on_pushButton_clicked()
{
    QString fileName = QFileDialog::getOpenFileName(this,
        tr("Open Image"), ".",
        tr("Image Files (*.png *.jpg *.jpeg *.bmp)"));
    image= cv::imread(fileName.toAscii().data());
    cv::namedWindow("Original Image");
    cv::imshow("Original Image", image);
}
```

You then create a new slot by right-clicking on the second button. This second slot will perform some processing on the selected input image. The following code will simply flip the image:

```
void MainWindow::on_pushButton_2_clicked()
{
    cv::flip(image,image,1);
    cv::namedWindow("Output Image");
    cv::imshow("Output Image", image);
}
```

You can now compile and run this program and your 2-button GUI will allow you to select an image and process it.

The input and output images are being displayed on the two `highgui` windows that we defined.

How it works...

Under the GUI programming framework of Qt, objects communicate using signals and slots. Whenever a widget changes state, or an event occurs, a signal is emitted. This signal has a pre-defined signature, and if another object wants to receive this signal it must define a slot with the same signature. A slot is therefore a special class method that is automatically called when the signal to which it is connected is emitted.

Signals and slots are defined as class methods but must be declared under the Qt access which specifies slots and signals. This is what Qt Creator did when you added a slot to your button, that is:

```
private slots:
   void on_pushButton_clicked();
```

Signals and slots are loosely coupled, that is, a signal does not know anything about the objects having slots connected to it, and a slot does not know if a signal is connected to it or not. Also, many slots can be connected to one signal and a slot can receive signals from many objects. The only requirement is that the signatures of the signal and the slot methods must match.

All classes that inherit from the `QObject` class can contain signals and slots. These will most often be subclasses of a widget class (subclass of `QWidget`) but any other class can define slots and signals. The signal-and-slot concept is, in fact, a very powerful class communication mechanism. It is however specific to the Qt framework.

In Qt, the main window is an instance of the class, `MainWindow`. You have access to it through the member variable `ui` that is declared within the `MainWindow` class definition. In addition, each widget of the GUI is also an object. When the GUI is created, a pointer to each of the widget instances you have added to the main window is associated with the `ui` variable. Therefore, you can access the properties and methods of each widget in your program. For example, if you want the **Process** button to be disabled until an input image is selected, all you need to do is call the following method when the GUI is initialized (that is in the `MainWindow` constructor):

```
ui->pushButton_2->setEnabled(false);
```

The pointer variable `pushbutton_2` corresponds here to the **Process** button. You then enable the button when an image is successfully loaded (in the **Open Image** button):

```
if (image.data) {
    ui->pushButton_2->setEnabled(true);
}
```

It is also worth noting that under Qt, the layout of your GUI is completely described in a XML file. This is the file with the `.ui` extension. If you go in your project directory and open the `.ui` file with a text editor, you will be able to read the XML content of this file. Several XML tags are defined. In the case of the example application presented in this recipe, you will find two widget class tags defined as `QPushButton`. A name is associated with these widget classes' tags that corresponds to the name of the pointer variable attached to the `ui` object. Each of these defines a geometry property that describes their position and size. Many other property tags are also defined. Qt Creator has a property tab that shows the value of the properties of each widget. Consequently, even if Qt Creator is the best tool to create your GUI, you can also edit the `.ui` XML file to create and modify your GUI.

There's more...

Displaying an image directly on the GUI is relatively easy with Qt. All you need to do is add a label object to your window. You then assign an image to this label in order to display this image. Remember, you have access to the label instance via the corresponding pointer attribute of the `ui` pointer (`ui->label` in our example). But this image must be of type `QImage`, the Qt data structure to handle images. The conversion is relatively straightforward except that the order of the three color channels needs to be inverted (from BGR in our `cv::Mat` to RGB in `QImage`). We can use the `cv::cvtColor` function for this. The **Process** button of our simple GUI application can then be changed to:

```
void MainWindow::on_pushButton_2_clicked()
{
    cv::flip(image,image,1); // process the image
    // change color channel ordering
    cv::cvtColor(image,image,CV_BGR2RGB);
    // Qt image
```

```
QImage img= QImage((const unsigned char*)(image.data),
    image.cols,image.rows,QImage::Format_RGB888);
// display on label
ui->label->setPixmap(QPixmap::fromImage(img));
// resize the label to fit the image
ui->label->resize(ui->label->pixmap()->size());
}
```

As a result, the output image is now displayed directly on the GUI as seen here:

See also

Consult the online Qt documentation located at `http://doc.trolltech.com` for more information on the Qt GUI module and on the signals and slots mechanism.

2

Manipulating the Pixels

In this chapter, we will cover:

- ► Accessing pixel values
- ► Scanning an image with pointers
- ► Scanning an image with iterators
- ► Writing efficient image scanning loops
- ► Scanning an image with neighbor access
- ► Performing simple image arithmetic
- ► Defining regions of interest

Introduction

In order to build computer vision applications, you must be able to access image content, and eventually modify or create images. This chapter will teach you how to manipulate the picture elements (a.k.a. **pixels**). You will learn how to scan an image and process each of its pixels. You will also learn how to do this efficiently since even images of modest dimensions can contain tens of thousands of pixels.

Fundamentally, an image is a matrix of numerical values. This is why OpenCV 2 manipulates them using the `cv::Mat` data structure. Each element of the matrix represents one pixel. For a gray-level image (a "black-and-white" image), pixels are unsigned 8-bit values where 0 corresponds to black and corresponds 255 to white. For a color image, three such values per pixel are required to represent the usual three primary color channels {Red, Green, Blue}. A matrix element is therefore made, in this case, of a triplet of values.

As we saw in the previous chapter, OpenCV also allows you to create matrices (or images) with pixel values of different types (for example, integer (CV_8U) and floating point (CV_32F) numbers). These are very useful to store for example, intermediate values in some image processing task. Most operations can be applied on matrices of any type, others require a specific type, or work only with a given number of channels. Therefore, a good understanding of a function's or method's preconditions is essential to avoid common programming errors.

Throughout this chapter, we use the following color image as input (see the book's website to view this image in color):

Accessing pixel values

In order to access each individual element of a matrix, you just need to specify its row and column numbers. The corresponding element, which can be a single numerical value or a vector of values in the case of a multi-channel image, will be returned.

Getting ready

To illustrate the direct access to pixel values, we will create a simple function that adds salt-and-pepper noise to an image. As the name suggests, **salt-and-pepper noise** is a particular type of noise in which some pixels are replaced by a white or a black pixel. This type of noise can occur in faulty communication when the value of some pixels is lost during transmission. In our case, we will simply randomly select a few pixels and assign them the white color.

How to do it...

We create a function that receives an input image. This is the image that will be modified by our function. To this end, we use the pass-by-reference mechanism. The second parameter is the number of pixels on which we want to overwrite white values:

```cpp
void salt(cv::Mat &image, int n) {

    for (int k=0; k<n; k++) {

        // rand() is the MFC random number generator
        // try qrand() with Qt
        int i= rand()%image.cols;
        int j= rand()%image.rows;

        if (image.channels() == 1) { // gray-level image

            image.at<uchar>(j,i)= 255;

        } else if (image.channels() == 3) { // color image

            image.at<cv::Vec3b>(j,i)[0]= 255;
            image.at<cv::Vec3b>(j,i)[1]= 255;
            image.at<cv::Vec3b>(j,i)[2]= 255;
        }
    }
}
```

The function is made of a single loop that assigns n times the value 255 to randomly selected pixels. Here, the pixel column i and row j are selected using a random number generator. Note that we distinguish the two cases of gray-level and color images by checking the number of channels associated with each pixel. In the case of a gray-level image, the number 255 is assigned to the single 8-bit value. For a color image, you need to assign 255 to the three primary color channels in order to obtain a white pixel.

You can call this function by passing it an image you have previously opened:

```cpp
// open the image
cv::Mat image= cv::imread("boldt.jpg");

// call function to add noise
salt(image,3000);

// display image
cv::namedWindow("Image");
cv::imshow("Image",image);
```

The resulting image will look as follows:

How it works...

The class `cv::Mat` includes several methods to access the different attributes of an image. The public member variables `cols` and `rows` give you the number of columns and rows in the image. For element access, `cv::Mat` has the method `at(int y, int x)`. However, the type returned by a method must be known at compile time, and since a `cv::Mat` can hold elements of any type, the programmer needs to specify the return type that is expected. This is why the `at` method has been implemented as a template method. So when you call it, you must specify the image element type as in:

```
image.at<uchar>(j,i)= 255;
```

It is important to note that it is the programmer's responsibility to make sure that the type specified matches the type contained in the matrix. The `at` method does not perform any type conversion.

In color images, each pixel is associated with three components: the red, green, and blue channels. Therefore, a `cv::Mat` containing a color image will return a vector of three 8-bit values. OpenCV has a defined type for such short vectors that is called `cv::Vec3b`. It is a vector of 3 `unsigned char`s. This explains why the element access to the pixels of a color pixel is written as:

```
image.at<cv::Vec3b>(j,i)[channel]= value;
```

The index `channel` designates one of the three color channels.

Similar vector types also exist for 2-element and 4-element vectors (cv::Vec2b and cv::Vec4b) and for other element types. In this later case, the last letter is replaced by s for short, i for int, f for float, and d for double. All of these types are defined using the template class cv::Vec<T,N> where T is the type and N is the number of vector elements.

There's more...

Using the at method of the cv::Mat class can sometimes be cumbersome because the returned type must be specified as a template argument for each call. In cases where the matrix type is known, it is possible to use the cv::Mat_ class which is a template subclass of cv::Mat. This class defines a few extra methods but no new data attributes, so that pointers or references to one class can be directly converted to the other class. Among the extra methods, there is the operator() allowing direct access to matrix elements. Therefore, if image is a reference to a uchar matrix, then one can write:

```
cv::Mat_<uchar> im2= image; // im2 refers to image
im2(50,100)= 0; // access to row 50 and column 100
```

Since the type of the cv::Mat_ elements is declared when the variable is created, the operator() method knows at compile-time which type to return. Other than being shorter to write, using the operator() method provides exactly the same result as the at method.

See also

The *Writing efficient image scanning loops* recipe for a discussion on the efficiency of this method.

Scanning an image with pointers

In most image processing tasks, one needs to scan all pixels of the image in order to perform a computation. Considering the large number of pixels that will need to be visited, it is essential to perform this task in an efficient way. This recipe, and the next one, will show you different ways of implementing an image scanning loop. This recipe uses pointer arithmetic.

Getting ready

We will illustrate the image scanning process by accomplishing a simple task: reducing the number of colors in an image.

Color images are composed of 3-channel pixels. Each of these channels corresponds to the intensity value of one of the three primary colors (red, green, blue). Since each of these values is an 8-bit `unsigned char`, the total number of colors is 256x256x256, which is more than 16 million colors. Consequently, to reduce the complexity of an analysis, it is sometimes useful to reduce the number of colors in an image. One simple way to achieve this goal is to simply subdivide the RGB space into cubes of equal sizes. For example, if you reduce the number of colors in each dimension by 8, then you would obtain a total of 32x32x32 colors. Each color in the original image is then assigned a new color value in the color-reduced image that corresponds to the value in the center of the cube to which it belongs.

Therefore, the basic color reduction algorithm is simple. If N is the reduction factor, then for each pixel in the image and for each channel of this pixel, divide the value by N (integer division, therefore the reminder is lost). Then multiply the result by N, this will give you the multiple of N just below the input pixel value. Just add N/2 and you obtain the central position of the interval between two adjacent multiples of N. If you repeat this process for each 8-bit channel value, then you will obtain a total of 256/N x 256/N x 256/N possible color values.

How to do it...

The signature of our color reduction function will be as follows:

```
void colorReduce(cv::Mat &image, int div=64);
```

The user provides an image and the per-channel reduction factor. Here, the processing is done **in-place**, that is the pixel values of the input image are modified by the function. See the *There's more...* section of this recipe for a more general function signature with input and output arguments.

The processing is simply done by creating a double loop that goes over all pixel values:

```
void colorReduce(cv::Mat &image, int div=64) {
        int nl= image.rows; // number of lines
        // total number of elements per line
        int nc= image.cols * image.channels();

        for (int j=0; j<nl; j++) {
            // get the address of row j
            uchar* data= image.ptr<uchar>(j);
            for (int i=0; i<nc; i++) {
                // process each pixel --------------------

                        data[i]=    data[i]/div*div + div/2;
                // end of pixel processing ---------------
```

```
        } // end of line
    }
}
```

This function can be tested using the following code snippet:

```
// read the image
image= cv::imread("boldt.jpg");
// process the image
colorReduce(image);
// display the image
cv::namedWindow("Image");
cv::imshow("Image",image);
```

This will give you, for example, the following image (see the book's website to view this image in color):

How it works...

In a color image, the first 3 bytes of the image data buffer gives the 3 color channel values of the upper left pixel, the next 3 bytes are the values of the second pixel of the first row, and so on (note that OpenCV uses, by default, BGR channel order, so blue is usually the first channel). An image of width W and height H would then require a memory block of WxHx3 `uchar`s. However, for efficiency reasons, the length of a row can be padded with few extra pixels. This is because some multimedia processor chips (for example, the Intel MMX architecture) can process images more efficiently when their rows are multiples of 4 or 8. Obviously, these extra pixels are not displayed or saved, their exact values are ignored. OpenCV designates the length of a padded row as the keyword. Obviously, if the image has not been padded with extra pixels, the effective width will be equal to the real image width. The data attribute `cols` gives you the image width (that is the number of columns), and the attribute `rows` gives you the image height while the `step` data attribute gives you the effective width in number of bytes. Even if your image is of a type other than `uchar`, `step` will still give you the number of bytes in a row. The size of a pixel element is given by method `elemSize` (for example, for a 3-channel short integer matrix (`CV_16SC3`), `elemSize` will return 6). The number of channels in the image is given by the `nchannels` method (which will be 1 for a gray-level image and 3 for a color image). Finally, method `total` returns the total number of pixels (that is matrix entries) in the matrix.

The number of pixel values per rows is then given by:

```
int nc= image.cols * image.channels();
```

To simplify the computation of the pointer arithmetic, the `cv::Mat` class offers a method which directly gives you the address of an image row. This is the `ptr` method. It is a template method that returns the address of row number `j`:

```
uchar* data= image.ptr<uchar>(j);
```

Note, that in the processing statement, we could have equivalently used pointer arithmetic to move from column to column. So we could have written:

```
*data++= *data/div*div + div2;
```

There's more...

The color reduction function presented in this recipe provides just one way of accomplishing this task. One could also use other color reduction formulas. A more general version of the function would also allow the specification of distinct input and output images. The image scanning can also be made more efficient by taking into account the continuity of the image data. Finally, it is also possible to use regular low-level pointer arithmetic to scan the image buffer. All of these elements are discussed in the following sub-sections.

Other color reduction formulas

In our example, color reduction is achieved by taking advantage of an integer division that floors the division result to the nearest lower integer:

```
data[i]= data[i]/div*div + div/2;
```

The reduced color could have also been computed using the modulo operator which brings us to the nearest multiple of `div` (the 1D reduction factor):

```
data[i]=    data[i] - data[i]%div + div/2;
```

But this computation is a bit slower because it requires reading each pixel value twice.

Another option would be to use bitwise operators. Indeed, if we restrict the reduction factor to a power of 2, that is, `div=pow(2,n)`, then masking the first n bits of the pixel value would give us the nearest lower multiple of `div`. This mask would be computed by a simple bit shift:

```
// mask used to round the pixel value
uchar mask= 0xFF<<n; // e.g. for div=16, mask= 0xF0
```

The color reduction would be given by:

```
data[i]=    (data[i]&mask) + div/2;
```

In general, bitwise operations lead to very efficient code, so they could constitute a powerful alternative when efficiency is a requirement.

Having input and output arguments

In our color reduction example, the transformation is directly applied to the input image, which is called an *in-place* transformation. This way, no extra image is required to hold the output result, which could save on the memory usage when it is a concern. However, in some applications, the user wants to keep the original image intact. The user would then be forced to create a copy of the image before calling the function. Note that the easiest way to create an identical deep copy of an image is to call the `clone` method, for example:

```
// read the image
image= cv::imread("boldt.jpg");
// clone the image
cv::Mat imageClone= image.clone();
// process the clone
// orginal image remains untouched
colorReduce(imageClone);
// display the image result
cv::namedWindow("Image Result");
cv::imshow("Image Result",imageClone);
```

This extra overload can be avoided by defining a function that gives the option to the user to either use or not use the in-place processing. The signature of the method would then be:

```
void colorReduce(const cv::Mat &image,   // input image
                 cv::Mat &result,         // output image
                 int div=64);
```

Note that the input image is now passed as a `const` reference, meaning that this image will not be modified by the function. When in-place processing is preferred, the same image is specified as input and output:

```
colorReduce(image,image);
```

If not, another `cv::Mat` instance can be provided, for example:

```
cv::Mat result;
colorReduce(image,result);
```

The key here is to first verify if the output image has an allocated data buffer with a size and pixel type that match the ones of the input image. Very conveniently, this check is encapsulated inside the `create` method of `cv::Mat`. This is the method to use when a matrix must be re-allocated with a new size and type. If, by chance, the matrix already has the size and type specified, then no operation is performed and the method simply returns without touching the instance. Therefore, our function should simply start with a call to `create` that builds a matrix (if necessary) of the same size and type than the input image:

```
result.create(image.rows,image.cols,image.type());
```

Note that `create` always creates a continuous image, that is an image with no padding. The memory block allocated has a size of `total()*elemSize()`.The looping is then done with two pointers:

```
for (int j=0; j<nl; j++) {
    // get the addresses of input and output row j
    const uchar* data_in= image.ptr<uchar>(j);
    uchar* data_out= result.ptr<uchar>(j);
    for (int i=0; i<nc; i++) {
        // process each pixel --------------------

                data_out[i]= data_in[i]/div*div + div/2;
        // end of pixel processing ----------------
    } // end of line
```

In the case where the same image is provided as input and output, this function becomes completely equivalent to the first version presented in this recipe. If another image is provided as output, the function will work correctly irrespective of whether the image has been or has not been allocated prior to the function call.

Efficient scanning of continuous images

We previously explained that, for efficiency reasons, an image can be padded with extra pixels at the end of each row. However, it is interesting to note that when the image is unpadded, the image can be seen as a long one-dimensional array of *WxH* pixels. A convenient `cv::Mat` method can tell us if the image has been padded or not. It is the `isContinuous` method that returns `true` if the image does not include padded pixels.

In some specific processing algorithms, one can take advantage of the continuity of the image by processing it in one single (longer) loop. Our processing function would then be written as follows:

```
void colorReduce(cv::Mat &image, int div=64) {

    int nl= image.rows; // number of lines
    int nc= image.cols * image.channels();

    if (image.isContinuous())
    {
        // then no padded pixels
        nc= nc*nl;
        nl= 1;  // it is now a 1D array
    }
    // this loop is executed only once
    // in case of continuous images
    for (int j=0; j<nl; j++) {
    uchar* data= image.ptr<uchar>(j);

        for (int i=0; i<nc; i++) {
            // process each pixel --------------------

                    data[i]= data[i]/div*div + div/2;

            // end of pixel processing ---------------
        } // end of line

    }

}
```

Now, when the continuity test tells us that the image does not contain padded pixels, we eliminate the outer loop by setting the width to 1 and the height to *WxH*. Note that there is also a `reshape` method that could have been used here. You would write the following in this case:

```
if (image.isContinuous())
{
    // no padded pixels
    image.reshape(1,                     // new number of channels
        image.cols*image.rows) ; // new number of rows
```

```
        }
        int nl= image.rows; // number of lines
        int nc= image.cols * image.channels();
```

The method `reshape` changes the matrix dimensions without requiring any memory copy or re-allocation. The first parameter is the new number of channels and the second one is the new number of rows. The number of columns is readjusted accordingly.

In these implementations, the inner loop processes all image pixels in sequence. This approach is mainly advantageous when several small images are scanned simultaneously into the same loop.

Low-level pointer arithmetics

In the `cv::Mat` class, the image data is contained into a memory block of `unsigned char`s. The address of the first element of this memory block is given by the data attribute which returns an unsigned char pointer. So, to start your loop at the beginning of the image, you could have written:

```
        uchar *data= image.data;
```

Moving from one row to the next could have been done by moving your row pointer using the effective width:

```
        data+= image.step;  // next line
```

The method `step` gives you the total number of bytes (including the padded pixels) in a line. In general, you can obtain the address of the pixel at row j and column i as follows:

```
        // address of pixel at (j,i) that is &image.at(j,i)
        data= image.data+j*image.step+i*image.elemSize();
```

However, even if this would work in our example, it is not recommended to proceed this way. In addition to being error-prone, this approach will not work with regions of interest. Regions of interest are discussed at the end of this chapter.

See also

The *Writing efficient image scanning loops* recipe for a discussion on the efficiency of the scanning methods presented here.

Scanning an image with iterators

In object-oriented programming, looping over a data collection is usually done using iterators. Iterators are specialized classes built to go over each element of a collection, hiding how the iteration over each element is specifically done for a given collection. This application of the information hiding principle makes scanning a collection easier. In addition, it makes it similar in form no matter what type of collection is used. The Standard Template Library (STL) has an iterator class associated with each of its collection classes. OpenCV then offers a `cv::Mat` iterator class compatible with the standard iterators found in the C++ STL.

Getting ready

In this recipe, we again use the color reduction example described in the previous recipe.

How to do it...

An iterator object for a `cv::Mat` instance can be obtained by first creating a `cv::MatIterator_` object. As in the case of the `cv::Mat_` subclass, the underscore indicates that this is a template method. Indeed, since image iterators are used to access the image elements, the return type must be known at compile time. The iterator is then declared as follows:

```
cv::MatIterator_<cv::Vec3b> it;
```

Alternatively, you can also use the `iterator` type defined inside the `Mat_` template class:

```
cv::Mat_<cv::Vec3b>::iterator it;
```

You then loop over the pixels using the usual `begin` and `end` iterator methods except that these ones are again template methods. Consequently, our color reduction function is now written as follows:

```
void colorReduce(cv::Mat &image, int div=64) {
    // obtain iterator at initial position
    cv::Mat_<cv::Vec3b>::iterator it=
            image.begin<cv::Vec3b>();
    // obtain end position
    cv::Mat_<cv::Vec3b>::iterator itend=
            image.end<cv::Vec3b>();
    // loop over all pixels
    for ( ; it!= itend; ++it) {
        // process each pixel ---------------------
        (*it)[0]= (*it)[0]/div*div + div/2;
```

```
        (*it)[1]= (*it)[1]/div*div + div/2;
        (*it)[2]= (*it)[2]/div*div + div/2;

        // end of pixel processing ----------------
    }
}
```

Remember that the iterator here returns a `cv::Vec3b` because we are processing a color image. Each color channel element is accessed using dereferencing `operator[]`.

How it works...

Working with iterators, no matter what kind of collection is scanned, always follows the same pattern.

First, you create your iterator object using the appropriate specialized class which is, in our example, `cv::Mat_<cv::Vec3b>::iterator` (or `cv::MatIterator_<cv::Vec3b>`).

You then obtain an iterator initialized at the starting position (in our example, the upper-left corner of the image). This is done using a `begin` method. With a `cv::Mat` instance, you obtain it as `image.begin<cv::Vec3b>()`. You can also use arithmetic on the iterator. For example, if you wish to start at the second row of an image, you can initialize your `cv::Mat` iterator at `image.begin<cv::Vec3b>()+image.rows`. The end position of your collection is obtained similarly but using the `end` method. However, the iterator thus obtained is just outside your collection. This is why your iterative process must stop when it reaches that end position. You can also use arithmetic on this iterator, for example, if you wish to stop before the last row, your final iteration would stop when the iterator reaches `image.end<cv::Vec3b>()-image.rows`.

Once your iterator is initialized, you create a loop that goes over all elements until the end is reached. A typical `while` loop will look like this:

```
    while (it!= itend) {

        // process each pixel ---------------------
        ...
        // end of pixel processing ----------------
        ++it;
    }
```

The `operator++` is the one to use to move to the next element. You can also specify larger step size. For example `it+=10` would process every 10 pixels.

Finally, inside the processing loop, you use the dereferencing `operator*` in order to access the current element, using which you can read (for example, `element= *it;`) or write (for example, `*it= element;`). Note that it is also possible to create constant iterators that you use if you receive a reference to a `const cv::Mat` or if you wish to signify that the current loop does not modify the `cv::Mat` instance. These are declared as follows:

```
cv::MatConstIterator_<cv::Vec3b> it;
```

or:

```
cv::Mat_<cv::Vec3b>::const_iterator it;
```

There's more...

In this recipe, the start and end positions of the iterator were obtained using the template methods `begin` and `end`. As we did in the first recipe of this chapter, we could have also obtained them using a reference to a `cv::Mat_` instance. This would avoid the need to specify the iterator type in the `begin` and `end` methods since this one is specified when the `cv::Mat_` reference is created.

```
cv::Mat_<cv::Vec3b> cimage= image;
cv::Mat_<cv::Vec3b>::iterator it= cimage.begin();
cv::Mat_<cv::Vec3b>::iterator itend= cimage.end();
```

See also

The *Writing efficient image scanning loops* recipe for a discussion on the efficiency of iterators when scanning an image.

Also, if you are not familiar with the concept of iterators in object-oriented programming and how they have been implemented in ANSI C++, you should read a tutorial on STL iterators. Simply search the web with the keywords "STL Iterator" and you will find numerous references on the subject.

Writing efficient image scanning loops

In the previous recipes of this chapter, we have presented different ways of scanning an image in order to process its pixels. In this recipe, we will compare the efficiency of these different approaches.

When you write an image processing function, efficiency is often a concern. When you design your function, you will frequently need to check the computational efficiency of your code in order to detect any bottleneck in your processing which might slow down your program.

However, it is important to note, that unless necessary, optimization should not be done at the price of reducing program clarity. Simple code is indeed always easier to debug and maintain. Only code portions that are critical to a program's efficiency should be heavily optimized.

How to do it...

In order to measure the execution time of a function or a portion of code, there exists a very convenient OpenCV function called `cv::getTickCount()`. This function gives you the number of clock cycles that occurred since the last time you started your computer. Since we want the execution time of a code portion given in milliseconds, we use another method, `cv::getTickFrequency()`. This gives us the number of cycles per seconds. The usual pattern to use in order to obtain the computational time of a given function (or portion of code) would then be:

```
double duration;
duration = static_cast<double>(cv::getTickCount());

colorReduce(image); // the function to be tested

duration = static_cast<double>(cv::getTickCount())-duration;
duration /= cv::getTickFrequency(); // the elapsed time in ms
```

The duration result should be averaged over several calls of the function.

In the testing of the `colorReduce` function, we also implemented a version of the function that uses the `at` method for pixel access. The main loop of this implementation would then read simply as:

```
for (int j=0; j<nl; j++) {
    for (int i=0; i<nc; i++) {

    // process each pixel ---------------------

    image.at<cv::Vec3b>(j,i)[0]=
         image.at<cv::Vec3b>(j,i)[0]/div*div + div/2;
    image.at<cv::Vec3b>(j,i)[1]=
        image.at<cv::Vec3b>(j,i)[1]/div*div + div/2;
    image.at<cv::Vec3b>(j,i)[2]=
        image.at<cv::Vec3b>(j,i)[2]/div*div + div/2;

    // end of pixel processing ----------------

    } // end of line
}
```

How it works...

The execution times of the different implementations of the `colorReduce` function from this chapter are reported here. The absolute runtime numbers would differ from one machine to another (here we used a Pentium dual core 2.2GHz). It is rather interesting to look at their relative difference. Our tests report the average time to reduce the colors of an image having a resolution of 4288x2848 pixels. The results are summarized in the following table and are discussed below:

Method	Average time
`data[i]= data[i]/div*div + div/2;`	37ms
`*data++= *data/div*div + div/2;`	37ms
`*data++= v - v%div + div/2;`	52ms
`*data++= *data&mask + div/2;`	35ms
`colorReduce(input, output);`	44ms
`i<image.cols*image.channels();`	65ms
`MatIterator`	67ms
`.at(j,i)`	80ms
`3-channel loop`	29ms

First, we compare the three ways of computing the color reduction (rows 1-4) as presented in the *There's more...* section of the *Scanning an image with pointers* recipe. As expected, the version that uses bitwise operators is the fastest with an execution time of 35ms. The version that uses integer division took 37ms, while the one with modulo is at 52ms. This represents a difference of almost 50% between the fastest and the slowest! It is therefore important to take the time to identify the most efficient way of computing a result in an image loop as the net impact can be very significant. Note that when an output image that needs to be re-allocated is specified instead of an in-place processing (row 5), the execution time becomes 44ms. The extra duration represents the overhead for memory allocation.

In a loop, you should avoid repetitive computations of values that could be precomputed. This obviously consumes time. For example, if you replace the following inner loop of the color reduction function:

```
int nc= image.cols * image.channels();
...
    for (int i=0; i<nc; i++) {
```

with this one:

```
    for (int i=0; i<image.cols * image.channels(); i++) {
```

that is a loop where you need to compute the total number of elements in a line again and again. You will obtain a runtime of 65ms which is 80% slower than the original version at 35ms (row 6).

The version of the color reduction function that uses iterators (row 7), as shown in recipe *Scanning an image with iterators*, gives slower results at 67ms. The main objective of iterators is to simplify the image scanning process and make it less error-prone. It is not necessarily to optimize this process.

The implementation that uses the at method presented at the end of the preceding section is much slower (row 8). A runtime of 80ms is obtained. This method should then be used for random access of image pixels but never when scanning an image.

A shorter loop with few statements is generally more efficiently executed than a longer loop over a single statement, even if the total number of elements processed is the same. Similarly, if you have *N* different computations to apply to a pixel, do all of them in one loop rather than writing *N* successive loops, one for each computation. You should then favor loops, doing more work over longer loops that do less computation. As an example, we could process all three channels inside the inner loop and have it iterating over the number of columns, instead of using the original version where the looping is over the total number of elements (that is 3 times the number of pixels). The color reduction function would then be written as follows (this is the fastest version):

```
void colorReduce(cv::Mat &image, int div=64) {
    int nl= image.rows; // number of lines
    int nc= image.cols ; // number of columns
    // is it a continous image?
    if (image.isContinuous())   {
       // then no padded pixels
       nc= nc*nl;
       nl= 1;   // it is now a 1D array
     }
    int n= static_cast<int>(
            log(static_cast<double>(div))/log(2.0));
    // mask used to round the pixel value
    uchar mask= 0xFF<<n; // e.g. for div=16, mask= 0xF0
    // for all pixels
    for (int j=0; j<nl; j++) {
          // pointer to first column of line j
          uchar* data= image.ptr<uchar>(j);
          for (int i=0; i<nc; i++) {

              // process each pixel --------------------
```

```
        *data++= *data&mask + div/2;
        *data++= *data&mask + div/2;
        *data++= *data&mask + div/2;
        // end of pixel processing ---------------
    } // end of line
}
}
```

With this modification, the execution time is now at 29ms (row 9). We also added the continuity test that produces one loop in case of continuous images, instead of the regular double loop over lines and columns. For a very large image, as the one we used in our tests, this optimization is not significant, but in general it is always a good practice to use this strategy since it can lead to significant gain in speed.

There's more...

Multi-threading is another way to increase the efficiency of your algorithms, especially since the advent of multi-core processors. OpenMP and the Intel Threading Building Blocks (TBB) are two popular APIs used in concurrent programming to create and manage your threads.

See also

Have a look at the *Performing simple image arithmetic* recipe for an implementation of the color reduction method that uses the OpenCV 2 arithmetic image operators.

Scanning an image with neighbor access

In image processing, it is common to have a processing function which computes a value at each pixel location based on the value of the neighboring pixels. When this neighborhood includes pixels of the previous and next lines, you then need to simultaneously scan several lines of the image. This recipe shows you how to do it.

Getting ready

To illustrate this recipe, we will apply a processing function that sharpens an image. It is based on the Laplacian operator (which will be discussed in *Chapter 6*). It is indeed a well-known result in image processing that if you subtract its Laplacian from an image, the image edges are amplified giving a sharper image. This sharpen operator is computed as follows:

```
sharpened_pixel= 5*current-left-right-up-down;
```

where `left` is the pixel immediately on the left of the current one, `up` is the corresponding one on the previous line, and so on.

How to do it...

This time, the processing cannot be accomplished in-place. Users need to provide an output image. The image scanning is done by using three pointers, one for the current line, one for the line above, and another one for the line below. Also, since each pixel computation requires access to the neighbors, it is not possible to compute a value for the pixels of the first and last row of the image as well as the pixels of the first and last column. The loop can then be written as follows:

```cpp
void sharpen(const cv::Mat &image, cv::Mat &result) {

    // allocate if necessary
    result.create(image.size(), image.type());

    for (int j= 1; j<image.rows-1; j++) { // for all rows
                                          // (except first and last)
        const uchar* previous=
            image.ptr<const uchar>(j-1); // previous row
        const uchar* current=
            image.ptr<const uchar>(j);      // current row
        const uchar* next=
            image.ptr<const uchar>(j+1); // next row

        uchar* output= result.ptr<uchar>(j); // output row

        for (int i=1; i<image.cols-1; i++) {

            *output++= cv::saturate_cast<uchar>(
                       5*current[i]-current[i-1]
                       -current[i+1]-previous[i]-next[i]);
        }
    }

    // Set the unprocess pixels to 0
    result.row(0).setTo(cv::Scalar(0));
    result.row(result.rows-1).setTo(cv::Scalar(0));
    result.col(0).setTo(cv::Scalar(0));
    result.col(result.cols-1).setTo(cv::Scalar(0));
}
```

If we apply this function on a gray-level version of our test image, the following sample is obtained:

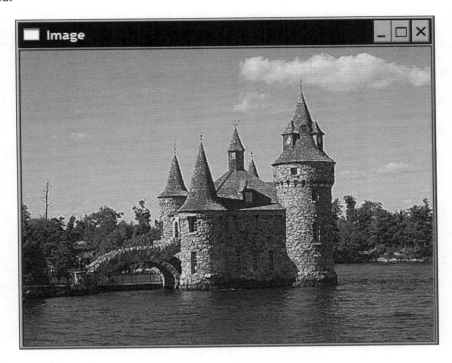

How it works...

In order to access the neighboring pixels of the previous and next row, one must simply define additional pointers that are jointly incremented. You then access the pixels of these lines inside the scanning loop.

In the computation of the output pixel value, the template function `cv::saturate_cast` is called on the result of the operation. This is because it often happens that a mathematical expression applied on pixels leads to a result that goes outside the range of the permitted pixel values (that is below 0 or over 255). The solution is then to bring back the values inside this 8-bit range. This is done by changing negative values to 0 and values over 255 to 255. This is exactly what the `cv::saturate_cast<uchar>` function is doing. In addition, if the input argument is a floating point number, then the result is rounded to the nearest integer. You can obviously use this function with other types in order to guarantee the result will remain within the limits defined by this type.

Border pixels that cannot be processed because their neighborhood is not completely defined need to be handled separately. Here, we simply set them to 0. In other cases, it could be possible to perform some special computation for these pixels, but most of the time there is no point in spending time processing these very few pixels. In our function, these border pixels are set to 0 using two special methods. The first one is `row` and its dual `col`. They return a special `cv::Mat` instance composed of a single line (or a single column) as specified in a parameter. No copy is made here because if the elements of this 1D matrix are modified, they will also be modified in the original image. That is what we do when the method `setTo` is called. This method assigns a value to all elements of a matrix. Therefore the statement:

```
result.row(0).setTo(cv::Scalar(0));
```

assigns the value 0 to all pixels of the first line of the result image. In the case of a 3-channel color image, you would use `cv::Scalar(a,b,c)` to specify the three values to assign to each channel of the pixel.

There's more...

When a computation is done over a pixel neighborhood, it is common to represent this with a kernel matrix. This kernel describes how the pixels involved in the computation are combined in order to obtain the desired result. For the sharpening filter used in this recipe, the kernel would be:

0	-1	0
-1	5	-1
0	-1	0

Unless stated otherwise, the current pixel corresponds to the center of the kernel. The value in each cell of the kernel represents a factor that multiplies the corresponding pixel. The result of the application of the kernel on a pixel is then given by the sum of all these multiplications. The size of the kernel corresponds to the size of the neighborhood (here, 3x3). Using this representation, it can be seen that, as required by the sharpening filter, the four horizontal and vertical neighbors of the current pixel are multiplied by -1, while the current one is multiplied by 5. Applying a kernel to an image is more than a convenient representation, it is the basis for the concept of convolution in signal processing. The kernel defines a filter that is applied to the image.

Since filtering is a common operation in image processing, OpenCV has defined a special function that performs this task: the `cv::filter2D` function. To use it, one just needs to define a kernel (in the form of a matrix). The function is then called with the image and the kernel, and returns the filtered image. Using this function, it is therefore easy to redefine our sharpening function as follows:

```
void sharpen2D(const cv::Mat &image, cv::Mat &result) {
    // Construct kernel (all entries initialized to 0)
    cv::Mat kernel(3,3,CV_32F,cv::Scalar(0));
    // assigns kernel values
    kernel.at<float>(1,1)= 5.0;
    kernel.at<float>(0,1)= -1.0;
    kernel.at<float>(2,1)= -1.0;
    kernel.at<float>(1,0)= -1.0;
    kernel.at<float>(1,2)= -1.0;

    //filter the image
    cv::filter2D(image,result,image.depth(),kernel);
}
```

This implementation produces exactly the same result as the previous one (and with the same efficiency). However, with a larger kernel, it is advantageous to use the `filter2D` method as it uses, in this case, a more efficient algorithm.

See also

Chapter 6, Filtering the Images has more explanations on the concept of image filtering.

Performing simple image arithmetic

Images can be combined in different ways. Since they are regular matrices, they can be added, subtracted, multiplied, or divided. OpenCV offers various image arithmetic operators and their use is discussed in this recipe.

Getting ready

Let's work with a second image that we will combine to our input image using an arithmetic operator. The following represents the second image:

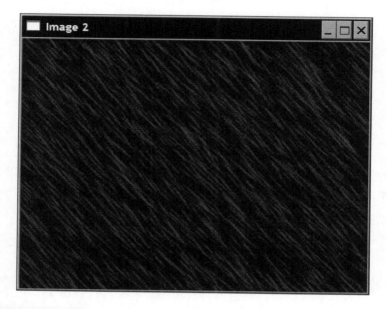

How to do it...

Here we add two images. This is useful when one wants to create some special effects or to overlay information over an image. We do this by calling the cv::add function, or more precisely here, the cv::addWeighted function since we want a weighted sum, that is:

```
cv::addWeighted(image1,0.7,image2,0.9,0.,result);
```

The operation results in a new image as seen in the following screenshot:

How it works...

All binary arithmetic functions work the same way. Two inputs are provided and a third parameter specifies the output. In some cases, weights can be specified that are used as scalar multipliers in the operation. Each of these functions comes in several flavors. `cv::add` is a good example of a function available in many forms:

```
// c[i]= a[i]+b[i];
cv::add(imageA,imageB,resultC);
// c[i]= a[i]+k;
cv::add(imageA,cv::Scalar(k),resultC);
// c[i]= k1*a[1]+k2*b[i]+k3;
cv::addWeighted(imageA,k1,imageB,k2,k3,resultC);
// c[i]= k*a[1]+b[i];
cv::scaleAdd(imageA,k,imageB,resultC);
```

For some functions, you can also specify a mask:

```
// if (mask[i]) c[i]= a[i]+b[i];
cv::add(imageA,imageB,resultC,mask);
```

If you apply a mask, the operation is performed only on pixels for which the mask value is not null (the mask must be 1-channel). Have a look at the different forms of cv::subtract, cv::absdiff, cv::multiply, and cv::divide functions. Bit-wise operators are also available: cv::bitwise_and, cv::bitwise_or, cv::bitwise_xor, and cv::bitwise_not. Operators cv::min and cv::max which find per-element maximum or minimum pixel value are also very useful.

In all cases, function cv::saturate_cast (see the preceding recipe) is always used to make sure the results stay within the defined pixel value domain (that is to avoid overflow or underflow).

The images must have the same size and type (the output image will be re-allocated if it does match the input size). Also, since the operation is performed per-element, one of the input images can be used as output.

Several operators that take a single image as input are also available: cv::sqrt, cv::pow, cv::abs, cv::cuberoot, cv::exp, and cv::log. In fact, there exists an OpenCV function for almost any operation you have to apply on your images.

There's more...

It is also possible to use the usual C++ arithmetic operator on the cv::Mat instances, or on the individual channels of cv::Mat instances. The two following sub-sections explain how to do it.

Overloaded image operators

Very conveniently, most arithmetic functions have their corresponding operator overloaded in OpenCV 2. Consequently, the call to cv::addWeighted can be written as:

```
result= 0.7*image1+0.9*image2;
```

which is a more compact form that is also easier to read. These two ways of writing the weighted sum are equivalent. In particular, function cv::saturate_cast will still be called in both cases.

Most C++ operators have been overloaded. Among them the bitwise operators &, |, ^, ~, the min, max, and abs functions, the comparison operators <, <=, ==,!=, >, >=; these later returning a 8-bit binary image. You will also find the matrix multiplication m1*m2 (where m1 and m2 are both cv::Mat instances), matrix inversion m1.inv(), transpose m1.t(), determinant m1.determinant(), vector norm, v1.norm(), cross-product v1.cross(v2), dot product v1.dot(v2), and so on. When this makes sense, you also have the op= operator (for example, +=) defined.

In the *Writing efficient image scanning loops* recipe, we presented a color reduction function that was written using loops scanning the image pixels to perform some arithmetic operations on them. From what we learned here, this function could be rewritten simply using arithmetic operators on the input image, that is:

```
image=(image&cv::Scalar(mask,mask,mask))
        +cv::Scalar(div/2,div/2,div/2);
```

The use of `cv::Scalar` is due to the fact that we are manipulating a color image. Performing the same test as we did in the *Writing efficient image scanning loops* recipe, we obtain an execution time of `89ms`. This is mainly because, as written, the expression requires calling two functions, the bitwise-and and the scalar sum (instead of performing the complete operation inside one image loop). Even if the resulting code is not always optimal, using the image operators makes the code so simple, and the programmer so productive, that you should consider their use in most situations.

Splitting the image channels

You'll sometimes want to process the different channels of an image independently. For example, you might want to perform an operation only on one channel of the image. You can, of course, achieve this in an image scanning loop. But you can also use the `cv::split` function that will copy the three channels of a color image into three distinct `cv::Mat` instances. Suppose we want to add our rain image to the blue channel only. The following is how we would proceed:

```
// create vector of 3 images
std::vector<cv::Mat> planes;
// split 1 3-channel image into 3 1-channel images
cv::split(image1,planes);
// add to blue channel
planes[0]+= image2;
// merge the 3 1-channel images into 1 3-channel image
cv::merge(planes,result);
```

The `cv::merge` function performs the dual operation, that is it creates a color image from three 1-channel image.

Defining regions of interest

Sometimes, a processing function needs to be applied on only a portion of the image. This recipe will teach you how to define a region of interest inside an image.

Getting ready

Suppose we want to combine two images of different sizes. For example, let's say we want to add the following small logo to our test image:

But function `cv::add` requires two images of same size. In this case, a region of interest (ROI) can be defined over which the `cv::add` can be applied. This will work as long as the ROI is of same size as our logo image. The position of the ROI will determined where in the image the logo will be inserted.

How to do it...

The first step consists of defining the ROI. Once defined, the ROI can be manipulated as a regular `cv::Mat` instance. The key is that the ROI points to the same data buffer as its parent image. Inserting the logo would then be accomplished as follows:

```
// define image ROI
cv::Mat imageROI;
imageROI= image(cv::Rect(385,270,logo.cols,logo.rows));
// add logo to image
cv::addWeighted(imageROI,1.0,logo,0.3,0.,imageROI);
```

The following image is then obtained:

Since the colors of the logo are added to the colors of the image (with possible saturation also applied), the visual result will not always be satisfactory. For this reason, it might be better to simply set the pixel values of the image to the logo values where this one appears. You do this by copying the logo to the ROI using a mask:

```
// define ROI
imageROI= image(cv::Rect(385,270,logo.cols,logo.rows));

// load the mask (must be gray-level)
cv::Mat mask= cv::imread("logo.bmp",0);

// copy to ROI with mask
logo.copyTo(imageROI,mask);
```

Then, the result image is:

How it works...

One way of defining an ROI is to use a `cv::Rect` instance. As the name indicates, it describes a rectangular region by specifying the position of the upper-left corner (the first two parameters of the constructor) and the size of the rectangle (width and height given in the last two parameters).

The ROI can also be described using row and column ranges. A range is a continuous sequence from a start index to an end index (excluded). The `cv::Range` structure is used to represent this concept. Therefore, an ROI can be defined from two ranges, for example, in our example, the ROI could have been equivalently defined as follows:

```
cv::Mat imageROI= image(cv::Range(270,270+logo.rows),
                        cv::Range(385,385+logo.cols))
```

The `operator()` of `cv::Mat` returns another `cv::Mat` instance that can then be used in subsequence calls. Any transformation of the ROI will affect the original image in the corresponding area because the image and the ROI share the same image data. Since the definition of an ROI does not copy data, it is executed in constant time, no matter the size of the ROI.

If one wants to define an ROI made of some lines of an image, the following call could be used:

```
cv::Mat imageROI= image.rowRange(start,end) ;
```

and similarly, for an ROI made of some image columns:

```
cv::Mat imageROI= image.colRange(start,end) ;
```

The methods `row` and `col` that were used in the recipe *Scanning an image with neighbor access* are a special case of these later methods in which the start and end index are equal in order to define a single-line or single-column ROI.

3
Processing Images with Classes

In this chapter, we will cover:

- ▶ Using the Strategy pattern in algorithm design
- ▶ Using a Controller to communicate with processing modules
- ▶ Using the Singleton design pattern
- ▶ Using the Model-View-Controller architecture to design an application
- ▶ Converting color spaces

Introduction

Good computer vision programs start with good programming practices. Building a bug-free application is just the beginning. What you really want is an application that you, and the programmers working with you, will be able to easily adapt and evolve as new requirements come in. This chapter will show you how to make best use of some of the object-oriented programming principles in order to build quality software programs. In particular, we will introduce some important design patterns that will help you build applications made of components that are easy to test, maintain, and reuse.

Design pattern is a well-known concept in software engineering. Basically, a **design pattern** is a sound, reusable solution to a generic problem that occurs frequently in software design. Many software patterns have been introduced and well documented. Good programmers should build a working knowledge of these existing patterns.

This chapter also has a secondary objective. It will teach you how to play with image colors. The example used throughout this chapter will show you how to detect pixels of a given color, and the last recipe will explain how to work with different color spaces.

Using the Strategy pattern in algorithm design

The objective of the Strategy design pattern is to encapsulate an algorithm into a class. This way it becomes easier to replace a given algorithm by another one, or to chain several algorithms together in order to build a more complex process. In addition, this pattern facilitates the deployment of an algorithm by hiding as much of its complexity as possible behind an intuitive programming interface.

Getting ready

Let's say we want to build a simple algorithm that will identify all of the pixels in an image which have a given color. The algorithm has then to accept an image and a color as input and returns a binary image showing the pixels having the specified color. The tolerance with which we want to accept a color will be another parameter to be specified before running the algorithm.

How to do it...

The core process of this algorithm is quite easy to build. It is a simple scanning loop that goes over each pixel, comparing its color with the target color. Using what we learned in the previous chapter, this loop can be written as:

```cpp
// get the iterators
cv::Mat_<cv::Vec3b>::const_iterator it=
                    image.begin<cv::Vec3b>();
cv::Mat_<cv::Vec3b>::const_iterator itend=
                  image.end<cv::Vec3b>();
cv::Mat_<uchar>::iterator itout=
                    result.begin<uchar>();
// for each pixel
for ( ; it!= itend; ++it, ++itout) {
   // process each pixel --------------------
   // compute distance from target color
   if (getDistance(*it)<minDist) {
      *itout= 255;
   } else {
      *itout= 0;
   }
   // end of pixel processing ----------------
}
```

The cv::Mat variable image refers to the input image while result refers to the binary output image. Therefore, the first step, consists of setting up the required iterators. The scanning for loop is then easy to implement. Each iteration checks if the distance between the current pixel color and the target color is within the tolerance defined by minDist. If that is the case, the value 255 (white) is then assigned to the output image, and if not, 0 (black) is assigned. To compute the distance between two color values, the getDistance method is used. There are different ways to compute this distance. One could, for example, calculate the Euclidean distance between the 3-vectors containing the RGB color values. In our case, to keep this computation simple and efficient, we simply sum the absolute difference of the RGB values (this is also known as the city block distance). The getDistance method is then simply defined as follows:

```cpp
// Computes the distance from target color.
int getDistance(const cv::Vec3b& color) const {

    return abs(color[0]-target[0])+
           abs(color[1]-target[1])+
           abs(color[2]-target[2]);
}
```

Note how we used the cv::Vec3d to hold the three unsigned chars representing the RGB values of a color. The variable target obviously refers to the specified target color, and as we will see, it is defined as a class variable in the class algorithm we are defining. Now let's complete the definition of the processing method. Users will provide an input image and the result will be returned once the image scanning is completed:

```cpp
cv::Mat ColorDetector::process(const cv::Mat &image) {
    // re-allocate binary map if necessary
    // same size as input image, but 1-channel
    result.create(image.rows,image.cols,CV_8U);
```

processing loop above goes here

```cpp
    ...
    return result;
}
```

Each time this method is called, it is important to check if the output image which will contain the resulting binary map needs to be re-allocated to fit the size of the input image. This is why we use the method create of cv::Mat. Remember, this one will only proceed to re-allocation if the specified size and depth do not correspond to the current image structure.

Now that we have the core processing method defined, let's see what additional methods should be added in order to deploy this algorithm. We previously determined what input and output data our algorithm requires. We will therefore first define class attributes that will hold this data:

```
class ColorDetector {

  private:

      // minimum acceptable distance
      int minDist;

      // target color
      cv::Vec3b target;

      // image containing resulting binary map
      cv::Mat result;
```

In order to create an instance of the class that encapsulates our algorithm (and that we have named `ColorDetector`), we need to define a constructor. Remember that one of the objectives of the Strategy design pattern is to make the algorithm deployment as easy as possible. The simplest constructor that can be defined is an empty one. It will create an instance of the class algorithm in a valid state. We then want the constructor to initialize all input parameters to their default values (or values that are known to generally give a good result). In our case, we decided that a distance of 100 is generally an acceptable tolerance. We also set a default target color. We chose black for no particular reason. The idea is to make sure we always start with predictable and valid input values:

```
      // empty constructor
      ColorDetector() : minDist(100) {

          // default parameter initialization here
          target[0]= target[1]= target[2]= 0;
      }
```

At this point, a user who creates an instance of our class algorithm can immediately call the process method with a valid image and obtain a valid output. This is another objective of the Strategy pattern, that is, to make sure the algorithm always runs with valid parameters. Obviously, a user of this class will want to use his own settings. This is done by providing the user with the appropriate getters and setters. Let's start by the color tolerance parameter:

```
      // Sets the color distance threshold.
      // Threshold must be positive,
      // otherwise distance threshold is set to 0.
      void setColorDistanceThreshold(int distance) {

          if (distance<0)
             distance=0;
          minDist= distance;
      }
      // Gets the color distance threshold
      int getColorDistanceThreshold() const {

          return minDist;
      }
```

Note how we first check the validity of the input. Again, this is to make sure that our algorithm will never be run in an invalid state. The target color can be set similarly:

```cpp
// Sets the color to be detected
void setTargetColor(unsigned char red,
                    unsigned char green,
                    unsigned char blue) {

    // BGR order
    target[2] = red;
    target[1] = green;
    target[0] = blue;
}
// Sets the color to be detected
void setTargetColor(cv::Vec3b color) {

    target= color;

}
// Gets the color to be detected
cv::Vec3b getTargetColor() const {

    return target;
}
```

This time it is interesting to note that we have provided the user with two definitions of the `setTagertColor` method. In the first one, the three color components are specified as three arguments, while in the second version, a `cv::Vec3b` is used to hold the color values. Again, the objective is to facilitate the use of our class algorithm. The user simply selects the setter that best fit the needs.

How it works...

Once an algorithm has been encapsulated into a class using the Strategy design pattern, it can be deployed by creating an instance of this class. Typically, the instance would be created when the program is initialized. The default value of the algorithm's parameters can be read and displayed. In the case of an application with a GUI, the parameter values can be read and set using different widgets (textfields, silders, and so on) so that a user can easily play with them. But before we introduce a GUI (this will be done later in this chapter), let's first write a simple main function that will run our color detection algorithm:

```cpp
int main()
{
    // 1. Create image processor object
    ColorDetector cdetect;

    // 2. Read input image
    cv::Mat image= cv::imread("boldt.jpg");
```

```
    if (!image.data)
        return 0;

    // 3. Set input parameters
    cdetect.setTargetColor(130,190,230); // here blue sky

    cv::namedWindow("result");

    // 4. Process the image and display the result
    cv::imshow("result",cdetect.process(image));

    cv::waitKey();

    return 0;
}
```

Running this program on the color version of the image presented in the previous chapter produces the following output:

Obviously, the algorithm we encapsulated in this class is relatively simple (just one scanning loop and one tolerance parameter). The Strategy design pattern becomes really powerful when the algorithm to be implemented is more complex, has many steps, and includes several parameters.

There's more...

To compute the distance between two color vectors, we used this simple formula:

```
    return abs(color[0]-target[0])+
           abs(color[1]-target[1])+
           abs(color[2]-target[2]);
```

However, OpenCV includes a function to compute the Euclidean norm of a vector. Consequently, we could have computed our distance as follows:

```
return static_cast<int>(
    cv::norm<int,3>(cv::Vec3i(color[0]-target[0],
                              color[1]-target[1],
                              color[2]-target[2])));
```

A very similar result would then be obtained using this definition of the `getDistance` method. Here, we use a `cv::Vec3i` (a 3-vector of integers) because the result of the subtraction is an integer value.

It is also interesting to recall from *Chapter 2* that the OpenCV matrix and vector data structures include a definition of the basic arithmetic operators. For example, if you want to add two `cv::Vec3i` vectors, `a` and `b`, and assign the result to `c`, you can simply write:

```
c= a+b;
```

Alternatively, one could have proposed the following definition for the distance computation:

```
return static_cast<int>(
    cv::norm<uchar,3>(color-target);
```

This definition may look right at first glance, however, it is wrong. This is because, all of these operators always include a call to `saturate_cast` (see recipe *Scanning an image with neighbor access* in the previous chapter) in order to make sure that the results stay within the domain of the input type (here, `uchar`). Therefore, in cases where the target value is greater than the corresponding color value, the value 0 will be assigned instead of the negative value one would have expected.

See also

The Policy-based class design introduced by *A. Alexandrescu*, is an interesting variant of the Strategy design pattern in which algorithms are selected at compile-time.

The book *Design Patterns*: *Elements of Reusable Object-Oriented Software* by *Erich Gamma et al, Addison-Wesley*, 1994, is one of the classic books on the subject.

Also see the *Building a GUI-based application using the Model-View-Controller pattern* recipe, to learn how to use the Strategy pattern in an application with a GUI.

Using a Controller to communicate with processing modules

As you will be building more complex applications, you will need to create multiple algorithms that can be combined together in order to accomplish some advanced tasks. Consequently, properly setting up the application, and having all classes communicating together, will become more and more complex. It then becomes advantageous to centralize the control of the application in a single class. This is the idea behind the **Controller**. It is a particular object in an application that plays an important role and we will explore it in this recipe.

Getting ready

Create a simple dialog-based application with two buttons, one to select an image and one to start the processing as seen below:

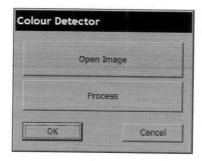

Here, we use the `ColorDetector` class of the previous recipe.

How to do it...

The role of the Controller is first to create the classes required to execute the application. Here, it is only one class. In addition, we need two member variables in order to hold a reference to the input and output results:

```
class ColorDetectController {

  private:

    // the algorithm class
    ColorDetector *cdetect;

    cv::Mat image;    // The image to be processed
    cv::Mat result;   // The image result

  public:

    ColorDetectController() {
```

```
        //setting up the application
        cdetect= new ColorDetector();
  }
```

You then need to define all of the setters and getters that a user would need to control the application:

```
        // Sets the color distance threshold
        void setColorDistanceThreshold(int distance) {

            cdetect->setColorDistanceThreshold(distance);
        }
        // Gets the color distance threshold
        int getColorDistanceThreshold() const {

            return cdetect->getColorDistanceThreshold();
        }
        // Sets the color to be detected
        void setTargetColor(unsigned char red,
            unsigned char green, unsigned char blue) {

            cdetect->setTargetColor(red,green,blue);
        }
        // Gets the color to be detected
        void getTargetColor(unsigned char &red,
            unsigned char &green, unsigned char &blue) const {

            cv::Vec3b color= cdetect->getTargetColor();

            red= color[2];
            green= color[1];
            blue= color[0];
        }
        // Sets the input image. Reads it from file.
        bool setInputImage(std::string filename) {

            image= cv::imread(filename);

            if (!image.data)
                return false;
            else
                return true;
        }
        // Returns the current input image.
        const cv::Mat getInputImage() const {

            return image;
        }
```

You also need a method that will be invoked to start the process:

```
// Performs image processing.
void process() {

    result= cdetect->process(image);
}
```

and a method to obtain the result of the processing:

```
// Returns the image result from the latest processing.
const cv::Mat getLastResult() const {

    return result;
}
```

Finally, it is important to clean up everything when the application terminates (and the controller is released):

```
// Deletes processor objects created by the controller.
~ColorDetectController() {

    delete cdetect;
}
```

How it works...

Using the Controller class above, a programmer can easily build an interface for an application that will execute your algorithm. There is no need for the programmer to understand how all of the classes are connected together, or to find out which methods in which class must called to have everything running properly. This is all done by the Controller class. The only requirement is to create an instance of that Controller class.

The setters and getters that are defined in the Controller are the ones that you would think are required to deploy your algorithm. These methods simply call the corresponding ones in the appropriate class. Again, the simple example here includes only one class algorithm, but in most cases, several class instances would be involved. Therefore, the role of the Controller is to redirect the request to the appropriate class and to simplify the interface to these classes. As an example of such simplifications, consider the methods `setTargetColor` and `getTargetColor`. They both use `uchar` to set and get the color of interest. This removes the necessity for the application programmer to know anything about the `cv::Vec3b` class.

In some cases, the Controller also prepares the data provided by the application programmer. This is what we did in the case of the `setInputImage` method, in which the image that corresponds to the given filename is loaded in memory. The method returns true or false depending on whether the loading operation was successful or not (one could also have thrown an exception to handle this situation).

Finally, the method `process` is the one that runs the algorithm. This method does not return the result and another method must be called in order to get the result of the latest processing performed.

Now, to create a very basic dialog-based application using this controller, you just add a `ColorDetectController` member variable to the dialog class (called `colordetect` here). In the case of a MFC dialog, the Open button would then look as follows:

```
// Callback method of "Open" button.
void OnOpen()
{
    // MFC widget to select a file of type bmp or jpg
    CFileDialog dlg(TRUE, _T("*.bmp"), NULL,
     OFN_FILEMUSTEXIST|OFN_PATHMUSTEXIST|OFN_HIDEREADONLY,
     _T("image files (*.bmp; *.jpg)
        |*.bmp;*.jpg|All Files (*.*)|*.*||"),NULL);

    dlg.m_ofn.lpstrTitle= _T("Open Image");

    // if a filename has been selected
    if (dlg.DoModal() == IDOK) {

      // get the path of the selected filename
      std::string filename= dlg.GetPathName();

      // set and display the input image
      colordetect.setInputImage(filename);
      cv::imshow("Input Image",colordetect.getInputImage());
    }
}
```

The second button executes the process and displays the result:

```
// Callback method of "Process" button.
void OnProcess()
{
    // target color is hard-coded here
    colordetect.setTargetColor(130,190,230);

    // process the input image and display result
    colordetect.process();
    cv::imshow("Output Result",colordetect.getLastResult());
}
```

Obviously, a more complete application would include additional widgets in order to allow the user to set the algorithm parameters.

See also

Also see the recipe *Building a GUI-based Application using the Model-View-Controller pattern* that presents a more expanded example of an application controlled by a GUI.

Using the Singleton design pattern

The **Singleton** is another popular design pattern that is used to facilitate access to a class instance and also to guarantee that only one instance of that class will exist during program execution. In this recipe, we use the Singleton to access a Controller object.

Getting ready

We use the `ColorDetectController` class of the previous recipe. This one will be modified in order to obtain a Singleton class.

How to do it...

The first thing to do is to add a private static member variable which will hold the reference to the single class instance. Also, in order to forbid the construction of additional class instances, the constructor is made private:

```
class ColorDetectController {

  private:

   // pointer to the singleton
    static ColorDetectController *singleton;

   ColorDetector *cdetect;

   // private constructor
   ColorDetectController() {

     //setting up the application
     cdetect= new ColorDetector();
   }
```

In addition, you can also make the copy constructor and the `operator=` private to make sure no one can create a copy of the Singleton's unique instance. The Singleton object is created on demand, when a user of the class asks for an instance of this class. This is done using a static method which creates the instance if it does not exist yet and then returns a pointer to this instance:

```
   // Gets access to Singleton instance
   static ColorDetectController *getInstance() {

     // Creates the instance at first call
```

```
    if (singleton == 0)
      singleton= new ColorDetectController;

    return singleton;
}
```

Note that this implementation of the Singleton is not thread-safe however. Therefore, it should not be used when concurrent threads need to access the Singleton instance.

Finally, since the Singleton instance has been created dynamically, the user must delete it when it is not required anymore. Again, this is done through a static method:

```
// Releases the singleton instance of this controller.
static void destroy() {

    if (singleton != 0) {
        delete singleton;
        singleton= 0;
    }
}
```

Since `singleton` is a static member variable, it must be defined in a `.cpp` file. This is done as follows:

```
#include "colorDetectController.h"

ColorDetectController *ColorDetectController::singleton=0;
```

How it works...

Since the Singleton can be obtained through a public static method, all classes that include the Singleton class declaration have access to the Singleton object. This is particularly useful for a Controller object that is accessed by several widget classes of some sophisticated GUI. There is no need for a member variable in one of the GUI class as was needed in the previous recipe. The two callback methods of the dialog class would then be written as follows:

```
// Callback method of "Open" button.
void OnOpen()
{
    ...

    // if a filename has beed selected
    if (dlg.DoModal() == IDOK) {

        // get the path of the selected filename
        std::string filename= dlg.GetPathName();

        // set and display the input image
        ColorDetectController::
            getInstance()->setInputImage(filename);
```

```
            cv::imshow("Input Image",
              ColorDetectController::
               getInstance()->getInputImage());
        }
    }
    // Callback method of "Process" button.
    OnProcess()
    {
        // target color is hard-coded here
        ColorDetectController::
          getInstance()->setTargetColor(130,190,230);

        // process the input image and display result
        ColorDetectController::getInstance()->process();
        cv::imshow("Output Result",
          ColorDetectController::getInstance()->getLastResult());
    }
```

and when the application is closed, the Singleton instance must be released:

```
    // Callback method of "Close" button.
    void OnClose()
    {
        // Releases the Singleton.
        ColorDetectController::getInstance()->destroy();
        OnOK();
    }
```

As shown here, when a Controller is encapsulated inside a Singleton, it becomes easier to obtain access to this instance from any class. However, a more serious implementation of this application would require a more elaborate GUI. This is done in next recipe which wraps up the discussion on the use of patterns in application design by presenting the Model-View-Controller architecture.

Using the Model-View-Controller architecture to design an application

The previous recipes let you discover three important design patterns: the Strategy, Controller, and Singleton patterns. This recipe introduces an architectural pattern in which these three patterns are used in combination with other classes. It is the **Model-View-Controller**, or **MVC**, that has the objective of producing an application that clearly separates the application logic from the user interface. In this recipe, we will use the MVC pattern to build a GUI-based application using Qt. However, before seeing it in action, let's give a brief description of the pattern.

Getting ready

As the name indicates, the MVC pattern involves three main components. We will now take a look at the role of each of them.

The **Model** contains the information concerning the application. It holds all of the data that is processed by the application. When new data is produced, it will inform the Controller, which in turn will ask the view to display the new results. Often, the Model will group together several algorithms, possibly implemented following the Strategy pattern. All of these algorithms are part of the Model.

The **View** corresponds to the user interface. It is composed of the different widgets that present the data to the user and allow the user to interact with the application. One of its roles is to send the commands issued by the user to the Controller. When new data is available, it refreshes itself in order to display the new information.

The **Controller** is the module that bridges the View and the Model together. It receives requests from the View and relays them to the appropriate methods in the model. It is also informed when the Model changes its state, and consequently asks the View to refresh in order to display this new information.

How to do it...

As we did in the previous recipes, we will use the `ColorDetector` class. This one will be our Model containing the application logic and underlying data. We have also implemented a Controller, it is the `ColorDetectController` class. It then becomes easy to build a more sophisticated GUI by choosing the most appropriate widget. For example, using Qt, one can build the following interface:

The **Open Image** button is used to select and open an image. The color to be detected can be selected by pushing the **Select Color** button. This one opens up a **Color Chooser** widget (printed below in black and white) that makes easy the selection of the desired color:

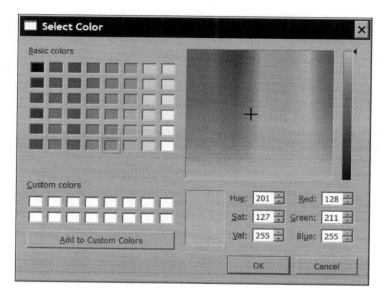

A slider is then used to select the right threshold to be used. Then, by pushing the **Process** button, the image is processed and the result is displayed.

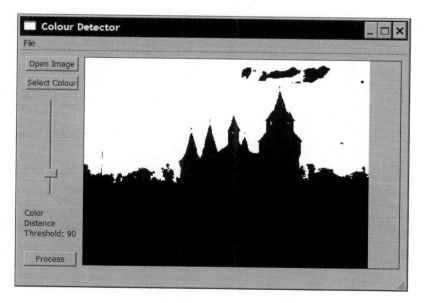

How it works...

Under the MVC architecture, the user interface simply calls the Controller methods. It does not contain any application data and does not implement any application logic. Consequently, it is easy to substitute an interface with another one. Here, a color chooser widget, the `QColorDialog`, has been added and once the color selected, the appropriate Controller method is called from the **Select Color** slot:

```
QColor color = QColorDialog::getColor(Qt::green, this);
if (color.isValid()) {
ColorDetectController::getInstance()
    ->setTargetColor(color.red(),color.green(),color.blue());
}
```

The threshold is set via the `QSlider` widget. This value is read when the **Process** button is clicked, which also triggers the processing and displays the result:

```
ColorDetectController::getInstance()
    ->setColorDistanceThreshold(
        ui->verticalSlider_Threshold->value());
ColorDetectController::getInstance()->process();
cv::Mat resulting =
    ColorDetectController::getInstance()->getLastResult();
if (!resulting.empty())
    displayMat(resulting);
```

In fact, the GUI library of Qt makes extensive use of the MVC pattern. It uses the concept of the concept of signals in order to keep all of the widgets of a GUI synchronized with the data model.

See also

The Qt online documentation can help you to learn more about Qt implementation of the MVC pattern (http://doc.qt.nokia.com).

The recipe *Creating a GUI application using Qt* of *Chapter 1* for a brief description of the Qt GUI framework and its signal and slot model.

Converting color spaces

This chapter taught you how to encapsulate an algorithm into a class. This way, the algorithm becomes easier to use through a simplified interface. Encapsulation also permits you to modify an algorithm's implementation without impacting the classes that use it. This principle is illustrated in this recipe where we will modify the `ColorDetector` class algorithm in order to use another color space. Therefore, this recipe will be an opportunity to introduce color conversion with OpenCV.

Getting ready

The RGB color space (or BGR depending on which order the colors are stored) is based on the use of the red, green, and blue additive primary colors. These have been selected because when they are combined they can produce a wide gamut of different colors. In fact, the human visual system is also based on a trichromatic perception of colors with cone cell sensitivity located around the red, green, and blue spectrum. It is often the default color space in digital imagery because that is the way they are acquired. Captured light goes through red, green, and blue filters. Additionally, in digital images, the red, green, and blue channels are adjusted such that when combined in equal amounts, a gray-level intensity is obtained, that is, from black (0,0,0) to white (255,255,255).

Unfortunately, computing the distance between colors using the RGB color space is not the best way to measure the similarity of two given colors. Indeed, RGB is not a **perceptually uniform color space**. This means that two colors at a given distance might look very similar, while two other colors separated by the same distance will look very different.

To solve this problem, other color spaces having the property of being perceptually uniform have been introduced. In particular, the CIE L*a*b* is one such color space. By converting our images to this space, the Euclidean distance between an image pixel and the target color will then meaningfully be a measure of the visual similarity between the two colors. We will show in this recipe how we can modify the previous application in order to work with the CIE L*a*b*.

How to do it...

Converting between different color spaces is easily done through the use of the OpenCV function `cv::cvtColor`. Let's convert the input image to CIE L*a*b* color space at the beginning of the process method:

```
cv::Mat ColorDetector::process(const cv::Mat &image) {
    // re-allocate binary map if necessary
    // same size as input image, but 1-channel
    result.create(image.rows,image.cols,CV_8U);
    // re-allocate intermediate image if necessary
    converted.create(image.rows,image.cols,image.type());
    // Converting to Lab color space
    cv::cvtColor(image, converted, CV_BGR2Lab);
    // get the iterators of the converted image
    cv::Mat_<cv::Vec3b>::iterator it=
            converted.begin<cv::Vec3b>();
    cv::Mat_<cv::Vec3b>::iterator itend=
            converted.end<cv::Vec3b>();
    // get the iterator of the output image
```

```
cv::Mat_<uchar>::iterator itout= result.begin<uchar>();

// for each pixel
for ( ; it!= itend; ++it, ++itout) {
    ...
```

The variable `converted` contains the image after color conversion. In the `ColorDetector` class, it is defined as a class attribute:

```
class ColorDetector {

  private:
      // image containing color converted image
      cv::Mat converted;
```

We also need to convert the input target color. We do this by creating a temporary image containing only 1 pixel. Note that you need to keep the same signature as in the previous recipes, that is, the user continues to supply the target color in RGB:

```
// Sets the color to be detected
void setTargetColor(unsigned char red,
        unsigned char green, unsigned char blue) {

    // Temporary 1-pixel image
    cv::Mat tmp(1,1,CV_8UC3);
    tmp.at<cv::Vec3b>(0,0)[0]= blue;
    tmp.at<cv::Vec3b>(0,0)[1]= green;
    tmp.at<cv::Vec3b>(0,0)[2]= red;

        // Converting the target to Lab color space
    cv::cvtColor(tmp, tmp, CV_BGR2Lab);

    target= tmp.at<cv::Vec3b>(0,0);
}
```

If the application of the preceding recipe is compiled with this modified class, it will now detect the pixels of the target color using the CIE L*a*b* color space.

How it works...

When an image is converted from one color space to another, a linear or non-linear transformation is applied on each input pixel to produce the output pixels. The pixel type of the output image will match the one of the input image. Even if most of the time you work with 8-bit pixels, you can also use color conversion with images of floats (in which case, pixel values are generally assumed to vary between 0 and 1.0) or with integer images (with pixel generally varying between 0 and 65535). But the exact domain of the pixel values depends on the specific color space. For example, with the CIE L*a*b* color space, the L channel varies between 0 and 100, while the a and b chromaticity components vary between -127 and 127.

Most commonly used color spaces are available. It is just a question of providing the right mask to the OpenCV function. Among them is the YCrCb, which is the color space used in JPEG compression. To convert from BGR to YCrCb, the mask would be `CV_BGR2YCrCb`. Note that the representation with the three regular primary colors, red, green, and blue, is available in the RGB order or BRG order.

The HSV and HLS color spaces are also interesting because they decompose the colors into their hue and saturation components, plus the value or luminance component, which is a more natural way for humans to describe colors.

You can also convert color images to gray-level. The output will be a 1-channel image:

```
cv::cvtColor(color, gray, CV_BGR2Gray);
```

It is also possible to do the conversion in the other direction, but the 3 channels of the resulting color image will then be identically filled with the corresponding values in the gray-level image.

See also

The recipe *Using the mean shift algorithm* to *find an object* in *Chapter 4* that uses the HSV color space in order to find an object in an image.

Many good references are available on color space theory. Among them, the following is a complete and up-to-date reference, *The Structure and Properties of Color Spaces and the Representation of Color Images* by E. Dubois, Morgan and Claypool, Oct. 2009.

4
Counting the Pixels with Histograms

In this chapter, we will cover:

- ▶ Computing the image histogram
- ▶ Applying look-up tables to modify image appearance
- ▶ Equalizing the image histogram
- ▶ Backprojecting a histogram to detect specific image content
- ▶ Using the mean shift algorithm to find an object
- ▶ Retrieving similar images using histogram comparison

Introduction

An image is composed of pixels of different values (colors). The distribution of pixels values across the image constitutes an important characteristic of this image. This chapter introduces the concept of image histograms. You will learn how to compute a histogram and how to use it to modify the image's appearance. Histograms can also be used to characterize the image's content and to detect specific objects or textures in an image. Some of these techniques will be presented in this chapter.

Computing the image histogram

An image is made of pixels, each of them having different values. For example, in a 1-channel gray-level image, each pixel has a value between 0 (black) and 255 (white). Depending on the picture content, you will find different amounts of each gray shade laid out inside the image.

A **histogram** is a simple table that gives the number of pixels that have a given value in an image (or sometime a set of images). The histogram of a gray-level image will therefore have 256 entries (or **bins**). Bin 0 gives the number of pixels having value 0, bin 1 the number of pixels having value 1, and so on. Obviously, if you sum all of the entries of a histogram, you should get the total number of pixels. Histograms can also be normalized such that sum of the bins equals 1. In that case, each bin gives the percentage of pixels having this specific value in the image.

Getting started

Define a simple console project and have an image like the following ready to be used:

How to do it...

Computing a histogram with OpenCV can be easily done by using the `cv::calcHist` function. This is a general function which can compute the histogram of multiple channel images of any pixel value type. Let's make it simpler to use by specializing a class for the case of 1-channel gray-level images:

```
class Histogram1D {

  private:

      int histSize[1];   // number of bins
      float hranges[2]; // min and max pixel value
      const float* ranges[1];
      int channels[1];   // only 1 channel used here

  public:

    Histogram1D() {

        // Prepare arguments for 1D histogram
        histSize[0]= 256;
        hranges[0]= 0.0;
```

```
      hranges[1]= 255.0;
      ranges[0]= hranges;
      channels[0]= 0; // by default, we look at channel 0
}
```

With the defined member variables, computing a gray-level histogram can then be accomplished using the following method:

```
// Computes the 1D histogram.
cv::MatND getHistogram(const cv::Mat &image) {

    cv::MatND hist;

    // Compute histogram
    cv::calcHist(&image,
        1,              // histogram from 1 image only
        channels,   // the channel used
        cv::Mat(), // no mask is used
        hist,          // the resulting histogram
        1,              // it is a 1D histogram
        histSize,   // number of bins
        ranges      // pixel value range
    );

    return hist;
}
```

Now, your program simply needs to open an image, create a `Histogram1D` instance, and to call the `getHistogram` method:

```
// Read input image
cv::Mat image= cv::imread("../group.jpg",
                          0); // open in b&w

// The histogram object
Histogram1D h;

// Compute the histogram
cv::MatND histo= h.getHistogram(image);
```

The `histo` object here is a simple one-dimensional array with 256 entries. Therefore, you can read each bin by simply looping over this array:

```
// Loop over each bin
for (int i=0; i<256; i++)
    cout << "Value " << i << " = " <<
                histo.at<float>(i) << endl;
```

With the image shown at the start of this chapter, some of the displayed values would read as:

```
. . .
Value 7 = 159
Value 8 = 208
Value 9 = 271
Value 10 = 288
Value 11 = 340
Value 12 = 418
Value 13 = 432
Value 14 = 472
Value 15 = 525
. . .
```

It is obviously difficult to extract any intuitive meaning from this sequence of values. For this reason, it is often convenient to display a histogram as a function, for example, using bar graphs. The following method creates such a graph:

```cpp
// Computes the 1D histogram and returns an image of it.
cv::Mat getHistogramImage(const cv::Mat &image){

    // Compute histogram first
    cv::MatND hist= getHistogram(image);

    // Get min and max bin values
    double maxVal=0;
    double minVal=0;
    cv::minMaxLoc(hist, &minVal, &maxVal, 0, 0);

    // Image on which to display histogram
    cv::Mat histImg(histSize[0], histSize[0],
                    CV_8U,cv::Scalar(255));

    // set highest point at 90% of nbins
    int hpt = static_cast<int>(0.9*histSize[0]);

    // Draw a vertical line for each bin
    for( int h = 0; h < histSize[0]; h++ ) {

        float binVal = hist.at<float>(h);
        int intensity = static_cast<int>(binVal*hpt/maxVal);

        // This function draws a line between 2 points
        cv::line(histImg,cv::Point(h,histSize[0]),
                         cv::Point(h,histSize[0]-intensity),
                         cv::Scalar::all(0));
    }

    return histImg;
}
```

Using this method, you can obtain an image of the histogram function in the form of a bar graph drawn using lines:

```
// Display a histogram as an image
cv::namedWindow("Histogram");
cv::imshow("Histogram",
          h.getHistogramImage(image));
```

The result is the following image:

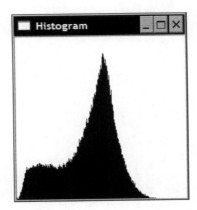

From this histogram, it can be seen that the image exhibits a large peak of mid-gray level values and a good quantity of darker pixels. These two groups mostly correspond to, respectively, the background and foreground of the image. This can be verified by thresholding the image at the transition between these two groups. A convenient OpenCV function can be used for this, namely, the cv::threshold function. This is the function to use when a threshold must be applied on an image in order to create a binary image. Here, we threshold the image at the minimum value just before the increase toward the high peak of the histogram (gray value 60):

```
cv::Mat thresholded;
cv::threshold(image,thresholded,60,255,cv::THRESH_BINARY);
```

The resulting binary image clearly shows the background/foreground segmentation:

How it works...

Function `cv::calcHist` has many parameters to permit its use in many contexts. Most of the time, your histogram will be one of a single 1-channel or 3-channel image. However, the function allows you to specify a multiple-channel image distributed over several images. This is why an array of images is input into this function. The 6th parameter specifies the dimensionality of the histogram, for example, 1 for a 1D histogram. The channels to be considered in the histogram computation are listed in an array having the specified dimensionality. In our class implementation, this single channel is by default the channel 0 (third parameter). The histogram itself is described by the number of bins in each dimension (seventh parameter, an array of integer) and by the minimum and maximum values in each dimension (eighth parameter, an array of 2-element arrays). It is also possible to define a non-uniform histogram in which case you need to specify the limits of each bin.

As for many OpenCV functions, a mask can be specified, indicating which pixels you want to include in the count (all pixels for which the mask value is 0 are then ignored). Two additional optional parameters can be specified, both which are Boolean values. The first one indicates if the histogram is uniform or not (uniform is the default). The second allows you to accumulate the result of several histogram computations. If this last parameter is true, then the pixel count of the image will be added to the current values found in the input histogram. This is useful when one wants to compute the histogram of a group of images.

The resulting histogram is stored in a `cv::MatND` instance. This is a general class used to manipulate N-dimensional matrices. Conveniently, this class has defined the `at` method for matrices of dimension 1, 2, and 3. This is why we were able to write:

```
float binVal = hist.at<float>(h);
```

when accessing each bin of the 1D histogram in the `getHistogramImage` method. Note that the values in the histogram are stored as `floats`.

There's more...

The class `Histogram1D` presented in this recipe has simplified the `cv::calcHist` function by restricting it to 1D histogram. This is useful for gray-level images. Similarly, we can define a class that could be used to compute histograms of color BGR images:

```
class ColorHistogram {

  private:

     int histSize[3];
     float hranges[2];
     const float* ranges[3];
     int channels[3];

  public:

   ColorHistogram() {

       // Prepare arguments for a color histogram
       histSize[0]= histSize[1]= histSize[2]= 256;
       hranges[0]= 0.0;      // BRG range
       hranges[1]= 255.0;
       ranges[0]= hranges;  // all channels have the same range
       ranges[1]= hranges;
       ranges[2]= hranges;
       channels[0]= 0;        // the three channels
       channels[1]= 1;
       channels[2]= 2;
   }
```

In this case, the histogram will be three-dimensional. Therefore, we need to specify a range for each of the three dimensions. In the case of a BGR image, the three channels have the same [0,255] range. With the arguments thus prepared, the color histogram is computed by the following method:

```
cv::MatND getHistogram(const cv::Mat &image) {

    cv::MatND hist;

    // Compute histogram
    cv::calcHist(&image,
        1,              // histogram of 1 image only
        channels,    // the channel used
        cv::Mat(),    // no mask is used
        hist,          // the resulting histogram
        3,              // it is a 3D histogram
```

```
        histSize,    // number of bins
        ranges       // pixel value range
    );

    return hist;
}
```

A three-dimensional `cv::Mat` instance is returned. This matrix has (256)*3 elements which represents more than 16 million entries. In many applications, it would be better to reduce the number of colors before computing such a large histogram (see *Chapter 2*). Alternatively, you can also use the `cv::SparseMat` data structure that is designed to represent large sparse matrices (that is, matrices with very few non-zero elements) without consuming too much memory. The `cv::calcHist` function has a version returning one such matrix. It is therefore simple to modify the previous method to use `cv::SparseMatrix`:

```
cv::SparseMat getSparseHistogram(const cv::Mat &image) {

    cv::SparseMat hist(3,histSize,CV_32F);

    // Compute histogram
    cv::calcHist(&image,
        1,              // histogram of 1 image only
        channels,       // the channel used
        cv::Mat(),      // no mask is used
        hist,           // the resulting histogram
        3,              // it is a 3D histogram
        histSize,       // number of bins
        ranges          // pixel value range
    );

    return hist;
}
```

See also

The recipe *Backprojecting a histogram to detect specific image content* later in this chapter that will make use of color histograms in order to detect specific image content.

Applying look-up tables to modify image appearance

Image histograms capture the way a scene is rendered using the available pixel intensity values. By analyzing the distribution of the pixel values over an image, it is possible to use this information to modify and possibly improve an image. This recipe explains how one can use a simple mapping function, represented by a look-up table, to modify the pixel values of an image.

How to do it...

A **look-up table** is a simple one-to-one (or many-to-one) function that defines how pixel values are transformed into new values. It is a 1D array with, in the case of regular gray-level images, 256 entries. Entry i of the table gives the new intensity value of the corresponding gray level, that is:

```
newIntensity= lookup[oldIntensity];
```

Function cv::LUT in OpenCV applies a look-up table to an image in order to produce a new image. We can add this function to our Histogram1D class:

```
cv::Mat applyLookUp(const cv::Mat& image, // input image
    const cv::Mat& lookup) { // 1x256 uchar matrix

    // the output image
    cv::Mat result;

    // apply lookup table
    cv::LUT(image,lookup,result);

    return result;
}
```

How it works...

When a look-up table is applied on an image, it results in a new image where the pixel intensity values have been modified as prescribed by the look-up table. A simple transformation like this could be the following:

```
// Create an image inversion table
int dim(256);
cv::Mat lut(1,   // 1 dimension
    &dim,        // 256 entries
    CV_8U);      // uchar
for (int i=0; i<256; i++) {
    lut.at<uchar>(i)= 255-i;
}
```

This transformation simply inverts the pixel intensities, that is, intensity 0 becomes 255, 1 becomes 254, and so on. Applying such a look-up table on an image will produce the negative of the original image. On the image of the previous recipe, the result is seen here:

There's more...

You can also define a look-up table that tries to improve an image's contrast. For example, if you observe the original histogram of the previous image shown in the first recipe, it is easy to notice that the full range of possible intensity values is not used (in particular, for this image, the brighter intensity values are not used in the image). One can therefore **stretch** the histogram in order to produce an image with an expanded contrast. The procedure is designed to detect the lowest (imin) and the highest (imax) intensity value with non-zero count in the image histogram. The intensity values can then be remapped such that the imin value is repositioned at intensity 0, and the imax is assigned value 255. The in-between intensities i are simply linearly remapped as follows:

```
255.0*(i-imin)/(imax-imin)+0.5);
```

Consequently, the complete image stretch method would look as follows:

```
cv::Mat stretch(const cv::Mat &image, int minValue=0) {
    // Compute histogram first
    cv::MatND hist= getHistogram(image);
    // find left extremity of the histogram
    int imin= 0;
    for( ; imin < histSize[0]; imin++ ) {
        std::cout<<hist.at<float>(imin)<<std::endl;
        if (hist.at<float>(imin) > minValue)
            break;
```

```
    }
    // find right extremity of the histogram
    int imax= histSize[0]-1;
    for( ; imax >= 0; imax-- ) {
        if (hist.at<float>(imax) > minValue)
            break;
    }
    // Create lookup table
    int dim(256);
    cv::Mat lookup(1,   // 1 dimension
            &dim,        // 256 entries
            CV_8U);      // uchar
    // Build lookup table
    for (int i=0; i<256; i++) {
        // stretch between imin and imax
        if (i < imin) lookup.at<uchar>(i)= 0;
        else if (i > imax) lookup.at<uchar>(i)= 255;
        // linear mapping
        else lookup.at<uchar>(i)= static_cast<uchar>(
                        255.0*(i-imin)/(imax-imin)+0.5);
    }
    // Apply lookup table
    cv::Mat result;
    result= applyLookUp(image,lookup);

    return result;
}
```

Note the call to our `applyLookUp` method once this one has been computed. Also, in practice, it could be advantageous to not only ignore bins with 0 value, but also entries with negligible count, for example, less than a given value (defined here as `minValue`). The method is called as follows:

```
// ignore starting and ending bins with less than 100 pixels
cv::Mat streteched= h.stretch(image,100);
```

The resulting image is then seen here:

With the following expanded histogram as seen in the following screenshot:

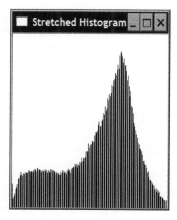

See also

The *Equalizing the image histogram* recipe shows you another way to improve the image contrast.

Equalizing the image histogram

In the previous recipe, we showed how the contrast of an image can be improved by stretching a histogram so that it occupies the full range of available intensity values. This strategy indeed constitutes an easy fix which can effectively improve an image. However, in many cases, the visual deficiency of an image is not that it uses too narrow a range of intensities. Rather, it is that some intensity values are used more frequently than others. The histogram shown in the first recipe of this chapter is a good example of this phenomenon. The middle-gray intensities are indeed heavily represented, while darker and brighter pixel values are rather rare. In fact, one can think that a good-quality image should make equal use of all available pixel intensities. This is the idea behind the concept of **histogram equalization**, that is making the image histogram as flat as possible.

How to do it...

OpenCV offers an easy-to-use function that performs histogram equalization. It can be called as follows:

```
cv::Mat equalize(const cv::Mat &image) {

    cv::Mat result;
    cv::equalizeHist(image,result);

    return result;
}
```

Applied on our image, the following screenshot is the result:

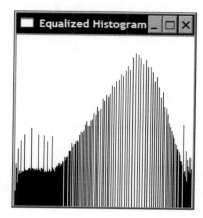

Of course, the histogram cannot be perfectly flat because the look-up table is a global many-to-one transformation. However, it can be seen that the general distribution of the histogram is now more uniform than the original one.

How it works...

In a perfectly uniform histogram, all bins have an equal number of pixels. This implies that 50% of the pixels have an intensity lower than 128, 25% have an intensity lower than 64, and so on. This observation can be expressed using the following rule: in a uniform histogram, *p%* of the pixels must have an intensity value lower than or equal to *255*p%*. This is the rule used to equalize a histogram: the mapping of intensity i should be at the intensity that corresponds to the percentage of pixels having an intensity value below i. Therefore, the required look-up table can be built from the following equation:

```
lookup.at<uchar>(i)= static_cast<uchar>(255.0*p[i]);
```

where p[i] is the number of pixels having an intensity lower than or equal to i. The function p[i] is often referred as a **cumulative histogram**, that is, it is a histogram that contains the count of pixels lower than or equal to a given intensity, instead of containing the count of pixels having a specific intensity value.

Generally, histogram equalization greatly improves the image's appearance. However, depending on the visual content, the quality of the result can vary from image to image.

Backprojecting a histogram to detect specific image content

A histogram is an important characteristic of an image's content. If you look at an image area showing a particular texture or a particular object, then the histogram of this area can be seen as a function giving the probability that a given pixel belongs to this specific texture or object. In this recipe, you will learn how the image histogram can be advantageously used to detect specific image content.

How to do it...

Suppose you have an image and you wish to detect specific content inside it (for example, in the following screenshot, the clouds in the sky). The first thing to do is to select a region of interest which contains a sample of what you are looking for. This region is the one inside the rectangle drawn on the following test screenshot:

In our program, the region of interest is obtained as follows:

```
cv::Mat imageROI;
imageROI= image(cv::Rect(360,55,40,50)); // Cloud region
```

You then extract the histogram of this ROI. This is easily accomplished using the Histogram1D class defined in the first recipe of this chapter:

```
Histogram1D h;
cv::MatND hist= h.getHistogram(imageROI);
```

By normalizing this histogram, we obtain a function that gives the probability of a pixel of a given intensity value to belong to the defined area:

```
cv::normalize(histogram,histogram,1.0);
```

Backprojecting a histogram consists in replacing each pixel value in an input image by its corresponding probability value read in the normalized histogram.

```
cv::calcBackProject(&image,
        1,              // one image
        channels,       // the channels used
        histogram,      // the histogram we are backprojecting
        result,         // the resulting back projection image
        ranges,         // the range of values, for each dimension
        255.0           // a scaling factor
);
```

The result is the following probability map, with probabilities from bright (low probability) to dark (high probability) of belonging to the reference area:

If we apply a threshold on this image, we obtain the most probable "cloud" pixels:

```
cv::threshold(result, result, 255*threshold,
                255, cv::THRESH_BINARY);
```

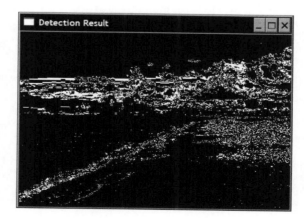

How it works...

The preceding result can be disappointing because, in addition to the clouds, other areas have been wrongly detected as well. It is important to understand that the probability function has been extracted from a simple gray-level histogram. Many other pixels in the image share the same intensities as the cloud pixels, and pixels of same intensity are replaced by the same probability value when backprojecting the histogram. One solution to improve the detection result would be to use color information. But in order to do this, we need to modify the call to cv::calBackProject.

Function cv::calBackProject is similar to the cv::calcHist function. The first parameter specifies the input image. You then need to list the channel numbers you wish to use. The histogram that is passed to the function is, this time, an input parameter. It should be normalized, and its dimension should match one of the channel list arrays, as well as one of the ranges parameters. This later is, as in cv::calcHist, an array of float arrays, each specifying the range (min and max values) of each channel. The resulting output is an image, the computed probability map. Since each pixel is replaced by the value found in the histogram at the corresponding bin position, the resulting image has values between 0.0 and 1.0 (assuming a normalized histogram has been provided as input). A last parameter allows you to optionally rescale these values by multiplying them by a given factor.

There's more...

Let's now see how we can use color information in the histogram backprojection algorithm. We first define a class that encapsulates the backprojection process. First, we define the required attributes and initialize the data:

```
class ContentFinder {

  private:

    float hranges[2];
    const float* ranges[3];
    int channels[3];

    float threshold;
    cv::MatND histogram;

  public:

  ContentFinder() : threshold(-1.0f) {

      ranges[0]= hranges; // all channels have same range
      ranges[1]= hranges;
      ranges[2]= hranges;
  }
```

Next, we define a threshold parameter that will be used to create the binary map showing the detection result. If this parameter is set to a negative value, the raw probability map will be returned:

```
// Sets the threshold on histogram values [0,1]
void setThreshold(float t) {

    threshold= t;
}
// Gets the threshold
float getThreshold() {

    return threshold;
}
```

The input histogram must be normalized:

```
// Sets the reference histogram
void setHistogram(const cv::MatND& h) {

    histogram= h;
    cv::normalize(histogram,histogram,1.0);
}
```

To backproject the histogram, you simply need to specify the image, the range (we assumed here that all channels have the same range), and the list of channels used:

```
cv::Mat find(const cv::Mat& image,
             float minValue, float maxValue,
             int *channels, int dim) {

    cv::Mat result;

    hranges[0]= minValue;
    hranges[1]= maxValue;

    for (int i=0; i<dim; i++)
        this->channels[i]= channels[i];

    cv::calcBackProject(&image, 1, // input image
            channels,         // list of channels used
            histogram,        // the histogram we are using
            result,           // the resulting backprojection
            ranges,           // the range of values
            255.0             // the scaling factor
    );
}

// Threshold back projection to obtain a binary image
if (threshold>0.0)
        cv::threshold(result, result,
```

```
                    255*threshold, 255, cv::THRESH_BINARY);

        return result;
    }
```

Let's now use a BGR histogram on the color version of the image we used above. This time, we will try to detect the blue sky area. We will first load the color image, reduce the number of color using the color reduction function of *Chapter 2*, and define the region of interest:

```
ColorHistogram hc;
// load color image
cv::Mat color= cv::imread("../waves.jpg");
// reduce colors
color= hc.colorReduce(color,32);
// blue sky area
cv::Mat imageROI= color(cv::Rect(0,0,165,75));
```

Next, you compute the histogram and use the find method to detect the sky portion of the image:

```
cv::MatND hist= hc.getHistogram(imageROI);

ContentFinder finder;
finder.setHistogram(hist);
finder.setThreshold(0.05f);

// Get back-projection of color histogram
Cv::Mat result= finder.find(color);
```

The result of the detection on the color version of the image, of the previous section is seen here:

See also

The next recipe will use the HSV color space to detect an object in an image. This is another of the many alternative solutions you can use in the detection of some image content.

Using the mean shift algorithm to find an object

The result of a histogram backprojection is a probability map that expresses the probability that a given image content is found at a specific image location. Suppose we now know the approximate location of an object in an image, the probability map can be used to find the exact location of the object. The most probable will be the one that maximizes this probability inside a given window. Therefore, if we start from an initial, location and iteratively move around, it should be possible to find the exact object location. This is what is accomplished by the mean shift algorithm.

How to do it...

Suppose we have identified an object of interest, here, a baboon's face, as shown in the following color screenshot (see the book's website to see this image in color):

This time, we will describe this object by using the hue channel of the HSV color space. This means we need to convert the image into an HSV one, then extract the hue channel and compute the 1D hue histogram of the defined ROI:

```
// Read reference image
cv::Mat image= cv::imread("../baboon1.jpg");
// Baboon's face ROI
cv::Mat imageROI= image(cv::Rect(110,260,35,40));
// Get the Hue histogram
int minSat=65;
ColorHistogram hc;
cv::MatND colorhist=
        hc.getHueHistogram(imageROI,minSat);
```

As it can be seen, the hue histogram is obtained using a convenient method that we have added to our ColorHistogram class:

```
// Computes the 1D Hue histogram with a mask.
// BGR source image is converted to HSV
// Pixels with low saturation are ignored
cv::MatND getHueHistogram(const cv::Mat &image,
                          int minSaturation=0) {

    cv::MatND hist;

    // Convert to HSV color space
    cv::Mat hsv;
    cv::cvtColor(image, hsv, CV_BGR2HSV);

    // Mask to be used (or not)
    cv::Mat mask;

    if (minSaturation>0) {

        // Spliting the 3 channels into 3 images
        std::vector<cv::Mat> v;
        cv::split(hsv,v);

        // Mask out the low saturated pixels
        cv::threshold(v[1],mask,minSaturation,255,
                              cv::THRESH_BINARY);
    }

    // Prepare arguments for a 1D hue histogram
    hranges[0]= 0.0;
    hranges[1]= 180.0;
    channels[0]= 0; // the hue channel

    // Compute histogram
    cv::calcHist(&hsv,
        1,              // histogram of 1 image only
```

```
            channels,    // the channel used
            mask,        // binary mask
            hist,        // the resulting histogram
            1,           // it is a 1D histogram
            histSize,    // number of bins
            ranges       // pixel value range
        );

        return hist;
    }
```

The resulting histogram is then input into our `ContentFinder` class instance:

```
        ContentFinder finder;
        finder.setHistogram(colorhist);
```

Let's now open a second image where we want to locate the new baboon's face position. This image needs to be converted to the HSV space:

```
        image= cv::imread("../baboon3.jpg");

        // Display image
        cv::namedWindow("Image 2");
        cv::imshow("Image 2",image);

        // Convert to HSV space
        cv::cvtColor(image, hsv, CV_BGR2HSV);

        // Split the image
        cv::split(hsv,v);

        // Identify pixels with low saturation
        cv::threshold(v[1],v[1],minSat,255,cv::THRESH_BINARY);
```

Next, let's obtain the backprojection of the hue channel of this image using the previously obtained histogram:

```
        // Get back-projection of hue histogram
        result= finder.find(hsv,0.0f,180.0f,ch,1);
        // Eliminate low stauration pixels
        cv::bitwise_and(result,v[1],result);
```

Now, from an initial rectangular area (that is, the position of the baboon's face in the initial image), the `cv::meanShift` algorithm of OpenCV will update the `rect` object at the new baboon face location:

```
        cv::Rect rect(110,260,35,40);
        cv::rectangle(image, rect, cv::Scalar(0,0,255));

        cv::TermCriteria criteria(cv::TermCriteria::MAX_ITER,
                                  10,0.01);
        cv::meanShift(result,rect,criteria);
```

The initial and new face locations are displayed in the following screenshot:

How it works...

In this example, we used the hue component of the HSV color space in order to characterize the object we were looking for. Therefore, the image must be converted first. The hue component being the first channel of the resulting image when the CV_BGR2HSV flag is used. This is an 8-bit component in which the hue varies from 0 to 180 (with cv::cvtColor, the converted image is of the same type as the source image). In order to extract the hue image, the 3-channel HSV image is split into three 1-channel images using the cv::split function. The three images are put into an std::vector instance, and the hue image is the first entry of the vector (that is at index 0).

When using the hue component of a color, it is always important to take its saturation into account (which is the second entry of the vector). Indeed, when the saturation of a color is low, the hue information becomes unstable and unreliable. This is due to the fact that for low-saturated color, the B, G, and R components are almost equal. This makes it difficult to determine the exact color represented. In consequence, we decided to ignore the hue component of colors with low saturation. That is, they are not counted in the histogram (using the parameter `minSat` that masks out pixels with saturation below this threshold in method `getHueHistogram`) and they are eliminated from the backprojection result (using the `cv::bitwise_and` operator that eliminates all positive detection pixels having low-saturated colors just before calling `cv::meanShift`).

The mean shift algorithm is an iterative procedure which locates the local maxima of a probability function. It does it by finding the centroid, or weighted mean, of the data point inside a predefined window. The algorithm then moves the window center to the centroid location and repeats the procedure until the window center converges to a stable point. The OpenCV implementation defines two stopping criteria: a maximum number of iterations and a window center displacement value below which the position is considered to have converged to a stable point. These two criteria are stored in a `cv::TermCriteria` instance. The `cv::meanShift` function returns the number of iterations performed. Obviously, the quality of the result depends on the quality of the probability map provided, and on the given initial position.

See also

The mean shift algorithm has been largely used for visual tracking. *Chapter 10* will explore the problem of object tracking in more detail.

OpenCV also offers an implementation of the CamShift algorithm that is an improved version of mean-shift in which the size and the orientation of the window can change.

Retrieving similar images using histogram comparison

Content-based image retrieval is an important problem in computer vision. It consists of finding a set of images presenting content similar to a given query image. Since we have learned that histograms constitute an effective way to characterize an image's content, it makes sense to think that they can be used to solve the content-based retrieval problem.

The key here is to be able to measure the similarity between two images by simply comparing their histograms. A measurement function which will estimate how different, or how similar, two histograms are will need to be defined. Various such measures have been proposed in the past, and OpenCV proposes few of them in its implementation of the `cv::compareHist` function.

How to do it...

In order to compare a reference image with a collection of images and find the ones that are the most similar to this query image, we created an `ImageComparator` class. This one contains a reference to a query image, and to an input image, together with their histograms (`cv::MatND` instances). In addition, since we will perform the comparison using color histograms, the `ColorHistogram` class is used:

```
class ImageComparator {

  private:

    cv::Mat reference;
    cv::Mat input;
    cv::MatND refH;
    cv::MatND inputH;

    ColorHistogram hist;
    int div;

  public:

    ImageComparator() : div(32) {

    }
```

To get a reliable similarity measure, the number of colors must be reduced. Therefore, the class includes a color reduction factor that will be applied to both the query and the input images:

```
    // Color reduction factor
    // The comparison will be made on images with
    // color space reduced by this factor in each dimension
    void setColorReduction( int factor) {

        div= factor;
    }
    int getColorReduction() {

        return div;
    }
```

The query image is specified using an appropriate setter that also color-reduces the image:

```
    void setReferenceImage(const cv::Mat& image) {

        reference= hist.colorReduce(image,div);
        refH= hist.getHistogram(reference);
    }
```

Finally, a `compare` method compares the reference image with a given input image. The method returns a score indicating how similar the two images are.

```
double compare(const cv::Mat& image) {

    input= hist.colorReduce(image,div);
    inputH= hist.getHistogram(input);

    return cv::compareHist(
                    refH,inputH,CV_COMP_INTERSECT);
    }
};
```

This class can be used to retrieve images similar to a given query image. This latter being initially provided to the class instance:

```
ImageComparator c;
c.setReferenceImage(image);
```

Here, the query image we used is the color version of the beach image shown in recipe *Backprojecting a histogram* to *detect specific image content* earlier in this chapter. This image was compared to a series of images shown below. The images are shown from the most similar, to the least:

How it works...

Most histogram comparison measures are based on a bin-by-bin comparison, that is, the neighboring bins are not used when comparing histograms' bins. Therefore, it important to reduce the color space before measuring the similarity of two color histograms. Other color spaces could be used as well.

The call to `cv::compareHist` is straightforward. You just input the two histograms and the function returns the measured distance. The specific measurement method you want to use is specified using a flag. In the `ImageComparator` class, the intersection method is used (with flag `CV_COMP_INTERSECT`). This method simply compares, for each bin, the two values in each histogram, and keeps the minimum one. The similarity measure is then simply the sum of these minimum values. Consequently, two images having histograms with no colors in common would get an intersection value of 0, while two identical histograms would get a value equal to the total number of pixels.

The other methods available are the Chi-Square (flag `CV_COMP_CHISQR`) which sums the normalized square difference between the bins, the correlation method (flag `CV_COMP_CORREL`) which is based on the normalized cross-correlation operator used in signal processing to measure the similarity between two signals, and the Bhattacharyya measure (flag `CV_COMP_BHATTACHARYYA`) used in statistics to estimate the similarity between two probabilistic distributions.

See also

The OpenCV documentation for a description of the exact formulas used in the different histogram comparison measures.

The Earth Mover Distance, which is also another popular histogram comparison method. The main advantage of this method is that it takes into account the values found in adjacent bins to evaluate the similarity of two histograms. It is described in the article *The Earth Mover's Distance as a Metric for Image Retrieval* by *Y.i Rubner, C. Tomasi,L. J. Guibas in Int. Journal of Computer Vision, Vol. 40, No. 2., 2000, pp. 99-121*

5
Transforming Images with Morphological Operations

In this chapter, we will cover:

- ▶ Eroding and dilating images using morphological filters
- ▶ Opening and closing images using morphological filters
- ▶ Detecting edges and corners using morphological filters
- ▶ Segmenting images using watersheds
- ▶ Extracting foreground objects with the GrabCut algorithm

Introduction

Morphological filtering is a theory developed in the 1960s for the analysis and processing of discrete images. It defines a series of operators which transform an image by probing it with a predefined shape element. The way this shape element intersects the neighborhood of a pixel determines the result of the operation. This chapter presents the most important morphological operators. It also explores the problem of image segmentation using algorithms working on the image morphology.

Eroding and dilating images using morphological filters

Erosion and dilation are the most fundamental morphological operators. Therefore, we will present them in this first recipe.

The fundamental instrument in mathematical morphology is the **structuring element**. A structuring element is simply defined as a configuration of pixels (a shape) on which an origin is defined (also called **anchor point**). Applying a morphological filter consists of probing each pixel of the image using this structuring element. When the origin of the structuring element is aligned with a given pixel, its intersection with the image defines a set of pixels on which a particular morphological operation is applied. In principle, the structuring element can be of any shape, but most often, a simple shape such as a square, circle, or diamond with the origin at the center is used (mainly for efficiency reasons).

Getting ready

As morphological filters usually work on binary images, we will use the binary image which was produced through thresholding in the first recipe of the previous chapter. However, since in morphology, the convention is to have foreground objects represented by high (white) pixel values and background by low (black) pixel values, we have negated the image. In morphological terms, the following image is said to be the **complement** of the image that was produced in the previous chapter:

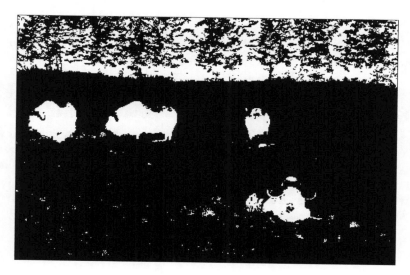

How to do it...

Erosion and dilation are implemented in OpenCV as simple functions which are `cv::erode` and `cv::dilate`. Their use is straightforward:

```cpp
// Read input image
cv::Mat image= cv::imread("binary.bmp");

// Erode the image
cv::Mat eroded;  // the destination image
cv::erode(image,eroded,cv::Mat());

// Display the eroded image
cv::namedWindow("Eroded Image");");
cv::imshow("Eroded Image",eroded);

// Dilate the image
cv::Mat dilated;  // the destination image
cv::dilate(image,dilated,cv::Mat());

// Display the dilated image
cv::namedWindow("Dilated Image");
cv::imshow("Dilated Image",dilated);
```

The two images produced by these function calls are seen in the following screenshot. Erosion is shown first:

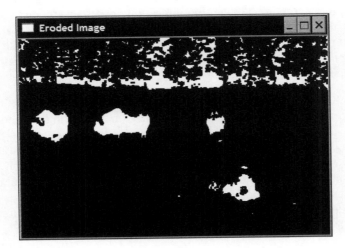

Followed by the dilation result:

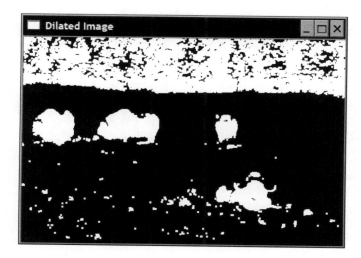

How it works...

As with all other morphological filters, the two filters of this recipe operate on the set of pixels (or neighborhood) around each pixel, as defined by the structuring element. Recall that when applied to a given pixel, the anchor point of the structuring element is aligned with this pixel location, and all pixels intersecting the structuring element are included in the current set. **Erosion** replaces the current pixel with the minimum pixel value found in the defined pixel set. **Dilation** is the complementary operator, and it replaces the current pixel with the maximum pixel value found in the defined pixel set. Since the input binary image contains only black (0) and white (255) pixels, each pixel is replaced by either a white or black pixel.

A good way to picture the effect of these two operators is to think in terms of background (black) and foreground (white) objects. With erosion, if the structuring element when placed at a given pixel location touches the background (that is, one of the pixels in the intersecting set is black), then this pixel will be sent to background. While in the case of dilation, if the structuring element on a background pixel touches a foreground object, then this pixel will be assigned a white value. This explains why in the eroded image, the size of the objects has been reduced. Observe how some of the very small objects (that can be considered as "noisy" background pixels) have also been completely eliminated. Similarly, the dilated objects are now larger and some of the "holes" inside of them have been filled.

By default, OpenCV uses a 3x3 square structuring element. This default structuring element is obtained when an empty matrix (that is `cv::Mat()`) is specified as the third argument in the function call, as it was done in the preceding example. You can also specify a structuring element of the size (and shape) you want by providing a matrix in which the non-zero element defines the structuring element. In the following example, a 7x7 structuring element is applied:

```
cv::Mat element(7,7,CV_8U,cv::Scalar(1));
cv::erode(image,eroded,element);
```

The effect is obviously much more destructive in this case as seen here:

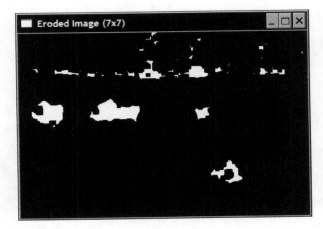

Another way to obtain the same result is to repetitively apply the same structuring element on an image. The two functions have an optional parameter to specify the number of repetitions:

```
// Erode the image 3 times.
cv::erode(image,eroded,cv::Mat(),cv::Point(-1,-1),3);
```

The origin argument `cv::Point(-1,-1)` means that the origin is at the center of the matrix (default), and it can be defined anywhere on the structuring element. The image obtained will be identical to the one we obtained with the 7x7 structuring element. Indeed, eroding an image twice is like eroding an image with a structuring element dilated with itself. This also applies to dilation.

Finally, since the notion of background/foreground is arbitrary, we can make the following observation (which is a fundamental property of the erosion/dilation operators). Eroding foreground objects with a structuring element can be seen as a dilation of the background part of the image. Or more formally:

▶ The erosion of an image is equivalent to the complement of the dilation of the complement image.

▶ The dilation of an image is equivalent to the complement of the erosion of the complement image.

There's more...

It is important to note that even if we applied our morphological filters on binary images here, these can also be applied on gray-level images with the same definitions.

Also note that the OpenCV morphological functions support in-place processing. This means you can use the input image as the destination image. So you can write:

```
cv::erode(image,image,cv::Mat());
```

OpenCV creates the required temporary image for you for this to work properly.

See also

The next recipe which applies erosion and dilation filters in cascade to produce new operators.

The *Detecting edges and corners using morphological filters* for the application of morphological filters on gray-level images.

Opening and closing images using morphological filters

The previous recipe introduced the two fundamental morphological operators: dilation and erosion. From these, other operators can be defined. The next two recipes will present some of them. The opening and closing operators are presented in this recipe.

How to do it...

In order to apply higher-level morphological filters, you need to use the `cv::morphologyEx` function with the appropriate function code. For example, the following call will apply the closing operator:

```
cv::Mat element5(5,5,CV_8U,cv::Scalar(1));
cv::Mat closed;
cv::morphologyEx(image,closed,cv::MORPH_CLOSE,element5);
```

Note that here we use a 5x5 structuring element to make the effect of the filter more apparent. If we input the binary image of the preceding recipe, we obtain:

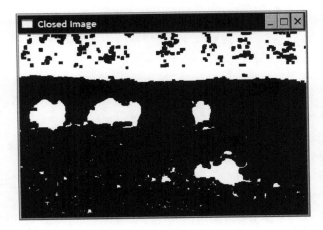

Similarly, applying the morphological opening operator will result in the following image:

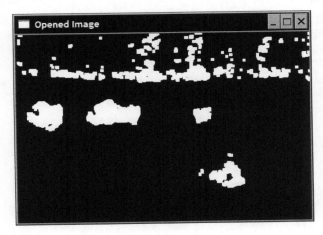

This one being obtained from the following code:

```
cv::Mat opened;
cv::morphologyEx(image,opened,cv::MORPH_OPEN,element5);
```

How it works...

The opening and closing filters are simply defined in terms of the basic erosion and dilation operations:

- ▶ **Closing** is defined as the erosion of the dilation of an image.
- ▶ **Opening** is defined as the dilation of the erosion of an image.

Consequently, one could compute the closing of an image using the following calls:

```
// dilate original image
cv::dilate(image,result,cv::Mat());
// in-place erosion of the dilated image
cv::erode(result,result,cv::Mat());
```

The opening would be obtained by inverting these two function calls.

While examining the result of the closing filter, it can be seen that the small holes of the white foreground objects have been filled. The filter also connects together several of the adjacent objects. Basically, any holes or gaps too small to completely contain the structuring element will be eliminated by the filter.

Reciprocally, the opening filter eliminated several of the small objects in the scene. All of the ones that were too small to contain the structuring element have been removed.

These filters are often used in object detection. The closing filter connects together objects erroneously fragmented into smaller pieces, while the opening filter removes the small blobs introduced by image noise. Therefore, it is advantageous to use them in sequence. If our test binary image is successively closed and opened, we obtain an image showing only the main objects in the scene, as shown below. You can also apply the opening filter before closing if you wish to prioritize noise filtering, but this can be at the price of eliminating some fragmented objects.

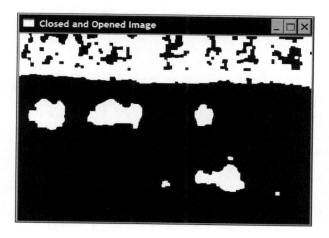

It should be noted that applying the same opening (and similarly the closing) operator on an image several times has no effect. Indeed, with the holes having been filled by the first opening, an additional application of this same filter will not produce any other changes to the image. In mathematical terms, these operators are said to be idempotent.

Detecting edges and corners using morphological filters

Morphological filters can also be used to detect specific features in an image. In this recipe, we will learn how to detect lines and corners in a gray-level image.

Getting started

In this recipe, the following image will be used:

How to do it...

Let's define a class named MorphoFeatures which will allow us to detect image features:

```
class MorphoFeatures {

  private:

      // threshold to produce binary image
      int threshold;
      // structuring elements used in corner detection
      cv::Mat cross;
      cv::Mat diamond;
      cv::Mat square;
      cv::Mat x;
```

Detecting lines is quite easy using the appropriate filter of the `cv::morphologyEx` function:

```
cv::Mat getEdges(const cv::Mat &image) {

   // Get the gradient image
   cv::Mat result;
   cv::morphologyEx(image,result,
                     cv::MORPH_GRADIENT,cv::Mat());

   // Apply threshold to obtain a binary image
   applyThreshold(result);

   return result;
}
```

The binary edge image is obtained through a simple private method of the class:

```
void applyThreshold(cv::Mat& result) {

   // Apply threshold on result
   if (threshold>0)
      cv::threshold(result, result,
                     threshold, 255, cv::THRESH_BINARY);
}
```

Using this class in a main function, you then obtain the edge image as follows:

```
// Create the morphological features instance
MorphoFeatures morpho;
morpho.setThreshold(40);

// Get the edges
cv::Mat edges;
edges= morpho.getEdges(image);
```

The result is the following image:

The detection of corners using morphological corners is a bit more complex since it is not directly implemented in OpenCV. This is a good example of the use of non-square structuring elements. Indeed, it requires the definition of four different structuring elements shaped as a square, diamond, cross, and an X-shape. This is done in the constructor (all of these structuring elements having a fixed 5x5 dimension for simplicity):

```
MorphoFeatures() : threshold(-1),
        cross(5,5,CV_8U,cv::Scalar(0)),
            diamond(5,5,CV_8U,cv::Scalar(1)),
        square(5,5,CV_8U,cv::Scalar(1)),
        x(5,5,CV_8U,cv::Scalar(0)){

    // Creating the cross-shaped structuring element
    for (int i=0; i<5; i++) {

        cross.at<uchar>(2,i)= 1;
        cross.at<uchar>(i,2)= 1;
    }
    // Creating the diamond-shaped structuring element
    diamond.at<uchar>(0,0)= 0;
    diamond.at<uchar>(0,1)= 0;
    diamond.at<uchar>(1,0)= 0;
    diamond.at<uchar>(4,4)= 0;
    diamond.at<uchar>(3,4)= 0;
    diamond.at<uchar>(4,3)= 0;
    diamond.at<uchar>(4,0)= 0;
```

```
        diamond.at<uchar>(4,1)= 0;
        diamond.at<uchar>(3,0)= 0;
        diamond.at<uchar>(0,4)= 0;
        diamond.at<uchar>(0,3)= 0;
        diamond.at<uchar>(1,4)= 0;
        // Creating the x-shaped structuring element
        for (int i=0; i<5; i++) {
          x.at<uchar>(i,i)= 1;
          x.at<uchar>(4-i,i)= 1;
        }
    }
```

In the detection of corner features, all of these structuring elements are applied in cascade to obtain the resulting corner map:

```
    cv::Mat getCorners(const cv::Mat &image) {

        cv::Mat result;

        // Dilate with a cross
        cv::dilate(image,result,cross);

        // Erode with a diamond
        cv::erode(result,result,diamond);

        cv::Mat result2;
        // Dilate with a X
        cv::dilate(image,result2,x);

        // Erode with a square
        cv::erode(result2,result2,square);

        // Corners are obtained by differencing
        // the two closed images
        cv::absdiff(result2,result,result);

        // Apply threshold to obtain a binary image
        applyThreshold(result);

        return result;
    }
```

In order to better visualize the result of the detection, the following method draws a circle on the image at each detected point on the binary map:

```
    void drawOnImage(const cv::Mat& binary,
                     cv::Mat& image) {

        cv::Mat_<uchar>::const_iterator it=
                        binary.begin<uchar>();
        cv::Mat_<uchar>::const_iterator itend=
```

```
                        binary.end<uchar>();
    // for each pixel
    for (int i=0; it!= itend; ++it,++i) {
        if (!*it)
            cv::circle(image,
                cv::Point(i%image.step,i/image.step),
                5,cv::Scalar(255,0,0));
    }
}
```

Corners are then detected on an image by using the following code:

```
// Get the corners
cv::Mat corners;
corners= morpho.getCorners(image);

// Display the corner on the image
morpho.drawOnImage(corners,image);
cv::namedWindow("Corners on Image");
cv::imshow("Corners on Image",image);
```

The image of detected corners is then, as follows.

How it works...

A good way to help understand the effect of morphological operators on a gray-level image is to consider an image as a topological relief in which gray-levels correspond to elevation (or altitude). Under this perspective, bright regions correspond to mountains, while the darker areas form the valleys of the terrain. Also, since edges correspond to a rapid transition between darker and brighter pixels, these can be pictured as abrupt cliffs. If an erosion operator is applied on such a terrain, the net result will be to replace each pixel by the lowest value in a certain neighborhood, thus reducing its height. As a result, cliffs will be "eroded" as the valleys expand. Dilation has the exact opposite effect, that is, cliffs will gain terrain over the valleys. However, in both cases, the plateaux (that is, area of constant intensity) will remain relatively unchanged.

The above observations lead to a simple way of detecting the edges (or cliffs) of an image. This could be done by computing the difference between the dilated image and the eroded image. Since these two transformed images differ mostly at the edge locations, the image edges will be emphasized by the differentiation. This is exactly what the `cv::morphologyEx` function is doing when the `cv::MORPH_GRADIENT` argument is inputted. Obviously, the larger the structuring element is, the thicker the detected edges will be. This edge detection operator is also called the **Beucher** gradient (the next chapter will discuss the concept of image gradient in more detail). Note that similar results could also be obtained by simply subtracting the original image from the dilated one, or the eroded image from the original. The resulting edges would simply be thinner.

Corner detection is a bit more complex since it uses four different structuring elements. This operator is not implemented in OpenCV but we present it here to demonstrate how structuring elements of various shapes can be defined and combined. The idea is to close the image by dilating and eroding it with two different structuring elements. These elements are chosen such that they leave straight edges unchanged, but because of their respective effect, edges at corner points will be affected. Let's use the simple following image made of a single white square to better understand the effect of this asymmetrical closing operation:

The first square is the original image. When dilated with a cross-shaped structuring element, the square edges are expanded, except at the corner points where the cross shape does not hit the square. This is the result illustrated by the middle square. This dilated image is then eroded by a structuring element that, this time, has a diamond shape. This erosion brings back most edges at their original position, but pushes the corners even further since they were not dilated. The left square is then obtained, which, as it can be seen, has lost its sharp corners. The same procedure is repeated with an X-shaped and a square-shaped structuring element. These two elements are the rotated version of the previous ones and will consequently capture the corners at a 45-degree orientation. Finally, differencing the two results will extract the corner features.

See also

The article, *Morphological gradients by J.-F. Rivest, P. Soille, S. Beucher, ISET's symposium on electronic imaging science and technology, SPIE, Feb. 1992,* for more on morphological gradient.

The article *A modified regulated morphological corner detector by F.Y. Shih, C.-F. Chuang, V. Gaddipati, Pattern Recognition Letters, volume 26, issue 7, May 2005,* for more information on morphological corner detection.

Segmenting images using watersheds

The watershed transformation is a popular image processing algorithm that is used to quickly segment an image into homogenous regions. It relies on the idea that when the image is seen as a topological relief, homogeneous regions correspond to relatively flat basins delimited by steep edges. As a result of its simplicity, the original version of this algorithm tends to over-segment the image which produces multiple small regions. This is why OpenCV proposes a variant of this algorithm that uses a set of predefined markers which guide the definition of the image segments.

How to do it...

The watershed segmentation is obtained through the use of the `cv::watershed` function. The input to this function is a 32-bit signed integer marker image in which each non-zero pixel represents a label. The idea is to mark some pixels of the image that are known to certainly belong to a given region. From this initial labeling, the watershed algorithm will determine the regions to which the other pixels belong. In this recipe, we will first create the marker image as a gray-level image, and then convert it into an image of integers. We conveniently encapsulated this step into a `WatershedSegmenter` class:

```
class WatershedSegmenter {

  private:
```

```
    cv::Mat markers;
public:
    void setMarkers(const cv::Mat& markerImage) {
     // Convert to image of ints
     markerImage.convertTo(markers,CV_32S);
    }
    cv::Mat process(const cv::Mat &image) {
     // Apply watershed
     cv::watershed(image,markers);
     return markers;
    }
```

The way these markers are obtained depends on the application. For example, some preprocessing steps might have resulted in the identification of some pixels belonging to an object of interest. The watershed would then be used to delimitate the complete object from that initial detection. In this recipe, we will simply use the binary image used throughout this chapter in order to identify the animals of the corresponding original image (this is the image shown at the beginning of *Chapter 4*).

Therefore, from our binary image, we need to identify pixels that certainly belong to the foreground (the animals) and pixels that certainly belong to the background (mainly the grass). Here, we will mark foreground pixels with label 255 and background pixels with label 128 (this choice is totally arbitrary, any label number other than 255 would work). The other pixels, that is the ones for which the labeling is unknown, are assigned value 0. As it is now, the binary image includes too many white pixels belonging to various parts of the image. We will then severely erode this image in order to retain only pixels belonging to the important objects:

```
    // Eliminate noise and smaller objects
    cv::Mat fg;
    cv::erode(binary,fg,cv::Mat(),cv::Point(-1,-1),6);
```

The result is the following image:

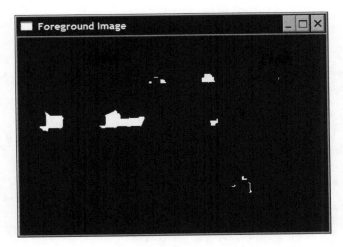

Note that a few pixels belonging to the background forest are still present. Let's simply keep them. Therefore, they will be considered to correspond to an object of interest. Similarly, we also select a few pixels of the background by a large dilation of the original binary image:

```
// Identify image pixels without objects
cv::Mat bg;
cv::dilate(binary,bg,cv::Mat(),cv::Point(-1,-1),6);
cv::threshold(bg,bg,1,128,cv::THRESH_BINARY_INV);
```

The resulting black pixels correspond to background pixels. This is why the thresholding operation immediately after the dilation assigns to these pixels the value 128. The following image is then obtained:

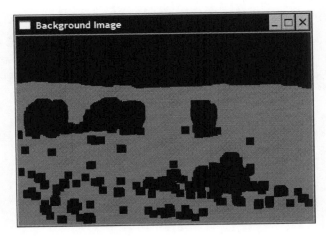

These images are combined to form the marker image:

```
// Create markers image
cv::Mat markers(binary.size(),CV_8U,cv::Scalar(0));
markers= fg+bg;
```

Note how we used the overloaded `operator+` here in order to combine the images. This is the image that will be used as input to the watershed algorithm:

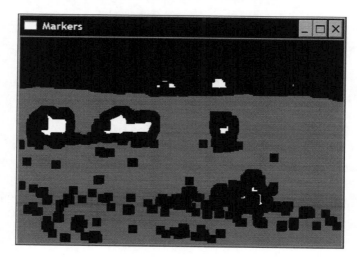

The segmentation is then obtained as follows:

```
// Create watershed segmentation object
WatershedSegmenter segmenter;

// Set markers and process
segmenter.setMarkers(markers);
segmenter.process(image);
```

The marker image is then updated such that each zero pixel is assigned one of the input labels, while the pixels belonging to the found boundaries have value -1. The resulting image of labels is then:

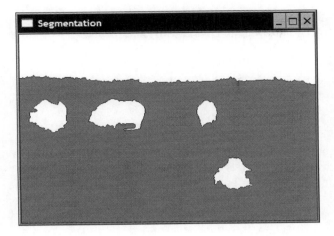

The boundary image is:

How it works...

As we did in the preceding recipe, we will use the topological map analogy in the description of the watershed algorithm. In order to create a watershed segmentation, the idea is to progressively flood the image starting at level 0. As the level of "water" progressively increases (to levels 1, 2, 3, and so on), catchment basins are formed. The size of these basins also gradually increase and, consequently, the water of two different basins will eventually merge. When this happens, a watershed is created in order to keep the two basins separated. Once the level of water has reached its maximal level, the sets of these created basins and watersheds form the watershed segmentation.

As one can expect, the flooding process initially creates many small individual basins. When all of these are merged, many watershed lines are created which results in an over-segmented image. To overcome this problem, a modification to this algorithm has been proposed in which the flooding process starts from a predefined set of marked pixels. The basins created from these markers are labeled in accordance with the values assigned to the initial marks. When two basins having the same label merge, no watersheds are created, thus preventing the over-segmentation.

This is what happens when the `cv::watershed` function is called. The input marker image is updated to produce the final watershed segmentation. Users can input a marker image with any number of labels with pixels of unknown labeling left to value 0. The marker image has been chosen to be an image of a 32-bit signed integer in order to be able to define more than 255 labels. It also allows the special value -1, to be assigned to pixels associated with a watershed. This is what is returned by the `cv::watershed` function. To facilitate the displaying of the result, we have introduced two special methods. The first one returns an image of the labels (with watersheds at value 0). This is easily done through thresholding:

```
// Return result in the form of an image
cv::Mat getSegmentation() {

 cv::Mat tmp;
 // all segment with label higher than 255
 // will be assigned value 255
 markers.convertTo(tmp,CV_8U);

 return tmp;
}
```

Similarly, the second method returns an image in which the watershed lines are assigned value 0, and the rest of the image is at 255. This time, the `cv::convertTo` method is used to achieve this result:

```
// Return watershed in the form of an image
cv::Mat getWatersheds() {

 cv::Mat tmp;
 // Each pixel p is transformed into
 // 255p+255 before conversion
 markers.convertTo(tmp,CV_8U,255,255);

 return tmp;
}
```

The linear transformation that is applied before the conversion allows -1 pixels to be converted into 0 (since -1*255+255=0).

Pixels with a value greater than 255 are assigned the value 255. This is due to the saturation operation that is applied when signed integers are converted into unsigned chars.

See also

The article *The viscous watershed transform by C. Vachier, F. Meyer, Journal of Mathematical Imaging and Vision, volume 22, issue 2-3, May 2005*, for more information on the watershed transform.

The next recipe which presents another image segmentation algorithm that can also segment an image into background and foreground objects.

Extracting foreground objects with the GrabCut algorithm

OpenCV proposes an implementation of another popular algorithm for image segmentation: the GrabCut algorithm. This algorithm is not based on mathematical morphology, but we present it here since it shows some similarities in its use with the watershed segmentation algorithm presented in the preceding recipe. GrabCut is computationally more expensive than watershed, but it generally produces a more accurate result. It is the best algorithm to use when one wants to extract a foreground object in a still image (for example, to cut and paste an object from one picture to another).

How to do it...

The `cv::grabCut` function is easy to use. You just need to input an image and label some of its pixels as belonging to the background or to the foreground. Based on this partial labeling, the algorithm will then determine a foreground/background segmentation for the complete image.

One way of specifying a partial foreground/background labeling for an input image is by defining a rectangle inside which the foreground object is included:

```
// Open image
image= cv::imread("../group.jpg");

// define bounding rectangle
// the pixels outside this rectangle
// will be labeled as background
cv::Rect rectangle(10,100,380,180);
```

All pixels outside of this rectangle will then be marked as background. In addition to the input image and its segmentation image, calling the `cv::grabCut` function requires the definition of two matrices which will contain the models built by the algorithm:

```
cv::Mat result; // segmentation (4 possible values)
cv::Mat bgModel,fgModel; // the models (internally used)
// GrabCut segmentation
cv::grabCut(image,     // input image
```

```
result,          // segmentation result
rectangle,       // rectangle containing foreground
bgModel,fgModel, // models
5,               // number of iterations
cv::GC_INIT_WITH_RECT); // use rectangle
```

Note how we specified that we are using the bounding rectangle mode using the `cv::GC_INIT_WITH_RECT` flag as the last argument of the function (the next section will discuss the other available mode). The input/output segmentation image can have one of the four values:

- ► `cv::GC_BGD`, for pixels certainly belonging to the background (for example, pixels outside the rectangle in our example)

- ► `cv::GC_FGD`, for pixels certainly belonging to the foreground (none in our example)

- ► `cv::GC_PR_BGD`, for pixels probably belonging to the background

- ► `cv::GC_PR_FGD` for pixels probably belonging to the foreground (that is the initial value for the pixels inside the rectangle in our example).

We get a binary image of the segmentation by extracting the pixels having a value equal to `cv::GC_PR_FGD`:

```
// Get the pixels marked as likely foreground
cv::compare(result,cv::GC_PR_FGD,result,cv::CMP_EQ);
// Generate output image
cv::Mat foreground(image.size(),CV_8UC3,
                   cv::Scalar(255,255,255));
image.copyTo(foreground,// bg pixels are not copied
             result);
```

To extract all foreground pixels, that is, with values equal to `cv::GC_PR_FGD` or `cv::GC_FGD`, it is possible to simply check the value of the first bit:

```
// checking first bit with bitwise-and
result= result&1; // will be 1 if FG
```

This is possible because these constants are defined as values 1 and 3, while the other two are defined as 0 and 2. In our example, the same result is obtained because the segmentation image does not contain `cv::GC_FGD` pixels (only `cv::GC_BGD` pixels have been inputted).

Finally, we obtain an image of the foreground objects (over a white background) by the following copy operation with mask:

```
// Generate output image
cv::Mat foreground(image.size(),CV_8UC3,
        cv::Scalar(255,255,255)); // all white image
image.copyTo(foreground,result); // bg pixels not copied
```

The resulting image is then:

How it works...

In the preceding example, the GrabCut algorithm was able to extract the foreground objects by simply specifying a rectangle inside which these objects (the four animals) were contained. Alternatively, one could also assign values `cv::GC_BGD` and `cv::GC_FGD` to some specific pixels of the segmentation image provided as the second argument of the `cv::grabCut` function. You would then specify `GC_INIT_WITH_MASK` as the input mode flag. These input labels could be obtained, for example, by asking a user to interactively mark a few elements of the image. It is also possible to combine these two input modes.

Using this input information, the GrabCut creates the background/foreground segmentation by proceeding as follows. Initially, a foreground label (`cv::GC_PR_FGD`) is tentatively assigned to all unmarked pixels. Based on the current classification, the algorithm groups the pixels into clusters of similar colors (that is K clusters for the background and K clusters for the foreground). The next step is to determine a background/foreground segmentation by introducing boundaries between foreground and background pixels. This is done through an optimization process that tries to connect pixels with similar labels, and that imposes a penalty for placing a boundary in regions of relatively uniform intensity. This optimization problem is efficiently solved using the **Graph Cuts** algorithm, a method that can find the optimal solution of a problem by representing it as a connected graph on which cuts are applied in order to compose an optimal configuration. The obtained segmentation produces new labels for the pixels. The clustering process can then be repeated and a new optimal segmentation is found again, and so on. Therefore, the GrabCut is an iterative procedure which gradually improves the segmentation result. Depending on the complexity of the scene, a good solution can be found in more or less iterations (in easy cases, one iteration can be enough!).

This explains the previous last argument of the function where the user can specify the number of iterations to apply. The two internal models maintained by the algorithm are passed as argument of the function (and returned) such that it is possible to call the function with the models of the last run again if one wishes to improve the segmentation result by performing additional iterations.

See also

The article by *C. Rother, V. Kolmogorov and A. Blake, GrabCut: Interactive Foreground Extraction using Iterated Graph Cuts in ACM Transactions on Graphics (SIGGRAPH) volume 23, issue 3, August 2004*, that describes in detail the GrabCut algorithm.

6

Filtering the Images

In this chapter, we will cover:

- ▶ Filtering images using low-pass filters
- ▶ Filtering images using a median filter
- ▶ Applying directional filters to detect edges
- ▶ Computing the Laplacian of an image

Introduction

Filtering is one of the fundamental tasks in signal and image processing. It is a process aimed at selectively extracting certain aspects of an image that are considered to convey important information in the context of a given application. Filtering removes noise in images, extracts interesting visual features, allows image resampling, and so on. It finds its roots in the general **Signals and Systems** theory. We will not cover this theory in details here. However, this chapter will present some of the important concepts related to filtering and will show how filters can be used in image processing applications. But first, let's begin with a brief explanation of the concept of frequency domain analysis.

When we look at an image, we observe how the different gray-level (or colors) are distributed over the image. Images differ from each others because they have a different gray-level distribution. But there exists another point of view under which an image can be analyzed. We can look at the gray-level variations that are present in an image. Some images contain large areas of almost constant intensity (for example, a blue sky) while in other images, the gray-level intensities vary rapidly over the image (for example, a busy scene crowded with many small objects). Therefore, observing the frequency of those variations in an image constitutes another way of characterizing an image. This point of view is referred to as the **frequency domain**, while characterizing an image by observing its gray-level distribution is referred to as the **spatial domain**.

The frequency domain analysis decomposes an image into its frequency content from the lowest to the highest frequencies. Low frequency corresponds to areas where the image intensities vary slowly, while high frequencies are generated by rapid changes in intensities. Several well-known transformations exist, such as the Fourier transform or the Cosine transform, which can be used to explicitly show the frequency content of an image. Note that since an image is a two-dimensional entity, it is made of both vertical frequencies (that is variations in the vertical directions) and horizontal frequencies (variations in the horizontal directions).

Under the frequency domain analysis framework, a **filter** is an operation that amplifies certain bands of frequencies of an image while blocking (or reducing) other image frequency bands. A low-pass filter is therefore a filter which eliminates the high-frequency components of an image and reciprocally, a high-pass filter eliminates the low-pass components. This chapter will present some filters that are frequently used in image processing and will explain their effect when applied on an image.

Filtering images using low-pass filters

In this first recipe, we will present some very basic low-pass filters. In the introductory section of this chapter, we learned that the objective of such filters is to reduce the amplitude of the image variations. One simple way to achieve this goal is to replace each pixel by the average value of the pixels around. By doing this, the rapid intensity variations will be smoothed out and thus replaced by a more gradual transition.

How to do it...

The objective of the `cv::blur` function is to smooth an image by replacing each pixel by the average pixel value computed over a rectangular neighborhood. This low-pass filter is applied as follows:

```
cv::blur(image,result,cv::Size(5,5));
```

This kind of filter is also called a box filter. Here, we applied it by using a 5x5 filter in order to make the filter's effect more visible. When this is applied on the following image:

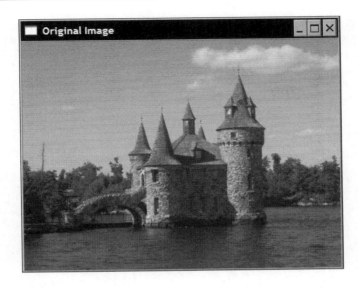

The result is:

In some cases, it might be desirable to give more importance to the closer pixels in the neighborhood of a pixel. It is therefore possible to compute a weighted average in which nearby pixels are assigned a larger weight than ones further away. This can be achieved by using a weighted scheme that follows a Gaussian function (a "bell-shaped" function). The `cv::GaussianBlur` function applies such a filter and it is called as follows:

```
cv::GaussianBlur(image,result,cv::Size(5,5),1.5);
```

The result is then seen in the following image:

How it works...

A filter is said to be linear if its application corresponds to replacing a pixel by a weighted sum of neighboring pixels. This is the case of the box filter in which a pixel is replaced by the sum of all pixels in a rectangular neighborhood and divided by the size of this neighborhood (to get the average value). This is like multiplying each neighboring pixel by 1 over the total number of pixels and summing all of these values. The different weights of a filter can be represented using a matrix that shows the multiplying factors associated with each pixel position in the considered neighborhood. The central element of the matrix corresponding to the pixel on which the filter is currently applied. Such a matrix is sometimes called a **kernel** or a **mask**. For a *3x3* box filter, the corresponding kernel would be:

1/9	1/9	1/9
1/9	1/9	1/9
1/9	1/9	1/9

Applying a linear filter then corresponds to moving a kernel over each pixel of an image and multiplying each corresponding pixel by its associated weight. Mathematically, this operation is called a **convolution**.

Looking at the output images produced in this recipe, it can be observed that the net effect of a low-pass filter is to blur or smooth the image. This is not surprising since this filter attenuates the high-frequency components that correspond to the rapid variations visible on an object's edge.

In the case of a Gaussian filter, the weight associated with a pixel is proportional to its distance from the central pixel. Recall that the 1D Gaussian function has the following form:

$$G(x) = Ae^{-x^2/2\sigma^2}$$

The normalizing coefficient A is chosen such that the different weights sum to one. The σ (sigma) value controls the width of the resulting Gaussian function. The greater this value is, the flatter the function will be. For example, if we compute the coefficients of the 1D Gaussian filter for the interval [-4,...,0,...4] with σ=0.5, we obtain:

```
[0.0 0.0 0.00026 0.10645 0.78657 0.10645 0.00026 0.0 0.0]
```

While for σ=1.5 these coefficients are:

```
[0.00761 0.036075 0.10959 0.21345 0.26666
  0.21345 0.10959 0.03608 0.00761 ]
```

Note that these values were obtained by calling the `cv::getGaussianKernel` function with the appropriate σ value:

```
cv::Mat gauss= cv::getGaussianKernel(9,sigma,CV_32F);
```

To apply a 2D Gaussian filter on an image, one can simply apply a 1D Gaussian filter on the image lines first (which will filter the horizontal frequencies) followed by the application of the same 1D Gaussian filter on the image columns (to filter the vertical frequencies). This is possible because the Gaussian filter is a **separable filter** (that is, the 2D kernel can be decomposed into two 1D filters). The function `cv::sepFilter2D` can be used to apply a general separable filter. It is also possible to directly apply a 2D kernel using `cv::filter2D` function.

With OpenCV, the Gaussian filter to be applied on an image is specified by providing to `cv::GaussianBlur` both the number of coefficients (third parameter, an odd number) and the value of σ (fourth parameter). You can also simply set the value of σ and let OpenCV determine the appropriate number of coefficients (you then input a value of 0 for the filter size). The opposite is also possible, where you input a size and a value of 0 for σ. The σ value that best fits the given size will be determined. However, it recommended that you input both values for a better control of the filter effect.

There's more...

Low-pass filters are also used when an image is resized. Suppose you want to reduce the size of an image by a factor of 2. You might think that this can simply be done by eliminating the even columns and rows of the image. Unfortunately, the resulting image will not look very nice. For example, an oblique edge in the original image will appear as a staircase on the reduced image. Other jagged distortions will also be visible on curves and textured parts of the image.

These undesirable artifacts are caused by a phenomenon called spatial **aliasing** that occurs when you try to include high-frequency components in an image that is too small to contain them. Indeed, smaller images (that is, images with fewer pixels) cannot represent fine textures and sharp edges as nicely as the higher resolution images (think of the difference between high-definition TV versus conventional TV). Since fine details in an image correspond to high frequencies, we'll need to remove those higher frequency components in an image before reducing its size. We learned in this recipe that this can be done through a low-pass filter. Consequently, to reduce the size of an image by half without adding annoying artifacts, you must first apply a low-pass filter to the original image and then throw away one column and row over two. This is exactly what the `cv::pyrDown` function does:

```
cv::Mat reducedImage;  // to contain reduced image
cv::pyrDown(image,reducedImage); // reduce image size by half
```

This one uses a 5x5 Gaussian filter to low-pass the image. The reciprocal `cv::pyrUp` function that doubles the size of an image also exists. Of course, if you downsize an image and then upsize it, you will not recover the exact original image. What was lost during the downsizing process cannot be recovered. These two functions are used to create **image pyramids**. This is a data structure made of stacked versions of an image at different sizes (often each level is half the size of the previous level) that is often built for efficient image analysis. For example, if one wishes to detect an object in an image, the detection can be first accomplished on the small image at the top of the pyramid, and as you locate the object of interest, you can refine the search by moving to the lower levels of the pyramid containing the higher resolution versions of the image.

Note that there is also a more general `cv:resize` function that allows you to specify the size you want for the resulting image. You simply call it by specifying a new size that could be smaller or larger than the original image:

```
cv::Mat resizedImage;  // to contain resized image
cv::resize(image,resizedImage,
    cv::Size(image.cols/3,image.rows/3)); // 1/3 resizing
```

Other options are available to specify resizing in terms of scale factors, or to select a particular interpolation method to be used in the resampling process.

See also

The function `cv::boxFilter` filters an image with a square kernel made of 1s only. It is similar to the mean filter but without dividing the result by the number of coefficients.

The *There's more...* section of the *Scanning an image with neighbor Access* in *Chapter 2* that introduces the `cv::filter2D` function. This function lets you apply a linear filter to an image by inputting the kernel of your choice.

Filtering images using a median filter

The first recipe of this chapter introduced the concept of linear filters. Non-linear filters also exist that can be advantageously used in image processing. One such filter is the median filter that we present in this recipe.

Since median filters are particularly useful to combat salt-and-pepper noise, we will use the image we created in the first recipe of *Chapter 2* and that is reproduced here:

How to do it...

The call to the median filtering function is done in a way similar to the other filters:

```
cv::medianBlur(image,result,5);
```

The resulting image is then as follows:

How it works...

Since the median filter is not a linear filter, it cannot be represented by a kernel matrix. However, it also operates on a pixel's neighborhood in order to determine the output pixel value. The pixel and its neighborhood form a set of values and, as the name suggests, the median filter will simply compute the median value of this set, and the current pixel is then replaced by this median value.

This explains why the filter is so efficient in eliminating of the salt-and-pepper noise. Indeed, when an outlier black or white pixel is present in a given pixel neighborhood, it is never selected as the median value (being rather maximal or minimal value) so it is always replaced by a neighboring value. In contrast, a simple mean filter would be greatly affected by such noise as it can be observed in the following image that represents the mean filtered version of our salt-and-pepper image:

Clearly, the noisy pixels shifted the mean value of neighboring pixels. As a result, the noise is still visible even if it has been blurred by the mean filter.

The median filter also has the advantage of preserving the sharpness of the edges. However, it washes out the textures in uniform regions (for example, the trees in the background).

Applying directional filters to detect edges

The first recipe of this chapter introduced the idea of linear filtering using kernel matrices. The filters used had the effect of blurring an image by removing or attenuating its high-frequency components. In this recipe, we will perform the opposite transformation that is amplifying the high-frequency content of an image. As a result, the high-pass filters introduced here will perform **edge detection**.

How to do it...

The filter we will use here is called the Sobel filter. It is said to be a directional filter because it only affects the vertical or the horizontal image frequencies depending on which kernel of the filter is used. OpenCV has a function that applies the Sobel operator on an image. The horizontal filter is called as follows:

```
cv::Sobel(image,sobelX,CV_8U,1,0,3,0.4,128);
```

While vertical filtering is achieved by the following (and very similar) call:

```
cv::Sobel(image,sobelY,CV_8U,0,1,3,0.4,128);
```

Several integer parameters are provided to the function and these will be explained in the next section. Simply note that these have been chosen to produce an 8-bit image (CV_8U) representation of the output.

The result of the horizontal Sobel operator is as follows:

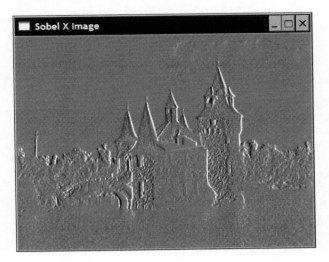

In this representation, a zero value corresponds to gray-level 128. Negative values are represented by darker pixels, while positive values are represented by brighter pixels. The vertical Sobel image is:

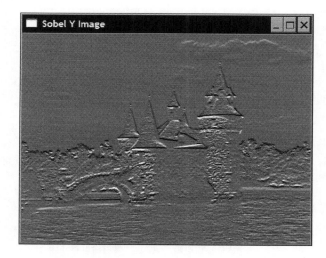

If you are familiar with photo-editing software, the preceding images may remind you of the *image emboss* effect, and indeed this image transformation is generally based on the use of directional filters.

Since its kernel contains positive and negative values, the result of the Sobel filter is generally computed in a 16-bit signed integer image (CV_16S). The two results (vertical and horizontal) are then combined to obtain the norm of the Sobel filter:

```
// Compute norm of Sobel
cv::Sobel(image,sobelX,CV_16S,1,0);
cv::Sobel(image,sobelY,CV_16S,0,1);
cv::Mat sobel;
//compute the L1 norm
sobel= abs(sobelX)+abs(sobelY);
```

The Sobel norm can be conveniently displayed in an image using the optional rescaling parameter of the convertTo method in order to obtain an image in which zero values correspond to white, and higher values are assigned darker gray shades:

```
// Find Sobel max value
double sobmin, sobmax;
cv::minMaxLoc(sobel,&sobmin,&sobmax);
// Conversion to 8-bit image
// sobelImage = -alpha*sobel + 255
cv::Mat sobelImage;
sobel.convertTo(sobelImage,CV_8U,-255./sobmax,255);
```

The result can be seen in the following image:

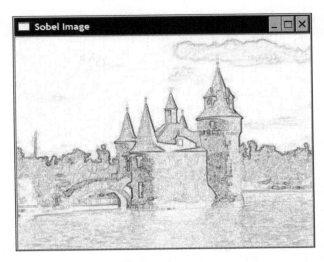

Looking at this image, it is now clear why this kind of operators are called edge detector. It is then possible to threshold this image in order to obtain a binary map showing the image contour. The following snippet creates the following image:

```
cv::threshold(sobelImage, sobelThresholded,
              threshold, 255, cv::THRESH_BINARY);
```

How it works...

The Sobel operator is a classic edge detection linear filter that is based on a simple *3x3* kernel which has the following structure:

-1	0	1
-2	0	2
-1	0	1

-1	-2	-1
0	0	0
1	2	1

If we view the image as a two-dimensional function, the Sobel operator can then be seen as a measure of the variation of the image in the vertical and horizontal directions. In mathematical terms, this measure is called a **gradient** and it is defined as a 2D vector made of the function's first derivatives in two orthogonal directions:

$$grad\,(I) = \left[\frac{\partial I}{\partial x}, \frac{\partial I}{\partial y} \right]^{\mathbf{T}}$$

Therefore, the Sobel operator gives an approximation of the image gradient by differencing pixels in the horizontal and in the vertical directions. It operates on a small window around the pixel of interest in order to reduce the influence of noise. The `cv::Sobel` function computes the result of the convolution of the image with a Sobel kernel. Its complete specification is as follows:

```
cv::Sobel(image,    // input
          sobel,    // output
          image_depth,    // image type
          xorder,yorder,  // kernel specification
          kernel_size,    // size of the square kernel
          alpha, beta);   // scale and offset
```

You therefore decide whether you wish to have the result written in an unsigned char, a signed integer, or a floating point image. Of course, if the result falls outside of the domain of the image pixel, saturation will be applied. This is where the last two parameters can be useful. Before storing the result in the image, the result can be scaled (multiplied) by `alpha` and an offset `beta` can be added. This is how we generated, in the previous section, an image for which the Sobel value 0 was represented by the mid-gray level 128. Each Sobel mask corresponds to a derivative in one direction. Therefore, two parameters are used to specify the kernel that will be applied, the order of the derivative in the *x* and the *y* directions.

For instance, the horizontal Sobel kernel is obtained by specifying 1 and 0 for the *x-order* and *y-order*, and the vertical kernel will be generated with 0 and 1. Other combinations are also possible, but these two are the ones that will be used most often (the case of second-order derivative is discussed in the next recipe). Finally, it is also possible to use kernels of size larger than *3x3*. Values 1, 3, 5, and 7 are possible choices for the kernel size. A kernel of size 1 corresponds to a 1D Sobel filter (1x3 or 3x1).

Since the gradient is a 2D vector, it has a norm and a direction. The norm of the gradient vector tells you what the amplitude of the variation is and it is normally computed as a Euclidean norm (also called *L2* norm):

$$|grad\,(I)| = \sqrt{\left(\frac{\partial I}{\partial x}\right)^2 + \left(\frac{\partial I}{\partial y}\right)^2}$$

However, in image processing, we generally compute this norm as the sum of the absolute values. This is called the *L1* norm and it gives values close to the *L2* norm but at a much lower computational cost. This is what we did in this recipe, that is:

```
//compute the L1 norm
sobel= abs(sobelX)+abs(sobelY);
```

The gradient vector always points in the direction of the steepest variation. For an image, this means that the gradient direction will be orthogonal to the edge, pointing in the darker to brighter direction. Gradient angular direction is given by:

$$\angle grad\,(I) = a\tan\left(-\frac{\partial I}{\partial y}\middle/\frac{\partial I}{\partial x}\right)$$

Most often, for edge detection, only the norm is computed. But if you require both the norm and the direction, then the following OpenCV function can be used:

```
// Sobel must be computed in floating points
cv::Sobel(image,sobelX,CV_32F,1,0);
cv::Sobel(image,sobelY,CV_32F,0,1);
// Compute the L2 norm and direction of the gradient
cv::Mat norm, dir;
cv::cartToPolar(sobelX,sobelY,norm,dir);
```

By default, the direction is computed in radians. Just add `true` as an additional argument in order to have them computed in degrees.

A binary edge map has been obtained by applying a threshold on the gradient magnitude. Choosing the right threshold is not an obvious task. If the threshold value is too low, too many (thick) edges will be retained, while if we select a more severe (higher) threshold, then broken edges will be obtained. As an illustration of this tradeoff situation, compare the preceding binary edge map with the following, obtained using a higher threshold value:

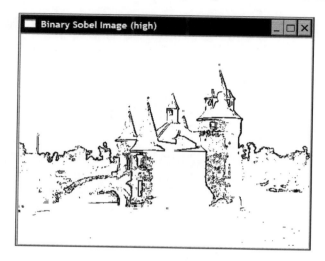

One possible alternative is to use the concept of hysteresis thresholding. This will be explained in the next chapter where we introduce the Canny operator.

There's more...

Other gradient operators also exists. For example, the Prewitt operator defines the following kernels:

-1	0	1
-1	0	1
-1	0	1

-1	-1	-1
0	0	0
1	1	1

The Roberts operator is based on these simple 2x2 kernels:

$$\begin{array}{cc} 1 & 0 \\ 0 & -1 \end{array}$$

$$\begin{array}{cc} 0 & 1 \\ -1 & 0 \end{array}$$

The Scharr operator is preferred when more accurate estimates of the gradient orientation is required:

$$\begin{array}{ccc} -3 & 0 & 3 \\ -10 & 0 & 10 \\ -3 & 0 & 3 \end{array}$$

$$\begin{array}{ccc} -3 & -10 & -3 \\ 0 & 0 & 0 \\ 3 & 10 & 3 \end{array}$$

Note that it is possible to use the Scharr kernels with the `cv::Sobel` function by calling it with the `CV_SCHARR` argument:

```
cv::Sobel(image,sobelX,CV_16S,1,0, CV_SCHARR);
```

or, equivalently, by calling the function `cv::Scharr`:

```
cv::Scharr(image,scharrX,CV_16S,1,0,3);
```

All of these directional filters try to estimate the first-order derivative of the image function. Therefore, high values are obtained at areas where large intensity variations in the filter direction are present, while flat areas produce low values. This is why filters that compute image derivatives are high-pass filters.

See also

The recipe *Detecting edges using the Canny operator* in *Chapter 7* where a binary edge map is obtained by using two different threshold values.

Computing the Laplacian of an image

The Laplacian is another high-pass linear filter that is based on the computation of the image derivatives. As it will be explained, it computes second-order derivatives to measure the curvature of the image function.

How to do it...

The OpenCV function `cv::Laplacian` computes the Laplacian of an image. It is very similar to the `cv::Sobel` function. In fact, it uses the same basic function `cv::getDerivKernels` in order to obtain its kernel matrix. The only difference is that there is no derivative order parameters since these ones are by definition second order derivatives.

For this operator, we will create a simple class that will encapsulate some useful operations related to the Laplacian. The basic methods are:

```cpp
class LaplacianZC {

  private:

      // original image
      cv::Mat img;

      // 32-bit float image containing the Laplacian
      cv::Mat laplace;
      // Aperture size of the laplacian kernel
      int aperture;

  public:

      LaplacianZC() : aperture(3) {}
      // Set the aperture size of the kernel
      void setAperture(int a) {

          aperture= a;
      }

      // Compute the floating point Laplacian
      cv::Mat computeLaplacian(const cv::Mat& image) {
          // Compute Laplacian
          cv::Laplacian(image,laplace,CV_32F,aperture);

          // Keep local copy of the image
          // (used for zero-crossings)
          img= image.clone();

          return laplace;
      }
```

The computation of the Laplacian is done here on a floating point image. To get an image of the result, we perform a rescaling as in the previous recipe. This rescaling is based on the Laplacian maximum absolute value, where value 0 is assigned gray-level 128. A method of our class allows this image representation to be obtained:

```
// Get the Laplacian result in 8-bit image
// zero corresponds to gray level 128
// if no scale is provided, then the max value will be
// scaled to intensity 255
// You must call computeLaplacian before calling this
cv::Mat getLaplacianImage(double scale=-1.0) {

    if (scale<0) {

        double lapmin, lapmax;
        cv::minMaxLoc(laplace,&lapmin,&lapmax);

        scale= 127/ std::max(-lapmin,lapmax);
    }

    cv::Mat laplaceImage;
    laplace.convertTo(laplaceImage,CV_8U,scale,128);

    return laplaceImage;
}
```

Using this class, the Laplacian image computed from a *7x7* kernel is obtained as follows:

```
// Compute Laplacian using LaplacianZC class
LaplacianZC laplacian;
laplacian.setAperture(7);
cv::Mat flap= laplacian.computeLaplacian(image);
laplace= laplacian.getLaplacianImage();
```

The resulting image is as follows:

How it works...

Formally, the **Laplacian** of a 2D function is defined as the sum of its second derivatives:

$$laplace\ (I) = \frac{\partial^2 I}{\partial x^2} + \frac{\partial^2 I}{\partial y^2}$$

In its simplest form, it can be approximated by the following *3x3* kernel:

0	1	0
1	-4	1
0	1	0

As for the Sobel operator, it is also possible to compute the Laplacian using larger kernels, and since this operator is even more sensitive to image noise, it is desirable to do so (unless computational efficiency is a concern). Note that the kernel values of the Laplacian always sum to 0. This guarantees that the Laplacian will be zero in areas of constant intensities. Indeed, since the Laplacian measures the curvature of the image function, it should be equal to 0 on flat areas.

At first glance, the effect of the Laplacian might be difficult to interpret. From the definition of the kernel, it is clear that any isolated pixel value (that is a value very different from its neighbors) will be amplified by the operator. This is a consequence of the operator's high sensitivity to noise. But it is more interesting to look at the Laplacian values around an image edge. The presence of an edge in an image is the result of a rapid transition between areas of different gray-level intensities. Following the evolution of the image function along an edge (for example, caused by a transition from dark to bright), one can observe that the gray-level ascension necessarily implies a gradual transition from a positive curvature (when the intensity values start to rise) to a negative curvature (when the intensity is about to reach its high plateau). Consequently, a transition between a positive and a negative Laplacian value (or reciprocally) constitutes a good indicator of the presence of an edge. Another way to express this fact is to say that edges will be located at the *zero-crossings* of the Laplacian function. We will illustrate this idea by looking at the values of a Laplacian in a small window of our test image. We select one that corresponds to an edge created by the bottom part of the roof of one of the castle's tower. A white box has been drawn in the following image to show the exact location of this region of interest:

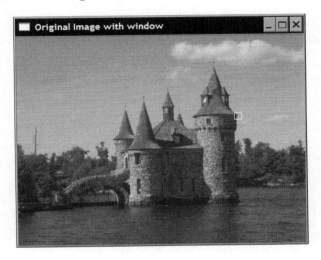

Now looking at the Laplacian values (7x7 kernel) inside this window, we have:

```
 25   -78  -140  -115   -59   -23    -5    -3    -6    -2    1    2
 46    -7  -127  -186  -148   -73   -21   -11   -12    -4    0   -1
-40    16   -46  -164  -213  -165   -84   -33   -10     4    2   -7
 -6    84   105     7  -121  -185  -158   -88   -29     0    2   -8
135   202   284   296   199   -20  -109  -106   -47   -10    3    0
124   193   316   438   442   251    16   -69   -41    -9    8    8
 39   111   216   287   254   123   -19   -69   -42   -12    6    8
 38   110   180    85  -131  -217  -161   -90   -37    -7    0   -3
 36   121   210    31  -299  -355  -183   -61   -12     5    0  -10
  1    95   210    43  -271  -293  -111   -17     0     6    1   -4
 -8   102   208    48  -227  -228   -62     4     3     2    2    3
 19   167   247    51  -225  -220   -57     6     3     0    0    0
```

If, as illustrated, you carefully follow the zero-crossings of the Laplacian (located between pixels of different signs), you obtain a curve which corresponds to the edge visible in the image window. Above, we drew dotted lines along the zero-crossings corresponding to the edge of the tower visible in the selected image window. This implies that, in principle, you can even detect the image edges at sub-pixel accuracy.

Following the zero-crossing curves in a Laplacian image is a delicate task. However, a simplified algorithm can be used to detect the approximate zero-crossing locations. This one proceeds as follows. Scan the Laplacian image and compare the current pixel with the one at its left. If the two pixels are of different signs, then declare a zero-crossing at the current pixel, if not, repeat the same test with the pixel immediately above. This algorithm is implemented by the following method which generates a binary image of zero-crossings:

```cpp
// Get a binary image of the zero-crossings
// if the product of the two adjacent pixels is
// less than threshold then this zero-crossing
// will be ignored
cv::Mat getZeroCrossings(float threshold=1.0) {

    // Create the iterators
    cv::Mat_<float>::const_iterator it=
        laplace.begin<float>()+laplace.step1();
    cv::Mat_<float>::const_iterator itend=
        laplace.end<float>();
    cv::Mat_<float>::const_iterator itup=
        laplace.begin<float>();

    // Binary image initialize to white
    cv::Mat binary(laplace.size(),CV_8U,cv::Scalar(255));
    cv::Mat_<uchar>::iterator itout=
        binary.begin<uchar>()+binary.step1();
```

```
    // negate the input threshold value
    threshold *= -1.0;

    for ( ; it!= iend; ++it, ++itup, ++itout) {

       // if the product of two adjascent pixel is
       // negative then there is a sign change
       if (*it * *(it-1) < threshold)
          *itout= 0; // horizontal zero-crossing
       else if (*it * *itup < threshold)
          *itout= 0; // vertical zero-crossing

    }

    return binary;

}
```

An additional threshold is also introduced to make sure that the current Laplacian values are significant enough to be considered an edge. The result is the following binary map:

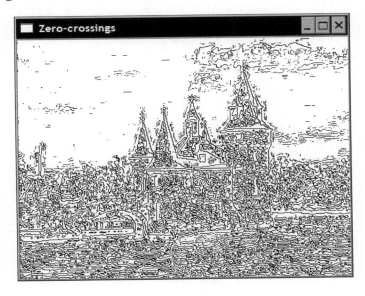

As you can see, the zero-crossings of the Laplacian detect all edges. No distinction is made between strong edges and weaker edges. We also mentioned that the Laplacian is very sensitive to noise. These two facts explain why so many edges are detected by the operator.

There's more...

The contrast of an image can be enhanced by subtracting its Laplacian from it. This is what we did in the recipe *Scanning an image with neighbor access* of *Chapter 2* where we introduced the kernel:

0	-1	0
-1	5	-1
0	-1	0

which is equal to 1 minus the Laplacian kernel (that is original image minus its Laplacian).

See also

The recipe *Detecting the scale-invariant SURF features* in *Chapter 8* that uses the Laplacian in the detection of scale-invariant features.

7

Extracting Lines, Contours, and Components

In this chapter, we will cover:

- ▶ Detecting image contours with the Canny operator
- ▶ Detecting lines in images with the Hough transform
- ▶ Fitting a line to a set of points
- ▶ Extracting the components' contours
- ▶ Computing components' shape descriptors

Introduction

In order to perform a content-based analysis of an image, it is necessary to extract meaningful features from the collection of pixels that constitute the image. Contours, lines, blobs, and so on, are fundamental image elements that define an image's content. This chapter will teach you how to extract some of these important image features.

Detecting image contours with the Canny operator

In the previous chapter, we learned how it is possible to detect the edges of an image. In particular, we showed that by applying a threshold on the gradient magnitude, a binary map of the main edges of an image can be obtained. Edges carry important visual information since they delineate the image elements. For this reason, they can be used, for example, in object recognition. However, simple binary edge maps suffer from two main drawbacks. First, the edges detected are unnecessarily thick. This means precise localization of an object limit cannot be done. Second, and more importantly, it is difficult to find a threshold that is sufficiently low to detect all important image edges of an image and that is, at the same time, sufficiently high to not include too many insignificant edges. This is a trade-off problem that the Canny algorithm tries to solve.

How to do it...

The Canny algorithm is implemented in OpenCV by the function `cv::Canny`. As will be explained, this algorithm requires the specification of two thresholds. The call to the function is therefore as follows:

```cpp
// Apply Canny algorithm
cv::Mat contours;
cv::Canny(image,     // gray-level image
          contours,  // output contours
          125,       // low threshold
          350);      // high threshold
```

When applied on the following image:

The result is as follows:

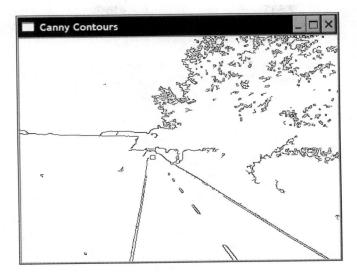

Note that to obtain an image as shown in the preceding screenshot, we had to invert the black and white values since the normal result represents contours by non-zero pixels. The inverted representation, which is nicer to print on a page, is simply produced as follows:

```
cv::Mat contoursInv; // inverted image
cv::threshold(contours,contoursInv,
            128,    // values below this
            255,    // becomes this
            cv::THRESH_BINARY_INV);
```

How it works...

The Canny operator is generally based on the Sobel operator, although other gradient operators can be used. The key idea here is to use two different thresholds in order to determine which point should belong to a contour: a low and a high threshold.

The low threshold should be chosen in a way that it includes all edge pixels that are considered to belong to a significant image contour. For example, using the low-threshold value specified in the example of the preceding section, and applying it on the result of a Sobel operator, the following edge map is obtained:

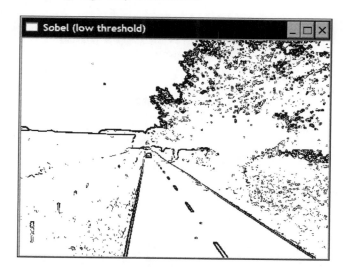

As it can be seen, the edges that delineate the road are very well defined. However, because a permissive threshold was used, more edges than what is ideally needed are also detected. The role of the second threshold is then to define the edges that belong to all important contours. It should exclude all edges considered as outliers. For example, the Sobel edge map corresponding to the high-threshold used in our example is:

We now have an image containing broken edges, but the ones visible certainly belong to the significant contours of the scene. The Canny algorithm combines these two edge maps in order to produce an "optimal" map of contours. It operates by keeping only the edge points of the low-threshold edge map for which a continuous path of edges exists, linking that edge point to an edge belonging to the high-threshold edge map. Consequently, all edge points of the high-threshold map are kept, while all isolated chains of edge points in the low-threshold map are removed. The solution obtained constitutes a good compromise allowing good quality contours to be obtained as long as appropriate threshold values are specified. This strategy, based on the use of two thresholds to obtain a binary map, is called **hysteresis thresholding** and can be used in any context where a binary map needs to be obtained from a thresholding operation. However, this is done at the cost of a higher computational complexity.

In addition, the Canny algorithm uses an extra strategy to improve the quality of the edge map. Prior to the application of the hysteresis thresholding, all edge points for which the gradient magnitude is not a maximum in the gradient direction are removed. Recall that the gradient orientation is always perpendicular to the edge. Therefore, the local maximum of the gradient in this direction corresponds to the point of maximum strength of the contour. This explains why thin edges are obtained in the Canny contour maps.

See also

The classic article by J. Canny, *A computational approach to edge detection, IEEE Transactions on Pattern Analysis and Image Understanding, vol. 18, issue 6, 1986.*

Detecting lines in images with the Hough transform

In our human-made world, planar and linear structures abound. As a result, straight lines are frequently visible in images. These are meaningful features that play an important role in object recognition and image understanding. Therefore, it is useful to detect these particular features in images. The **Hough transform** is a classic algorithm that achieves this goal. It was initially developed to detect lines in images and, as we will see, it can also be extended to detect other simple image structures.

Getting ready

With the Hough transform, lines are represented using the following equation:

$$p = x \cos \theta + y \sin \theta$$

The parameter ρ is the distance between the line and the image origin (upper-left corner), and θ is the angle of the perpendicular to the line. Under this representation, the lines visible in an image have a θ angle between 0 and π radians, while the radius ρ can have a maximum value that equals to the length of the image diagonal. Consider, for example, the following set of lines:

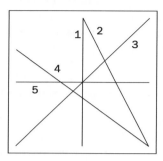

A vertical line like line 1 has a θ angle value equal to zero, while a horizontal line (for example, line 5) has its θ value equal to $\pi/2$. Therefore, line 3 has an angle θ equal to $\pi/4$, and line 4 is at approximately 0.7π. In order to be able to represent all possible lines with θ in the interval $[0,\pi]$, the radius value can be made negative. This is the case of line 2 which has a θ value equal to 0.8π with a negative value for ρ.

How to do it...

OpenCV offers two implementations of the Hough transform for line detection. The basic version is `cv::HoughLines`. Its input is a binary map containing a set of points (represented by non-zero pixels), some of them being aligned to form lines. Usually, it is an edge map obtained, for example, from the Canny operator. The output of the `cv::HoughLines` function is a vector of `cv::Vec2f` elements, each of them being a pair of floating point values which represents the parameters of a detected line (ρ, θ). Here is an example of using this function where we first apply the Canny operator to obtain the image contours, and then detect the lines using the Hough transform:

```
// Apply Canny algorithm
cv::Mat contours;
cv::Canny(image,contours,125,350);
// Hough tranform for line detection
std::vector<cv::Vec2f> lines;
cv::HoughLines(test,lines,
     1,PI/180,  // step size
     80);        // minimum number of votes
```

Parameters 3 and 4 correspond to the step size for the line search. In our example, the function will search for lines of all possible radii by step of 1 and of all possible angles by step of π/180. The role of the last parameter will be explained in the next section. With this particular choice of parameter values, fifteen lines are detected on the road image of the preceding recipe. In order to visualize the result of the detection, it is interesting to draw these lines on the original image. However, it is important, to note that this algorithm detects lines in an image, not line segments since the end points of each lines are not given. Consequently, we will draw lines that traverse the entire image. To do this, for an almost vertical line, we calculate its intersection with the horizontal limits of the image (that is, first and last rows) and draw a line between these two points. We proceed similarly with almost horizontal lines but using first and last columns. Lines are drawn using the `cv::line` function. Note that this function works well even with point coordinates outside the image limits. Therefore, do not need to check if the computed intersection points fall within the image. Lines are then drawn by iterating over the lines vector as follows:

```cpp
std::vector<cv::Vec2f>::const_iterator it= lines.begin();
while (it!=lines.end()) {

    float rho= (*it)[0];    // first element is distance rho
    float theta= (*it)[1]; // second element is angle theta

    if (theta < PI/4.
        || theta > 3.*PI/4.) { // ~vertical line

        // point of intersection of the line with first row
        cv::Point pt1(rho/cos(theta),0);
        // point of intersection of the line with last row
        cv::Point pt2((rho-result.rows*sin(theta))/
                                cos(theta),result.rows);
        // draw a white line
        cv::line( image, pt1, pt2, cv::Scalar(255), 1);

    } else { // ~horizontal line

        // point of intersection of the
        // line with first column
        cv::Point pt1(0,rho/sin(theta));
        // point of intersection of the line with last column
        cv::Point pt2(result.cols,
                (rho-result.cols*cos(theta))/sin(theta));
        // draw a white line
        cv::line(image, pt1, pt2, cv::Scalar(255), 1);
    }
    ++it;
}
```

The following result is then obtained:

As it can be seen, the Hough transform simply looks for an alignment of edge pixels across the image. This can potentially create some false detection due to an incidental pixel alignment, or multiple detections when several lines pass through the same alignment of pixels.

To overcome some of these problems, and to allow line segments to be detected (that is, with end points), a variant of the transform has been proposed. This is the Probabilistic Hough transform and it is implemented in OpenCV as function `cv::HoughLinesP`. We use it here to create our `LineFinder` class that encapsulates the function parameters:

```
class LineFinder {

  private:

    // original image
    cv::Mat img;

    // vector containing the end points
    // of the detected lines
    std::vector<cv::Vec4i> lines;

    // accumulator resolution parameters
    double deltaRho;
    double deltaTheta;

    // minimum number of votes that a line
    // must receive before being considered
    int minVote;

    // min length for a line
    double minLength;
```

```
    // max allowed gap along the line
    double maxGap;
public:
    // Default accumulator resolution is 1 pixel by 1 degree
    // no gap, no mimimum length
    LineFinder() : deltaRho(1), deltaTheta(PI/180),
                   minVote(10), minLength(0.), maxGap(0.) {}
```

With the corresponding setter methods:

```
    // Set the resolution of the accumulator
    void setAccResolution(double dRho, double dTheta) {

        deltaRho= dRho;
        deltaTheta= dTheta;
    }
    // Set the minimum number of votes
    void setMinVote(int minv) {

        minVote= minv;
    }
    // Set line length and gap
    void setLineLengthAndGap(double length, double gap) {

        minLength= length;
        maxGap= gap;
    }
```

The method that performs Hough line segment detection is then simply:

```
    // Apply probabilistic Hough Transform
    std::vector<cv::Vec4i> findLines(cv::Mat& binary) {

        lines.clear();
        cv::HoughLinesP(binary,lines,
                        deltaRho, deltaTheta, minVote,
                        minLength, maxGap);

        return lines;
    }
```

This method returns a vector of `cv::Vec4i`, each containing the start and end point coordinates of each detected segment. The detected lines can then be drawn on an image by the following method:

```
    // Draw the detected lines on an image
    void drawDetectedLines(cv::Mat &image,
            cv::Scalar color=cv::Scalar(255,255,255)) {
```

```
          // Draw the lines
          std::vector<cv::Vec4i>::const_iterator it2=
                                              lines.begin();

          while (it2!=lines.end()) {

            cv::Point pt1((*it2)[0],(*it2)[1]);
            cv::Point pt2((*it2)[2],(*it2)[3]);

            cv::line( image, pt1, pt2, color);

            ++it2;
          }
        }
```

Now, using the same input image, lines can be detected by the following sequence:

```
      // Create LineFinder instance
      LineFinder finder;

      // Set probabilistic Hough parameters
      finder.setLineLengthAndGap(100,20);
      finder.setMinVote(80);

      // Detect lines and draw them
      std::vector<cv::Vec4i> lines= finder.findLines(contours);
      finder.drawDetectedLines(image);
      cv::namedWindow("Detected Lines with HoughP");
      cv::imshow("Detected Lines with HoughP",image);
```

Which gives the following result:

How it works...

The objective of the Hough transform is to find all lines in a binary image that pass through a sufficient number of points. It proceeds by considering each individual pixel point in the input binary map and identifying all possible lines passing through it. When the same line passes through many points, it means that this line is significant enough to be considered.

The Hough transform uses a 2-dimensional accumulator in order to count how many times a given line is identified. The size of this accumulator is defined by the specified step sizes (as mentioned in the preceding section) of the (ρ, θ) parameters of the adopted line representation. To illustrate the functioning of the transform, let's create a *180* by *200* matrix (corresponding to a step size of $\pi/180$ for θ and *1* for ρ):

```
// Create a Hough accumulator
// here a uchar image; in practice should be ints
cv::Mat acc(200,180,CV_8U,cv::Scalar(0));
```

This accumulator is a mapping of different (ρ, θ) values. Therefore, each entry of this matrix corresponds to one particular line. Now if we consider one point, let's say one at coordinate `(50, 30)`, then it is possible to identify all lines passing through this point by looping over all possible θ angles (with a step size of $\pi/180$) and compute the corresponding (rounded) ρ value:

```
// Choose a point
int x=50, y=30;
// loop over all angles
for (int i=0; i<180; i++) {

    double theta= i*PI/180.;

    // find corresponding rho value
    double rho= x*cos(theta)+y*sin(theta);
    // j corresponds to rho from -100 to 100
    int j= static_cast<int>(rho+100.5);

    std::cout << i << "," << j << std::endl;

    // increment accumulator
    acc.at<uchar>(j,i)++;
}
```

The entries of the accumulator corresponding to the computed (ρ, θ) pairs are then incremented, signifying that all of these lines pass through one point of the image (or, to say it another way, each point votes for a set of possible candidate lines). If we display the accumulator as an image (multiply by `100` to make the count of 1 visible), we obtain:

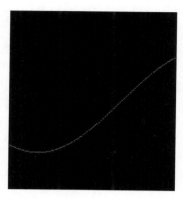

This curve represents the set of all lines passing through the considered point. Now, if we repeat the same exercise with, let's say point `(30, 10)`, we now have the following accumulator:

As it can be seen, the two resulting curves intersect at one point. The point that corresponds to the line passing by these two points. The corresponding entry of the accumulator receives two votes, indicating that two points pass through this line. If the same process is repeated for all points of a binary map, then points aligned along a given line will increment a common entry of the accumulator many times. At the end, one just needs to identify the local maxima in this accumulator that receives a significant number of votes in order to detect the lines (that is, point alignments) in the image. The last parameter specified in the `cv::HoughLines` function corresponds to the minimum number of votes that a line must receive to be considered as detected. For example, if we lower this value at 60, that is:

```
cv::HoughLines(test,lines,1,PI/180,60);
```

Then more lines will be accepted for the example of the preceding section as seen here:

The probabilistic Hough transform adds few modifications to the basic algorithm. First, instead of systematically scanning the image row-by-row, points are chosen in random order in the binary map. Whenever an entry of the accumulator reaches the specified minimum value, the image is scanned along the corresponding line and all points passing through it are removed (even if they have not voted yet). This scanning also determines the length of the segments that will be accepted. For this, the algorithm defines two additional parameters. One is the minimum length for a segment to be accepted, and the other is the maximum pixel gap that is permitted to form a continuous segment. This additional step increases the complexity of the algorithm, but this is partly compensated by the fact that fewer points will be involved in the voting process as some of them are eliminated by the line scanning process.

There's more...

The Hough transform can also be used to detect other geometrical entities. In fact, any entity that can be represented by a parametric equation is a good candidate for the Hough transform.

Detecting circles

In the case of circles, the corresponding parametric equation is:

$$r^2 = (x - x_0)^2 + (y - y_0)^2$$

This equation includes three parameters (the circle radius and center coordinates) which means that a 3-dimensional accumulator would be required. However, it is generally found that the Hough transform becomes less reliable as the dimensionality of its accumulator increases. Indeed, in this case, a large number of entries of the accumulator will be incremented for each point and, in consequence, the accurate localization of local peaks becomes more difficult. Therefore, different strategies have been proposed in order to overcome this problem. The one used in the OpenCV implementation of the Hough circle detection uses two passes. During the first pass, a 2-dimensional accumulator is used to find candidate circle locations. Since the gradient of points on the circumference of a circle should point in the direction of the radius, then, for each point, only the entries in the accumulator along the gradient direction are incremented (based on predefined minimum and maximum radius values). Once a possible circle center is detected (that is, received a predefined number of votes), then an 1D histogram of possible radius is built during the second pass. The peak value in this histogram corresponds to the radius of the detected circles.

The function `cv::HoughCircles` that implements the strategy above integrates both the Canny detection and the Hough transform. It is called as follows:

```
cv::GaussianBlur(image,image,cv::Size(5,5),1.5);
std::vector<cv::Vec3f> circles;
cv::HoughCircles(image, circles, CV_HOUGH_GRADIENT,
    2,   // accumulator resolution (size of the image / 2)
    50,  // minimum distance between two circles
    200, // Canny high threshold
    100, // minimum number of votes
    25, 100); // min and max radius
```

Note that it is always recommended to smooth the image before calling the `cv::HoughCircles` function in order to reduce the image noise that could cause several false circle detections. The result of the detection is given in a vector of `cv::Vec3f` instances. The first two values are the circle center and the third is the radius. The argument `CV_HOUGH_GRADIENT` was the only option available at the time of writing this book. It corresponds to the two-pass circle detection methods. The fourth parameter defines the accumulator resolution. It is a divider factor, for example, specifying a value of 2 makes the accumulator half the size of the image. The next parameter is the minimum distance in pixels between two detected circles. The other parameter corresponds to the high-threshold of the Canny edge detector. The low-threshold value is set at half this value. The seventh parameter is the minimum number of votes that a center location must receive during the first pass to be considered as a candidate circle for the second pass. Finally, the last two parameters are the minimum and maximum radius values for the circles to be detected. As can be seen, the function includes many parameters which make it difficult to tune.

Once the vector of detected circles is obtained, these can be drawn on the image by iterating over the vector and calling the `cv::circle` drawing function with the found parameters:

```
std::vector<cv::Vec3f>::
      const_iterator itc= circles.begin();

while (itc!=circles.end()) {

  cv::circle(image,
     cv::Point((*itc)[0], (*itc)[1]), // circle centre
     (*itc)[2],          // circle radius
     cv::Scalar(255), // color
     2);                 // thickness

  ++itc;
}
```

Here is the result obtained on a test image with the chosen arguments:

Generalized Hough transform

For some shapes, it is difficult to find a compact parametric representation, for example, triangles, octagons, polygons, object profiles, and so on. However, it is still possible to use the Hough transform to locate these shapes in an image. The principle remains the same. A 2-dimensional accumulator is created which represents all possible locations for the targeted shape. Therefore, a reference point must be defined on the shape, and each feature point on the image votes for possible reference point locations. Since a point can be anywhere on the contour of the shape, the locus of all possible reference positions will trace a shape in the accumulator that is the mirror of the shape of interest. Again, points that belong to the same shape in the image will generate a peak in the accumulator at an intersection point that corresponds to that shape's location.

This is illustrated in the following figure where the shape of interest is a triangle (shown on right) on which the reference is defined at the bottom-left corner. On the accumulator is shown a feature point that will increment all entries at the drawn locations as they correspond to possible positions for the reference points of a triangle passing through this feature point:

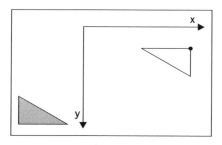

This approach is often referred to as the **Generalized Hough transform**. Obviously, it does not take into account possible scale change or rotations of the shape. This would require a search in higher dimension.

See also

The article *Gradient-based Progressive Probabilistic Hough Transform by C. Galambos, J. Kittler, and J. Matas, IEE Vision Image and Signal Processing, vol. 148 no 3, pp. 158-165, 2002*. It is one of the numerous reference on the Hough transform and describes the probabilistic algorithm implemented in OpenCV.

The article by *H.K. Yuen, J. Princen, J. Illingworth, and J Kittler, Comparative Study of Hough Transform Methods for Circle Finding, Image and Vision Computing, vol. 8 no 1, pp. 71-77, 1990* that describes different strategies for circle detection using the Hough transform.

Fitting a line to a set of points

In some applications, it could be important to not only detect lines in an image, but also to obtain an accurate estimate of the line's position and orientation. This recipe will show you how to find the line that best fits a given set of points.

How to do it...

The first thing to do is to identify points in an image that seem to be aligned along a straight line. Let's then use one of the lines we detected in the preceding recipe. Suppose the lines detected using `cv::HoughLinesP` are contained in a `std::vector` called `lines`. To extract the set of points that seem to belong to, let's say, the first of these line, we can proceed as follows. We draw a white line on a black image and intersect it with the Canny image of contours used to detect our lines. This is simply achieved by the following statements:

```
int n=0; // we select line 0
// black image
cv::Mat oneline(contours.size(),CV_8U,cv::Scalar(0));
// white line
cv::line(oneline,
         cv::Point(lines[n][0],lines[n][1]),
         cv::Point(lines[n][2],lines[n][3]),
         cv::Scalar(255),
         5);
// contours AND white line
cv::bitwise_and(contours,oneline,oneline);
```

The result is an image containing only the points that could be associated with the specified line. In order to introduce some tolerance, we draw a line of a certain thickness (here 5). All points inside the defined neighborhood are therefore accepted. Here is the image obtained (inverted for better viewing):

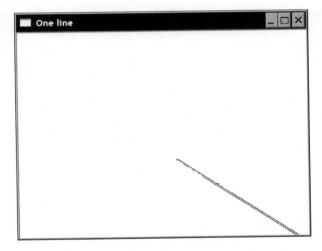

The coordinates of the points in this set can then be inserted in a std::vector of cv::Points (floating point coordinates, that is, cv::Point2f, can also be used) by the following double loop:

```
std::vector<cv::Point> points;

// Iterate over the pixels to obtain all point positions
for( int y = 0; y < oneline.rows; y++ ) {
    // row y
    uchar* rowPtr = oneline.ptr<uchar>(y);

    for( int x = 0; x < oneline.cols; x++ ) {
        // column x
```

```
            // if on a contour
            if (rowPtr[x]) {

                points.push_back(cv::Point(x,y));
            }
        }
    }
```

The best fit line is easily found by calling the OpenCV function `cv::fitLine`:

```
cv::Vec4f line;
cv::fitLine(cv::Mat(points),line,
            CV_DIST_L2, // distance type
            0,          // not used with L2 distance
            0.01,0.01); // accuracy
```

This gives us the parameters of the line equation in the form of a unit directional vector (the first two values of the `cv::Vec4f`) and the coordinates of one point on the line (the last two values of the `cv::Vec4f`). For our example, these values are (0.83, 0.55) for the directional vector and (366.1, 289.1) for the point coordinates. The last two parameters specify the requested accuracy for the line parameters. Note that the input points contained in a `std::vector` are transferred in a `cv::Mat` as required by the function.

In general, the line equation will be used in the calculation of some properties (calibration is a good example where precise parametric representation is required). As an illustration, and to make sure we calculated the right line, let's draw the estimated line on the image. Here, we simply draw an arbitrary black segment having a length of 200 pixels and a thickness of 3 pixels:

```
int x0= line[2];        // a point on the line
int y0= line[3];
int x1= x0-200*line[0]; // add a vector of length 200
int y1= y0-200*line[1]; // using the unit vector
image= cv::imread("../road.jpg",0);
cv::line(image,cv::Point(x0,y0),cv::Point(x1,y1),
        cv::Scalar(0),3);
```

The result is then seen in the following image:

How it works...

Fitting lines to a set of points is a classic problem in mathematics. The OpenCV implementation proceeds by minimizing the sum of the distances from each point to the line. Several distance functions are proposed, and the fastest option is to use the Euclidean distance, specified by CV_DIST_L2. This choice corresponds to the standard least-squares line fitting. When outliers (that is, points not belonging to the line) might be included in the point set, other distance functions that give less influence to far points can be selected. The minimization is based on the M-estimator technique that iteratively solves a weighted least-squares problem with weights inversely proportional to the distance from the line.

Using this function, it is also possible to fit a line to a 3D point set. The input is, in this case, a set of cv::Point3i or cv::Point3f and the output is a std::Vec6f.

There's more...

The function cv::fitEllipse fits an ellipse to a set of 2D points. It returns a rotated rectangle (a cv::RotatedRect instance) inside which the ellipse is inscribed. In this case, you would write:

```
cv::RotatedRect rrect= cv::fitEllipse(cv::Mat(points));
cv::ellipse(image,rrect,cv::Scalar(0));
```

The function cv::ellipse is the one you would use to draw the computed ellipse.

Extracting the components' contours

Images generally contain representation of objects. One of the goals of image analysis is to identify and extract those objects. In object detection/recognition applications, the first step is to produce a binary image showing where certain objects of interest could be located. No matter how this binary map has been obtained (for example, could be from the histogram back projection as we did in *Chapter 4*, or from motion analysis as we will learn in *Chapter 10*), the next step is to then extract the objects which are contained in this collection of 1s and 0s. Consider for example, the image of buffaloes in binary form that we manipulated in *Chapter 5* as seen here:

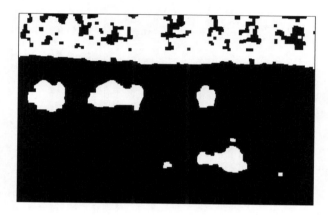

We obtained this image from a simple thresholding operation followed by the application of open and close morphological filters. This recipe will show you how to extract the objects of such images. More specifically, we will extract the **connected components**, that is, shapes made of a set of connected pixels in a binary image.

How to do it...

OpenCV offers a simple function which extracts the contours of the connected components of an image. It is the `cv::findContours` function:

```
std::vector<std::vector<cv::Point>> contours;
cv::findContours(image,
    contours, // a vector of contours
    CV_RETR_EXTERNAL, // retrieve the external contours
    CV_CHAIN_APPROX_NONE); // all pixels of each contours
```

The input is obviously the binary image. The output is a vector of contours, each contour being represented by a vector of `cv::Points`. This explains why the output parameter is defined as a `std::vector` of `std::vectors`. In addition, two flags are specified. The first one indicates that only the external contours are required, that is, holes in object will be ignored; (the *There's more...* section will discuss the other options). The second flag is there to specify the format of the contour. With the current option, the vector will list all of the points in the contour. With the flag `CV_CHAIN_APPROX_SIMPLE`, only the end points would be included for horizontal, vertical, or diagonal contours. Other flags would give more sophisticated chain approximation of the contours in order to obtain a more compact representation. With the preceding image, nine contours are obtained as given by `contours.size()`. Fortunately, there is a very convenient function that can draw those contours on an image (here, a white image):

```
// Draw black contours on a white image
cv::Mat result(image.size(),CV_8U,cv::Scalar(255));
cv::drawContours(result,contours,
    -1, // draw all contours
    cv::Scalar(0), // in black
    2); // with a thickness of 2
```

If the third parameter of this function is a negative value, then all contours are drawn. Otherwise, it is possible to specify the index of the contour to be drawn. The result is seen in the following screenshot:

How it works...

The contours are extracted by a simple algorithm that consists of systematically scanning the image until a component is hit. From this starting point on the component, its contour is followed, marking the pixels on its border. When the contour is completed, the scanning resumes at the last position until a new component is found.

The identified connected components can then be individually analyzed. For example, if some prior knowledge is available about the expected size of the objects of interest, it becomes possible to eliminate some of the components. Let's then use a minimum and a maximum value for the perimeter of the components. This is done by iterating over the vector of contours and eliminating the invalid components:

```
// Eliminate too short or too long contours
int cmin= 100;  // minimum contour length
int cmax= 1000; // maximum contour length
std::vector<std::vector<cv::Point>>::
          const_iterator itc= contours.begin();
while (itc!=contours.end()) {

   if (itc->size() < cmin || itc->size() > cmax)
      itc= contours.erase(itc);
   else
      ++itc;
}
```

Note that this loop could have been made more efficiently since each erasing operation in a `std::vector` is O(N). But considering the size of this vector, this operation is not too costly. This time we draw the remaining contours on the original image and obtain the following result:

We were lucky enough to find a simple criterion that allowed us to identify all objects of interest in this image. In more complex situations, a more refined analysis of the components' properties is required. This is the object of the next recipe.

There's more...

With the `cv::findContours` function, it is also possible to include all closed contours in the binary map, including the ones formed by holes in the components. This is done by specifying another flag in the function call:

```
cv::findContours(image,
      contours, // a vector of contours
      CV_RETR_LIST, // retrieve all contours
      CV_CHAIN_APPROX_NONE); // all pixels of each contours
```

With this call, the following contours are obtained:

Notice the extra contours that were added in the background forest. It is also possible to have these contours organized into a hierarchy. The main component is the parent, holes in it are its children, and if there are components inside these holes, they become the children of the previous children, and so on. This hierarchy is obtained by using the flag `CV_RETR_TREE`, as follows:

```
std::vector<cv::Vec4i> hierarchy;
cv::findContours(image,
      contours, // a vector of contours
      hierarchy, // hierarchical representation
      CV_RETR_TREE, // retrieve all contours in tree format
      CV_CHAIN_APPROX_NONE); // all pixels of each contours
```

In this case, each contour has a corresponding hierarchy element at the same index made of four integers. The first two integers give the index of the next and the previous contours of the same level, and the next two integers give the index of the first child and the parent of this contour. A negative index indicates the end of a contour list. The flag CV_RETR_CCOMP is similar but limits the hierarchy at two levels.

Computing components' shape descriptors

A connected component often corresponds to the image of some object in a pictured scene. To identify this object, or to compare it with other image elements, it can be useful to perform some measurements on the component in order to extract some of its characteristics. In this recipe, we will look at some of the shape descriptors available in OpenCV that can be used to describe the shape of a connected component.

How to do it...

Many OpenCV functions are available when it comes to shape description. We will apply some of them on the components that we have extracted in the preceding recipe. In particular, we will use our vector of four contours corresponding to the four buffaloes we previously identified. In the following code snippets, we compute a shape descriptor on the contours (contours[0] to contours[3]) and draw the result (with a thickness of 2) over the image of the contours (with a thickness of 1). This image is shown at the end of this section.

The first one is the bounding box, applied to the bottom right component:

```
// testing the bounding box
cv::Rect r0= cv::boundingRect(cv::Mat(contours[0]));
cv::rectangle(result,r0,cv::Scalar(0),2);
```

The minimum enclosing circle is similar. It is applied on the upper-right component:

```
// testing the enclosing circle
float radius;
cv::Point2f center;
cv::minEnclosingCircle(cv::Mat(contours[1]),center,radius);
cv::circle(result,cv::Point(center),
          static_cast<int>(radius),cv::Scalar(0),2);
```

The polygonal approximation of a component's contour is computed as follows (on the left component):

```
// testing the approximate polygon
std::vector<cv::Point> poly;
cv::approxPolyDP(cv::Mat(contours[2]),poly,
                5,      // accuracy of the approximation
                true); // yes it is a closed shape
```

Drawing the result on an image requires more work:

```
// Iterate over each segment and draw it
std::vector<cv::Point>::const_iterator itp= poly.begin();
while (itp!=(poly.end()-1)) {
    cv::line(result,*itp,*(itp+1),cv::Scalar(0),2);
    ++itp;
}
// last point linked to first point
cv::line(result,
            *(poly.begin()),
            *(poly.end()-1),cv::Scalar(20),2);
```

The convex hull is another form of polygonal approximation:

```
// testing the convex hull
std::vector<cv::Point> hull;
cv::convexHull(cv::Mat(contours[3]),hull);
```

Finally, the computation of the moments is another powerful descriptor:

```
// testing the moments

// iterate over all contours
itc= contours.begin();
while (itc!=contours.end()) {

    // compute all moments
    cv::Moments mom= cv::moments(cv::Mat(*itc++));

    // draw mass center
    cv::circle(result,
        // position of mass center converted to integer
        cv::Point(mom.m10/mom.m00,mom.m01/mom.m00),
        2,cv::Scalar(0),2); // draw black dot

}
```

The resulting image is as follows:

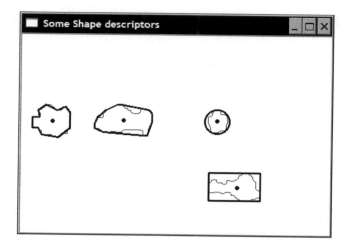

How it works...

The **bounding box** of a component is probably the most compact way to represent and localize a component in an image. It is defined as the upright rectangle of minimum size that completely contains the shape. Comparing the height and width of the box gives an indication about the vertical or horizontal orientation of the object (for example, to distinguish the image of a car from the one of a pedestrian). The minimum enclosing circle is generally used when only component size and location is required.

The polygonal approximation of a component is useful when one wants to manipulate a more compact representation that resembles the component's shape. It is created by specifying an accuracy parameter giving the maximal acceptable distance between a shape and its simplified polygon. It is the fourth parameter in the cv::approxPolyDP function. The result is a vector of cv::Point corresponding to the vertices of the polygon. To draw this polygon, we need to iterate over the vector and link each point with the next one by drawing a line between them.

The **convex hull**, or convex envelop, of a shape is the minimal convex polygon that encompass a shape. It can be visualized as the shape that an elastic band would take if placed around the component.

Moments are commonly used mathematical entities in the structural analysis of shapes. OpenCV has defined a data structure which encapsulates all computed moments of a shape. It is the object returned by the cv::moments function. We simply use this structure to obtain the mass center of each component that is here computed from the first three spatial moments.

There's more...

Other structural properties can be computed using the available OpenCV functions. Function `cv::minAreaRect` computes the minimum enclosing rotated rectangle. Function `cv::contourArea` estimates the area of (number of pixel inside) a contour. Function `cv::pointPolygonTest` determines if a point is inside or outside a contour, and `cv::matchShapes` measure the resemblance between two contours.

8
Detecting and Matching Interest Points

In this chapter, we will cover:

- ▶ Detecting Harris corners
- ▶ Detecting FAST features
- ▶ Detecting the scale-invariant SURF features
- ▶ Describing SURF features

Introduction

In computer vision, the concept of **interest points**, also called **keypoints** or **feature points**, has been largely used to solve many problems in object recognition, image registration, visual tracking, 3D reconstruction, and more. It relies on the idea that instead of looking at the image as a whole, it could be advantageous to select some special points in the image and perform a local analysis on these ones. These approaches work well as long as a sufficient number of such points are detected in the images of interest and these points are distinguishing and stable features that can be accurately localized. This chapter will introduce a few interest point detectors and show you how to use them in image matching.

Detecting Harris corners

When searching for interesting feature points in images, corners come out as an interesting solution. They indeed are local features that can be easily localized in an image, and in addition, they should abound in scenes of man-made objects (where they are produced by walls, doors, windows, tables, and so on). Corners are also interesting because they are two-dimensional features that can be accurately localized (even at sub-pixel accuracy) as they are at the junction of two edges. This is in contrast to points located on a uniform area or on the contour of an object and that would be difficult to repeatedly localize precisely on other images of the same object.

The Harris feature detector is a classical approach to detect corners in an image. We will explore this operator in this recipe.

How to do it...

The basic OpenCV function for detecting Harris corners is called `cv::cornerHarris` and is straightforward to use. You call it on an input image and the result is an image of floats which gives the corner strength at each pixel location. A threshold is then applied on this output image in order to obtain a set of detected corners. This is accomplished by the following code:

```cpp
// Detect Harris Corners
cv::Mat cornerStrength;
cv::cornerHarris(image,cornerStrength,
          3,      // neighborhood size
          3,      // aperture size
          0.01); // Harris parameter
// threshold the corner strengths
cv::Mat harrisCorners;
double threshold= 0.0001;
cv::threshold(cornerStrength,harrisCorners,
          threshold,255,cv::THRESH_BINARY);
```

Here is the original image:

The result is a binary map image shown in the following screenshot which is inverted for better viewing (that is, we used `cv::THRESH_BINARY_INV` instead of `cv::THRESH_BINARY` to get the detected corners in black):

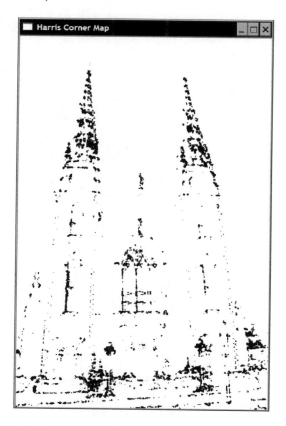

From the preceding function call, we observe that this interest point detector requires several parameters (these will be explained in the next section) which may make it difficult to tune. In addition, the corner map that is obtained contains many clusters of corner pixels which contradict the fact that we would like to detect well-localized points. Therefore, we will try to improve the corner detection method by defining our own class to detect Harris corners.

The class encapsulates the Harris parameters with their default values and corresponding getter and setter methods (which are not shown here):

```
class HarrisDetector {

  private:

      // 32-bit float image of corner strength
      cv::Mat cornerStrength;
      // 32-bit float image of thresholded corners
      cv::Mat cornerTh;
```

```
        // image of local maxima (internal)
        cv::Mat localMax;
        // size of neighborhood for derivatives smoothing
        int neighbourhood;
        // aperture for gradient computation
        int aperture;
        // Harris parameter
        double k;
        // maximum strength for threshold computation
        double maxStrength;
        // calculated threshold (internal)
        double threshold;
        // size of neighborhood for non-max suppression
        int nonMaxSize;
        // kernel for non-max suppression
        cv::Mat kernel;
    public:
        HarrisDetector() : neighbourhood(3), aperture(3),
                        k(0.01), maxStrength(0.0),
                        threshold(0.01), nonMaxSize(3) {
            // create kernel used in non-maxima suppression
            setLocalMaxWindowSize(nonMaxSize);
        }
```

To detect the Harris corners on an image, we proceed with two steps. First, the Harris values at each pixel are computed:

```
        // Compute Harris corners
        void detect(const cv::Mat& image) {
            // Harris computation
            cv::cornerHarris(image,cornerStrength,
                    neighbourhood,// neighborhood size
                    aperture,     // aperture size
                    k);           // Harris parameter

            // internal threshold computation
            double minStrength; // not used
            cv::minMaxLoc(cornerStrength,
                &minStrength,&maxStrength);

            // local maxima detection
            cv::Mat dilated;  // temporary image
            cv::dilate(cornerStrength,dilated,cv::Mat());
            cv::compare(cornerStrength,dilated,
                        localMax,cv::CMP_EQ);
        }
```

Next, the feature points are obtained based on a specified threshold value. Since the range of possible values for Harris depends on the particular choices of its parameters, the threshold is specified as a quality level defined as a fraction of the maximal Harris value computed in the image:

```
// Get the corner map from the computed Harris values
cv::Mat getCornerMap(double qualityLevel) {

    cv::Mat cornerMap;

    // thresholding the corner strength
    threshold= qualityLevel*maxStrength;
    cv::threshold(cornerStrength,cornerTh,
                threshold,255,cv::THRESH_BINARY);

    // convert to 8-bit image
    cornerTh.convertTo(cornerMap,CV_8U);

    // non-maxima suppression
    cv::bitwise_and(cornerMap,localMax,cornerMap);

    return cornerMap;
}
```

This method returns a binary corner map of the detected features. The fact that the detection of the Harris features has been split into two methods allows us to test the detection with a different threshold (until an appropriate number of feature points are obtained) without needing to repeat costly computations. It is also possible to obtain the Harris features in the form of a `std::vector` of `cv::Point`:

```
// Get the feature points from the computed Harris values
void getCorners(std::vector<cv::Point> &points,
                double qualityLevel) {

    // Get the corner map
    cv::Mat cornerMap= getCornerMap(qualityLevel);
    // Get the corners
    getCorners(points, cornerMap);
}

// Get the feature points from the computed corner map
void getCorners(std::vector<cv::Point> &points,
                const cv::Mat& cornerMap) {

    // Iterate over the pixels to obtain all features
    for( int y = 0; y < cornerMap.rows; y++ ) {

        const uchar* rowPtr = cornerMap.ptr<uchar>(y);

        for( int x = 0; x < cornerMap.cols; x++ ) {

            // if it is a feature point
            if (rowPtr[x]) {
```

```
                    points.push_back(cv::Point(x,y));
                }
            }
        }
    }
```

This class improves the detection of the Harris corners by adding a non-maxima suppression step which will be explained in the next section. The detected points can now be drawn on an image using the `cv::circle` function as demonstrated by the following method:

```
// Draw circles at feature point locations on an image
void drawOnImage(cv::Mat &image,
    const std::vector<cv::Point> &points,
    cv::Scalar color= cv::Scalar(255,255,255),
    int radius=3, int thickness=2) {

    std::vector<cv::Point>::const_iterator it=
                                    points.begin();

    // for all corners
    while (it!=points.end()) {

        // draw a circle at each corner location
        cv::circle(image,*it,radius,color,thickness);
        ++it;
    }
}
```

Using this class, the detection of the Harris points is accomplished as follows:

```
// Create Harris detector instance
HarrisDetector harris;
 // Compute Harris values
harris.detect(image);
 // Detect Harris corners
std::vector<cv::Point> pts;
harris.getCorners(pts,0.01);
// Draw Harris corners
harris.drawOnImage(image,pts);
```

Which results in the following image:

How it works...

To define the notion of corners in images, Harris looks at the average directional intensity change in a small window around a putative interest point. If we consider a displacement vector (u,v), the average intensity change is given by:

$$R = \sum (I(x + u, y + v) - I(x,y))^2$$

The summation is over a defined neighborhood around the considered pixel (the size of this neighborhood corresponds to the third parameter in the `cv::cornerHarris` function). This average intensity change can then be computed in all possible directions which leads to the definition of a corner as a point for which the average change is high in more than one direction. From this definition, the Harris test is performed as follows. We first obtain the direction of maximal average intensity change. Next, check if the average intensity change in the orthogonal direction is also high. If it is the case, then we have a corner.

Mathematically, this condition can be tested by using an approximation of the preceding formula using Taylor expansion:

$$R \approx \sum \left[I(x,y) + \frac{\partial I}{\partial x} u + \frac{\partial I}{\partial y} v - I(x,y) \right] = \sum \left[\left(\frac{\partial I}{\partial x} u \right)^2 + \left(\frac{\partial I}{\partial y} v \right)^2 + 2 \frac{\partial I}{\partial x} \frac{\partial I}{\partial y} uv \right]$$

Which is then rewritten in matrix form:

$$R \approx [u \quad v] \begin{bmatrix} \sum \left(\frac{\delta I}{\delta x} \right)^2 & \sum \frac{\delta I}{\delta x} \frac{\delta I}{\delta y} \\ \sum \frac{\delta I}{\delta x} \frac{\delta I}{\delta y} & \sum \left(\frac{\delta I}{\delta y} \right)^2 \end{bmatrix} \begin{bmatrix} u \\ v \end{bmatrix}$$

This matrix is a covariance matrix that characterizes the rate of intensity change in all directions. This definition involves the image's first derivatives that are often computed using the Sobel operator. This is the case of the OpenCV implementation, the fourth parameter of the function corresponding to the aperture used for the computation of the Sobel filters. It can be shown that the two eigenvalues of the covariance matrix gives the maximal average intensity change and the average intensity change for the orthogonal direction. It then follows that if these two eigenvalues are low, we are in a relatively homogenous region. If one eigenvalue is high and the other is low, we must be on an edge. Finally, if both eigenvalues are high, then we are at a corner location. Therefore, the condition for a point to be accepted as a corner is to have the smallest eigenvalue of the covariance matrix higher than a given threshold.

The original definition of the Harris corner algorithm uses some properties of the eigendecomposition theory in order to avoid the cost of explicitly computing the eigenvalues. These properties are:

▸ The product of the eigenvalues of a matrix is equal to its determinant

▸ The sum of the eigenvalues of a matrix is equal to the sum of the diagonal of the matrix (also known as the **trace** of the matrix)

It then follows that we can verify that two eigenvalues are high by computing the following score:

$$Det\ (C) - k \bullet Trace^2\ (C)$$

One can easily verify that this score will indeed be high only if both eigenvalues are also high. This is the score that is computed by the cv::cornerHarris function at each pixel location. The value of k is specified as the fifth parameter of the function. It could be difficult to determine what would be the best value for this parameter. However, in practice, it has been shown that a value in the range of 0.05 and 0.5 generally gives good results.

To improve the result of the detection, the class described in the previous section adds an additional non-maxima suppression step. The goal here is to exclude Harris corners that are adjacent to others. Therefore, to be accepted, the Harris corner must not only have a score higher than the specified threshold, but it must also be a local maximum. This condition is tested by using a simple trick which consists of dilating the image of Harris score in our `detect` method:

```
cv::dilate(cornerStrength,dilated,cv::Mat());
```

Since the dilation replaces each pixel value by the maximum in the defined neighborhood, then the only points that will not be modified are the local maxima That is what is verified by the following equality test:

```
cv::compare(cornerStrength,dilated,
            localMax,cv::CMP_EQ);
```

The `localMax` matrix will therefore be true (that is non-zero) only at local maxima locations. We then use it in our `getCornerMap` method to suppress all non-maximal features (using the `cv::bitwise_and` function).

There's more...

Additional improvements can be made to the original Harris corner algorithm. This section describes another corner detector found in OpenCV which expands the Harris detector to make its corners more uniformly distributed across the image. As we will see, this operator has an implementation in the new OpenCV 2 common interface for feature detector.

Good features to track

With the advent of the floating-point processor, the mathematical simplification introduced to avoid the eigenvalue decomposition has become negligible, and consequently the detection of Harris can be made based on the explicitly computed eigenvalues. In principle, this modification should not significantly affect the result of the detection, but it avoids the use of the arbitrary *k* parameter.

A second modification addresses the problem of feature point clustering. Indeed, in spite of the introduction of the local maxima condition, interest points tend to be unevenly distributed across an image, showing concentrations at locations highly textured. A solution to this problem is to impose a minimum distance between two interest points. This can be achieved by the following algorithm. Starting from the point with the strongest Harris score (that is with the largest minimum eigenvalue), only accept interest points if they are located at at least, a given distance from the already accepted points. This solution is implemented in OpenCV in the function `cv::goodFeaturesToTrack` thus named because the features it detects can be used as a good starting set in visual tracking application. It is called as follows:

```
// Compute good features to track
std::vector<cv::Point2f> corners;
```

```
cv::goodFeaturesToTrack(image,corners,
    500,    // maximum number of corners to be returned
    0.01,   // quality level
    10);    // minimum allowed distance between points
```

In addition to the quality-level threshold value, and the minimum tolerated distance between interest points, the function also uses a maximum number of points to be returned (this is possible since points are accepted in order of strength). The preceding function call produces the following result:

This approach increases the complexity of the detection since it requires the interest points to be sorted by their Harris score, but it also clearly improves the distribution of the points across the image. Note that this function also includes an optional flag to request Harris corners to be detected using the classical corner score definition (using covariance matrix determinant and trace).

Feature detector common interface

OpenCV 2 has introduced a new common interface for its different interest point detectors. This interface allows easy testing of different interest point detectors within the same application.

The interface defines a `Keypoint` class that encapsulates the properties of each detected feature point. For the Harris corners, only the position of the keypoints is relevant. The recipe *Detecting scale-invariant SURF points* will discuss the other properties that could be associated to a keypoint.

The `cv::FeatureDetector` abstract class basically imposes the existence of a `detect` operation with the following signatures:

```
void detect( const Mat& image, vector<KeyPoint>& keypoints,
             const Mat& mask=Mat() ) const;

void detect( const vector<Mat>& images,
             vector<vector<KeyPoint> >& keypoints,
             const vector<Mat>& masks=
                              vector<Mat>() ) const;
```

The second method allows interest points to be detected in a vector of images. The class also includes other methods to read and write the detected points in a file.

The `cv::goodFeaturesToTrack` function has a wrapper class called `cv::GoodFeatureToTrackDetector` , which inherits from the `cv::FeatureDetector` class. It can be used in a way similar to what we did with our Harris Corners class, that is:

```
// vector of keypoints
std::vector<cv::KeyPoint> keypoints;
// Construction of the Good Feature to Track detector
cv::GoodFeaturesToTrackDetector gftt(
    500,    // maximum number of corners to be returned
    0.01,   // quality level
    10);    // minimum allowed distance between points
// point detection using FeatureDetector method
gftt.detect(image,keypoints);
```

The results are the same as the one obtained before, since the same function is ultimately called by the wrapper.

See also

The classical article describing the Harris operator: *C. Harris and M.J. Stephens, A combined corner and edge detector,* by *Alvey Vision Conference, pp. 147–152, 1988.*

The article by J. Shi and C. Tomasi, *Good features to track, Int. Conference on Computer Vision and Pattern Recognition, pp. 593-600, 1994* which introduced these features.

The article by *K. Mikolajczyk* and *C. Schmid, Scale and Affine invariant interest point detectors, International Journal of Computer Vision, vol 60, no 1, pp. 63-86, 2004,* which proposes a multi-scale and affine-invariant Harris operator.

Detecting FAST features

The Harris operator proposed a formal mathematical definition for corners (or more generally, interest points) based on the rate of intensity changes in two perpendicular directions. Although this constitutes a sound definition, it requires the computation of the image derivatives which is a costly operation, especially considering the fact that interest point detection is often just the first step in a more complex algorithm.

In this recipe, we present another feature point operator. This one has been specifically designed to allow quick detection of interest points in an image. The decision to accept or not to accept a keypoint being based on only a few pixel comparisons.

How to do it...

Using the OpenCV 2 common interface for feature point detection makes the deployment of any feature point detectors easy. The one presented in this recipe is the FAST detector. As the name suggests, it has been designed to be quick to compute:

```
// vector of keypoints
std::vector<cv::KeyPoint> keypoints;
// Construction of the Fast feature detector object
cv::FastFeatureDetector fast(
        40); // threshold for detection
// feature point detection
fast.detect(image,keypoints);
```

Note that OpenCV also proposes a generic function to draw keypoints on an image:

```
cv::drawKeypoints(image,      // original image
    keypoints,                 // vector of keypoints
    image,                     // the output image
    cv::Scalar(255,255,255),   // keypoint color
    cv::DrawMatchesFlags::DRAW_OVER_OUTIMG); //drawing flag
```

By specifying the chosen drawing flag, the keypoints are drawn over the output image, thus producing the following result:

An interesting option is to specify a negative value for the keypoint color. In that case, a different random color will be selected for each drawn circle.

How it works...

As in the case of the Harris point, the FAST (Features from Accelerated Segment Test) feature algorithm derives from the definition of what constitutes a "corner". This time, this definition is based on the image intensity around a putative feature point. The decision to accept a keypoint is done by examining a circle of pixels centered at a candidate point. If an arc of contiguous points of length greater than 3/4 of the circle perimeter is found in which all pixels significantly differ from the intensity of the center point, then a keypoint is declared.

This is a simple test that can quickly be computed. Moreover, the algorithm uses an additional trick to further speed-up the process. Indeed, if we first test four points separated by 90° on the circle (for example, top, bottom, right, and left points) it can be easily shown that to satisfy the condition expressed above, at least three of these points must all be brighter or darker than the central pixel. If it is not the case, the point can immediately be rejected without inspecting additional points on the circumference. This is a very effective test since, in practice, most of the image points will be rejected by this simple 4-comparison test.

In principle, the radius of the circle of examined pixels should be a parameter of the method. However, it has been found that, in practice, a radius of 3 gives both good results and high efficiency. There are then 16 pixels to consider on the circumference of the circle as seen below:

```
              16   1    2
         15              3
     14                    4
     13           0        5
     12                    6
         11              7
              10   9    8
```

The four points used for the pretest are pixels 1, 5, 9, and 13.

As for Harris features, it is often better to perform non-maxima suppression on the corners found. Therefore, a corner strength measure needs to be defined. Several alternatives could have been considered, and the one that has been retained is the following. The strength of a corner is given by the sum of absolute difference between the central pixel and the pixels on the identified contiguous arc.

This algorithm results in very fast interest point detection and should then be used when speed is a concern. For example, this is often the case in visual tracking applications where several points must be tracked in a video sequence with high frame rates.

See also

The article by *E. Rosten and T. Drummond, Machine learning for high-speed corner detection, in In European Conference on Computer Vision, pp. 430-443, 2006* that describes the FAST feature algorithm in detail.

Detecting the scale-invariant SURF features

When trying to match features across different images, we are often faced with the problem of scale changes. That is, the different images to be analyzed can be taken at a different distance from the objects of interest, and consequently, these objects will be pictured at different sizes. If we try to match the same feature from two images using a fixed size neighborhood then, because of the scale change, their intensity patterns will not match.

To solve this problem, the concept of scale-invariant features has been introduced in computer vision. The main idea here is to have a scale factor associated with each of the detected feature points. In recent years, several scale-invariant features have been proposed and this recipe presents one of them, the SURF features. SURF stands for Speeded Up Robust Features, and as we will see, they are not only scale-invariant features, but they also offer the advantage of being computed very efficiently.

How to do it...

The OpenCV implementation of SURF features also use the `cv::FeatureDetector` interface. Therefore, the detection of these features is similar to what we demonstrated in the previous recipes of this chapter:

```cpp
// vector of keypoints
std::vector<cv::KeyPoint> keypoints;
// Construct the SURF feature detector object
cv::SurfFeatureDetector surf(
    2500.); // threshold
// Detect the SURF features
surf.detect(image,keypoints);
```

To draw these features, we again use the `cv::drawKeypoints` OpenCV function, but this time with another mask because we also want to show the scale factor associated with each feature:

```cpp
// Draw the keypoints with scale and orientation information
cv::drawKeypoints(image,        // original image
    keypoints,                  // vector of keypoints
    featureImage,               // the resulting image
    cv::Scalar(255,255,255),    // color of the points
    cv::DrawMatchesFlags::DRAW_RICH_KEYPOINTS); //flag
```

The resulting image with the detected feature that is produced by the drawing function is:

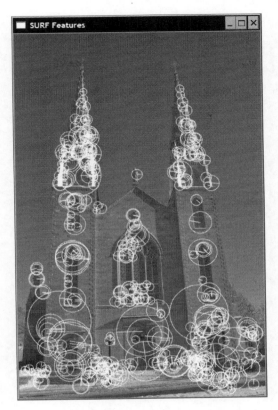

As can be seen in the preceding screenshot, the size of the keypoint circles resulting from the use of the DRAW_RICH_KEYPOINTS flag is proportional to the computed scale of each feature. The SURF algorithm also associates an orientation with each feature to make them rotation-invariant. This orientation is illustrated by a radial line inside each drawn circle.

If we take another picture of the same object but at a different scale, the feature detection results in:

By carefully observing the detected keypoints, it can be seen that the change in size of corresponding circles is proportional to the scale change. As an example, consider the bottom part of the upper-right window. In both images, a SURF feature has been detected at that location and the two corresponding circles (of different sizes) contain the same visual elements. Of course, this is not the case for all features, but as we will discover in the next chapter, the repeatability rate is sufficiently high to allow good matching between the two images.

How it works...

In *Chapter 6*, we learned that the image derivatives of an image can be estimated using Gaussian filters. Those filters make use of a σ parameter defining the aperture (size) of the kernel. As we saw, this σ corresponds to the variance of the Gaussian function used to construct the filter, and it then implicitly defines a scale at which the derivative is evaluated. Indeed, a filter having a larger σ value smoothed out the finer details of the image. This is why we can say that it operates at a coarser scale.

Now, if we compute, for instance, the Laplacian of a given image point using Gaussian filters at different scales, then different values are obtained. Looking at the evolution of the filter response for different scale factors, we obtain a curve which eventually reaches a maximum value at some σ value. If we extract this maximum value for two images of the same object taken at two different scales, the ratio of these two σ maxima will correspond to the ratio of the scales at which the images were taken. This important observation is at the core of the scale-invariant feature extraction process. That is, scale-invariant features should be detected as local maxima in both the spatial space (in the image) and the scale space (as obtained from the derivative filters applied at different scales).

SURF implements this idea by proceeding as follows. First, to detect the features, the Hessian matrix is computed at each pixel. This matrix measures the local curvature of a function and is defined as:

$$H(x,y) = \begin{bmatrix} \dfrac{\delta^2 I}{\delta x^2} & \dfrac{\delta^2 I}{\delta x\,\delta y} \\[2ex] \dfrac{\delta^2 I}{\delta x\,\delta y} & \dfrac{\delta^2 I}{\delta y^2} \end{bmatrix}$$

The determinant of this matrix gives the strength of this curvature. The idea is therefore to define corners as image points with high local curvature (that is, high variation in more than one direction). Since it is composed of second-order derivatives, this matrix can be computed using Laplacian Gaussian kernels of different scale σ. This Hessian then becomes a function of three variables: $H(x,y,\sigma)$. A scale-invariant feature is therefore declared when the determinant of this Hessian reaches a local maximum in both spatial and scale space (that is, 3x3x3 non-maxima suppression needs to be performed). However, this determinant must have a minimum value as specified by the first parameter in the constructor of the `cv::SurfFeatureDetector` class.

The calculation of all of these derivatives at different scales is computationally costly. The objective of the SURF algorithm is to make this process as efficient as possible. This is achieved by using approximated Gaussian kernels involving only few integer additions. These have the following structure:

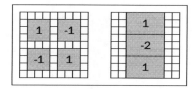

The kernel on the left is used to estimate the mixed second derivatives, while the right one estimates the second derivative in the vertical direction. A rotated version of this second kernel estimates the second derivative in the horizontal direction. The smallest kernels have a size of 9x9 pixels corresponding to $\sigma \approx 1.2$. Kernels of increasing size are successively applied. The exact amount of filter that is applied can be specified by additional parameters of the SURF class. By default, 12 different sizes of kernels are used (going up to size 99x99). Note that the fact that integral images are used guarantees that the sum inside each lob can be computed by using only 3 additions independently of the size of the filter.

Once the local maxima is identified, the precise position of each detected interest point is obtained through interpolation in both scale and image space. The result is then a set of feature points localized at sub-pixel accuracy and to which is associated a scale value.

There's more...

The SURF algorithm has been developed as an efficient variant of another well-known scale-invariant feature detector called SIFT (for Scale-Invariant Feature Transform). SIFT also detects features as local maxima in image and scale space, but uses the Laplacian filter response instead of the Hessian determinant. This Laplacian at different scales is computed using difference of Gaussian filters. OpenCV has a wrapper class that detects these features and it is called in a way similar to the SURF features:

```cpp
// vector of keypoints
std::vector<cv::KeyPoint> keypoints;
// Construct the SURF feature detector object
cv::SiftFeatureDetector sift(
    0.03,  // feature threshold
    10.);  // threshold to reduce
           // sensitivity to lines
// Detect the SURF features
sift.detect(image,keypoints);
```

The results are also very similar:

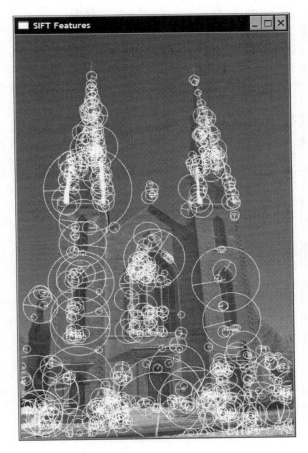

However, since the computation of the feature point is based on floating-point kernels, it is generally considered to be more accurate in terms of feature localization in space and scale. Although, for the same reason, it is also more computationally expensive.

See also

The article *SURF: Speeded Up Robust Features by H. Bay, A. Ess, T. Tuytelaars and L. Van Gool in Computer Vision and Image Understanding, vol. 110, No. 3, pp. 346–359, 2008* that describes the SURF features.

The pioneer work by *D. Lowe, Distinctive Image Features from Scale Invariant Features in International Journal of Computer Vision, Vol. 60, No. 2, 2004, pp. 91-110*, describing the SIFT algorithm.

Describing SURF features

The SURF algorithm, discussed in the preceding recipe, defines a location and a scale for each of the detected features. This scale factor can be used to define the size of a window around the feature point such that the defined neighborhood would include the same visual information no matter what scale the object to which the feature belongs has been pictured. In addition, the visual information included in this neighborhood can be used to characterize the feature point to make it distinguishable from the others.

This recipe will show you how to describe a feature point's neighborhood using compact descriptors. In feature matching, **feature descriptors** are usually N-dimensional vectors that describe a feature point, ideally in a way that is invariant to change in lighting and to small perspective deformations. In addition, good descriptors can be compared using a simple distance metric (for example, Euclidean distance). Therefore, they constitute a powerful tool to use in feature matching algorithms.

How to do it...

The following code is a pattern similar to the one used for feature detection. OpenCV 2 proposes a general class which defines a common interface for the extraction of the various feature point descriptors that are available. To follow up on the preceding recipe, here we use the one proposed in the SURF algorithm. Based on the `std::vector` of `cv::Keypoint` instances obtained from feature detection, the descriptors are obtained as follows:

```
// Construction of the SURF descriptor extractor
cv::SurfDescriptorExtractor surfDesc;
// Extraction of the SURF descriptors
cv::Mat descriptors1;
surfDesc.compute(image1,keypoints1,descriptors1);
```

The result is a matrix (that is, a `cv::Mat` instance) which will contain as many rows as the number of elements in the keypoint vector. Each of these rows is an N-dimensional descriptor vector. In the case of the SURF descriptor, by default, it has a size of 64. This vector characterizes the intensity pattern surrounding a feature point. The more similar the two feature points, the closer their descriptor vectors should be.

These descriptors are particularly useful in image matching. Suppose, for example, that two images of the same scene are to be matched. This can be accomplished by first detecting features on each image, and then extracting the descriptors of these features. Each feature descriptor vector in the first image is then compared to all feature descriptors in the second image. The pair that obtains the best score (that is, the lowest distance between the two vectors) is then kept as the best match for that feature. This process is repeated for all features in the first image. This is the most basic scheme that has been implemented in OpenCV as the `cv::BruteForceMatcher`. It is used as follows:

```
// Construction of the matcher
cv::BruteForceMatcher<cv::L2<float>> matcher;
// Match the two image descriptors
std::vector<cv::DMatch> matches;
matcher.match(descriptors1,descriptors2, matches);
```

This class is a subclass of the `cv::DescriptorMatcher` class defining the common interface for different matching strategies. The result is a vector of `cv::DMatch` instances which is the structure used to represent a match pair. Essentially, the `cv::DMatch` data structure contains a first index referring to an element in the first vector of descriptors, and a second index referring to the matching feature in the second vector of descriptors. It also contains a real value representing the distance between the two matched descriptors. This distance value is used in the definition of `operator<` comparing two `cv::DMatch` instances.

In order to visualize the result of the matching operation, OpenCV offers a drawing function that produces an image made of the concatenation of the two input images and on which matching points are linked by a line. In the preceding recipe, we obtained 340 SURF points for the first image. The brute-force approach will then produce the same number of matches. Drawing all of these lines on an image would make the results unreadable. Therefore, we will only display the 25 matches with the lowest distance. This is easily accomplished by using the `std::nth_element` that positions the nth element in sorted order at the nth position, with all elements smaller placed before this element. Once this is done, the vector is simply purged of its remaining elements:

```
std::nth_element(matches.begin(),    // initial position
    matches.begin()+24, // position of the sorted element
    matches.end());      // end position
// remove all elements after the 25th
matches.erase(matches.begin()+25, matches.end());
```

Recall that the preceding code works because the `operator<` has been defined in the `cv::DMatch` class. These 25 matches can then be visualized through the following call:

```
cv::Mat imageMatches;
cv::drawMatches(
    image1,keypoints1, // 1st image and its keypoints
    image2,keypoints2, // 2nd image and its keypoints
    matches,            // the matches
    imageMatches,       // the image produced
    cv::Scalar(255,255,255)); // color of the lines
```

That produces the following image:

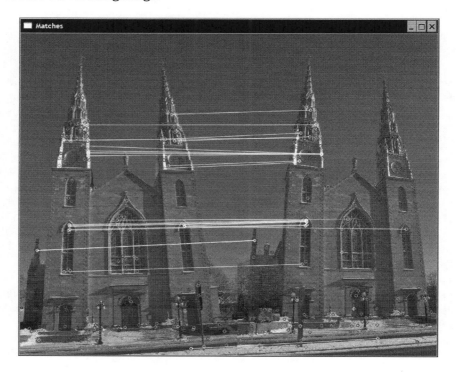

As can be seen, most of these matches correctly link a point on the left with its corresponding image point on the right. One can notice some errors due to the fact that the observed building has a symmetrical façade which makes some of the local matches ambiguous (the topmost match is one example of wrongly matched features).

How it works...

Good feature descriptors must be invariant to small changes in illumination, in viewpoint, and to the presence of image noise. Therefore, they are often based on local intensity differences. This is the case of the SURF descriptors which apply the following simple kernels inside a larger neighborhood around a keypoint:

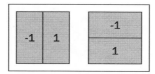

The first one simply measures the local intensity difference in the horizontal direction (designated as *dx*), and the second measures this difference in the vertical direction (designated as *dy*). The size of the neighborhood used to extract the descriptor vector is defined as 20 times the scale factor of the feature (that is, 20σ). This square region is then split into 4x4 smaller square sub-regions. For each sub-region, the kernel responses *dx* and *dy* are computed at 5x5 regularly spaced locations (the kernel size being 2σ). All of these responses are summed as follows in order to extract four descriptor values for each subregion:

$$[\sum dx \quad \sum dy \quad \sum |dx| \quad \sum |dy|]$$

Since there are 4x4=16 sub-regions, we have a total of 64 descriptor values. Note that in order to give more importance to the neighboring pixel values closer to the keypoint, the kernel responses are weighted by a Gaussian centered at the keypoint location (with a $\sigma=3.3$).

The *dx* and *dy* responses are also used to estimate the orientation of the feature. These values are computed (with a kernel size of 4σ) within a circular neighborhood of radius 6σ at locations regularly spaced by intervals of σ. For a given orientation, the responses inside a certain angular interval ($\pi/3$) are summed, and the orientation giving the longest vector is defined as the dominant orientation.

With the SURF features and descriptors, scale-invariant matching can be achieved. Here is an example showing the 25 best matches in a match pair containing two images at different scales:

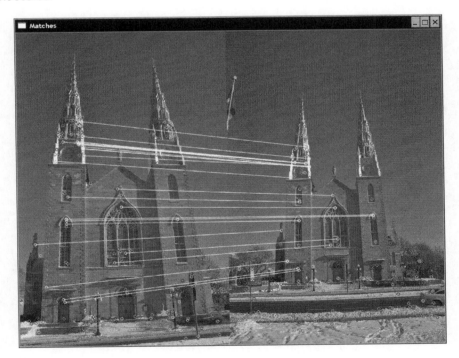

There's more...

The SIFT algorithm also defines its own descriptor. It is based on the gradient magnitude and orientation computed at the scale of the considered keypoint. As for the SURF descriptors, the scaled neighborhood of the keypoint is divided into 4x4 sub-regions. For each of these regions, an 8-bin histogram of gradient orientations (weighted by their magnitude and by a global Gaussian window centered at the keypoint) is built. Therefore, the descriptor vector is made of the entries of these histograms. There are 4x4 regions and 8 bins per histogram, which leads to a descriptor of length 128.

As for feature detection, the difference between SURF and SIFT descriptors is mainly speed and accuracy. Since SURF descriptors are mostly based on intensity differences, they are faster to compute. However, SIFT descriptors are generally considered to be more accurate in finding the right matching feature.

See also

The previous recipe for more on the SURF and SIFT features.

9
Estimating Projective Relations in Images

In this chapter, we will cover:

- ▶ Calibrating a camera
- ▶ Computing the fundamental matrix of an image pair
- ▶ Matching images using random sample consensus
- ▶ Computing a homography between two images

Introduction

Images are generally produced using a digital camera that captures a scene by projecting light onto an image sensor going through its lens. The fact that an image is formed through the projection of a 3D scene onto a 2D plane imposes the existence of important relations between a scene and its image, and between different images of the same scene. Projective geometry is the tool that is used to describe and characterize, in mathematical terms, the process of image formation. In this chapter, you will learn some of the fundamental projective relations that exist in multi-view imagery and how these can be used in computer vision programming. We will also pursue the discussion we initiated in the final recipe of the previous chapter about two-view feature matching. You will learn new strategies to improve the matching results. But before we start the recipes, let's explore the basic concepts related to scene projection and image formation.

Image formation

Fundamentally, the process used to produce images has not changed since the beginning of photography. The light coming from an observed scene is captured by a camera through a frontal **aperture** and the captured light rays hit an **image plane** (or **image sensor**) located on the back of the camera. Additionally, a lens is used to concentrate the rays coming from the different scene elements. This process is illustrated by the following figure:

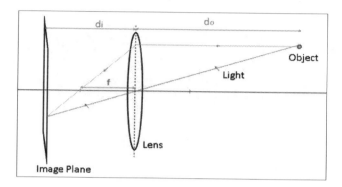

Here, **do** is the distance from the lens to the observed object, **di** is the distance from the lens to the image plane, and **f** is the **focal length** of the lens. These quantities are related by the so-called **thin lens equation**:

$$\frac{1}{f} = \frac{1}{do} + \frac{1}{di}$$

In computer vision, this camera model can be simplified in a number of ways. First, we can neglect the effect of the lens by considering a camera with an infinitesimal aperture since, in theory, this does not change the image. Only the central ray is therefore considered. Second, since most of the time we have $do >> di$, we can assume that the image plane is located at the focal distance. Finally, we can notice from the geometry of the system, that the image on the plane is inverted. We can obtain an identical but upright image by simply positioning the image plane in front of the lens. Obviously, this is not physically feasible, but from a mathematical point of view, this is completely equivalent. This simplified model is often referred to as the **pin-hole camera** model and it is represented as follows:

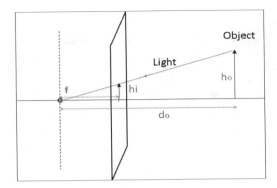

From this model, and using the law of similar triangles, we can easily derive the basic projective equation:

$$hi = f \frac{ho}{do}$$

The size (**hi**) of the image of an object (of height **ho**) is therefore inversely proportional to its distance (**do**) from the camera which is naturally true. This relation allows the position of the image of a 3D scene point to be predicted onto the image plane of a camera.

Calibrating a camera

From the introduction of this chapter, we learned that the essential parameters of a camera under the pin-hole model are its focal length and the size of the image plane (which defines the field of view of the camera). Also, since we are dealing with digital images, the number of pixels on the image plane is another important characteristic of a camera. Finally, in order to be able to compute the position of an image's scene point in pixel coordinates, we need one additional piece of information. Considering the line coming from the focal point that is orthogonal to the image plane, we need to know at which pixel position this line pierces the image plane. This point is called the **principal point**. It could be logical to assume that this principal point is at the center of the image plane, but in practice, this one might be off by few pixels depending at which precision the camera has been manufactured.

Camera calibration is the process by which the different camera parameters are obtained. One can obviously use the specifications provided by the camera manufacturer, but for some tasks, such as 3D reconstruction, these specifications are not accurate enough. Camera calibration will proceed by showing known patterns to the camera and analyzing the obtained images. An optimization process will then determine the optimal parameter values that explain the observations. This is a complex process but made easy by the availability of OpenCV calibration functions.

How to do it...

To calibrate a camera, the idea is show to this camera a set of scene points for which their 3D position is known. You must then determine where on the image these points project. Obviously, for accurate results, we need to observe several of these points. One way to achieve this would be to take one picture of a scene with many known 3D points. A more convenient way would be to take several images from different viewpoints of a set of some 3D points. This approach is simpler but requires computing the position of each camera view, in addition to the computation of the internal camera parameters which fortunately is feasible.

OpenCV proposes to use a chessboard pattern to generate the set of 3D scene points required for calibration. This pattern creates points at the corners of each square, and since this pattern is flat, we can freely assume that the board is located at Z=0 with the X and Y axes well aligned with the grid. In this case, the calibration process simply consists of showing the chessboard pattern to the camera from different viewpoints. Here is one example of a calibration pattern image:

The nice thing is that OpenCV has a function that automatically detects the corners of this chessboard pattern. You simply provide an image and the size of the chessboard used (number of vertical and horizontal inner corner points). The function will return the position of these chessboard corners on the image. If the function fails to find the pattern, then it simply returns false:

```
// output vectors of image points
std::vector<cv::Point2f> imageCorners;
// number of corners on the chessboard
cv::Size boardSize(6,4);
// Get the chessboard corners
bool found = cv::findChessboardCorners(image,
                        boardSize, imageCorners);
```

Note that this function accepts additional parameters if one needs to tune the algorithm, which are not discussed here. There is also a function that draws the detected corners on the chessboard image with lines connecting them in sequence:

```
//Draw the corners
cv::drawChessboardCorners(image,
          boardSize, imageCorners,
          found); // corners have been found
```

The image obtained is seen here:

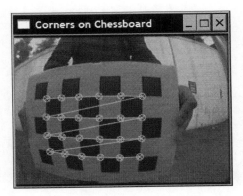

The lines connecting the points shows the order in which the points are listed in the vector of detected points. Now to calibrate the camera, we need to input a set of such image points together with the coordinate of the corresponding 3D points. Let's encapsulate the calibration process in a CameraCalibrator class:

```
class CameraCalibrator {

    // input points:
    // the points in world coordinates
    std::vector<std::vector<cv::Point3f>> objectPoints;
    // the point positions in pixels
    std::vector<std::vector<cv::Point2f>> imagePoints;
    // output Matrices
    cv::Mat cameraMatrix;
    cv::Mat distCoeffs;
    // flag to specify how calibration is done
    int flag;
    // used in image undistortion
    cv::Mat map1,map2;
    bool mustInitUndistort;

  public:
    CameraCalibrator() : flag(0), mustInitUndistort(true) {};
```

As mentioned previously, the 3D coordinates of the points on the chessboard pattern can be easily determined if we conveniently place the reference frame on the board. The method that accomplishes this takes a vector of the chessboard image filename as input:

```cpp
// Open chessboard images and extract corner points
int CameraCalibrator::addChessboardPoints(
          const std::vector<std::string>& filelist,
          cv::Size & boardSize) {

   // the points on the chessboard
    std::vector<cv::Point2f> imageCorners;
    std::vector<cv::Point3f> objectCorners;

   // 3D Scene Points:
   // Initialize the chessboard corners
   // in the chessboard reference frame
   // The corners are at 3D location (X,Y,Z)= (i,j,0)
   for (int i=0; i<boardSize.height; i++) {
      for (int j=0; j<boardSize.width; j++) {

         objectCorners.push_back(cv::Point3f(i, j, 0.0f));
      }
   }

   // 2D Image points:
   cv::Mat image; // to contain chessboard image
   int successes = 0;
   // for all viewpoints
   for (int i=0; i<filelist.size(); i++) {

      // Open the image
      image = cv::imread(filelist[i],0);

      // Get the chessboard corners
      bool found = cv::findChessboardCorners(
                     image, boardSize, imageCorners);

      // Get subpixel accuracy on the corners
      cv::cornerSubPix(image, imageCorners,
              cv::Size(5,5),
              cv::Size(-1,-1),
         cv::TermCriteria(cv::TermCriteria::MAX_ITER +
                     cv::TermCriteria::EPS,
          30,        // max number of iterations
          0.1));  // min accuracy

      //If we have a good board, add it to our data
      if (imageCorners.size() == boardSize.area()) {

         // Add image and scene points from one view
         addPoints(imageCorners, objectCorners);
```

```
                    successes++;
            }
        }
    return successes;
}
```

The first loop inputs the 3D coordinates of the chessboard, which are specified in an arbitrary square size unit here. The corresponding image points are the ones provided by the `cv::findChessboardCorners` function. This is done for all available viewpoints. Moreover, in order to obtain a more accurate image point location, the function `cv::cornerSubPix` can be used and as the name suggests, the image points will then be localized at sub-pixel accuracy. The termination criterion that is specified by the `cv::TermCriteria` object defines a maximum number of iterations and a minimum accuracy in sub-pixel coordinates. The first of these two conditions that is reached will stop the corner refinement process.

When a set of chessboard corners has been successfully detected, these points are added to our vector of image and scene points:

```
// Add scene points and corresponding image points
void CameraCalibrator::addPoints(const std::vector<cv::Point2f>&
imageCorners, const std::vector<cv::Point3f>& objectCorners) {

    // 2D image points from one view
    imagePoints.push_back(imageCorners);
    // corresponding 3D scene points
    objectPoints.push_back(objectCorners);
}
```

The vectors contains `std::vector` instances. Indeed, each vector element being a vector of points from one view.

Once a sufficient number of chessboard images have been processed (and consequently a large number of 3D scene point/2D image point correspondences are available), we can initiate the computation of the calibration parameters:

```
// Calibrate the camera
// returns the re-projection error
double CameraCalibrator::calibrate(cv::Size &imageSize)
{
    // undistorter must be reinitialized
    mustInitUndistort= true;
    //Output rotations and translations
    std::vector<cv::Mat> rvecs, tvecs;
    // start calibration
    return
        calibrateCamera(objectPoints, // the 3D points
```

```
        imagePoints,   // the image points
        imageSize,     // image size
        cameraMatrix,  // output camera matrix
        distCoeffs,    // output distortion matrix
        rvecs, tvecs,  // Rs, Ts
        flag);         // set options
}
```

In practice, 10 to 20 chessboard images are sufficient, but these must be taken from different viewpoints at different depths. The two important outputs of this function are the camera matrix and the distortion parameters. The camera matrix will be described in the next section. For now, let's consider the distortion parameters. So far, we have mentioned that with the pin-hole camera model, we can neglect the effect of the lens. But this is only possible if the lens used to capture an image does not introduce too important optical distortions. Unfortunately, this is often the case with lenses of lower quality or with lenses having a very short focal length. You may have already noticed that in the image we used for our example, the chessboard pattern shown is clearly distorted. The edges of the rectangular board being curved in the image. It can also be noticed that this distortion becomes more important as we move far from the center of the image. This is a typical distortion observed with fish-eye lens and it is called **radial distortion**. The lenses that are used in common digital cameras do not exhibit such a high degree of distortion, but in the case of the lens used here, these distortions cannot certainly be ignored.

It is possible to compensate for these deformations by introducing an appropriate model. The idea is to represent the distortions induced by a lens by a set of mathematical equations. Once established, these equations can then be reverted in order to undo the distortions visible on the image. Fortunately, the exact parameters of the transformation that will correct the distortions can be obtained together with the other camera parameter during the calibration phase. Once this is done, any image from the newly calibrated camera can be undistorted:

```
// remove distortion in an image (after calibration)
cv::Mat CameraCalibrator::remap(const cv::Mat &image) {

    cv::Mat undistorted;

    if (mustInitUndistort) { // called once per calibration

     cv::initUndistortRectifyMap(
        cameraMatrix,   // computed camera matrix
        distCoeffs,     // computed distortion matrix
        cv::Mat(),      // optional rectification (none)
        cv::Mat(),      // camera matrix to generate undistorted
            image.size(),   // size of undistorted
            CV_32FC1,       // type of output map
            map1, map2);    // the x and y mapping functions
     mustInitUndistort= false;
    }
```

```
    // Apply mapping functions
    cv::remap(image, undistorted, map1, map2,
        cv::INTER_LINEAR); // interpolation type
    return undistorted;
}
```

Which results in the following image:

As you can see, once the image is undistorted, we obtain a regular perspective image.

How it works...

In order to explain the result of the calibration, we need to go back to the figure in the introduction which describes the pin-hole camera model. More specifically, we want to demonstrate the relation between a point in 3D at position (X,Y,Z) and its image (x,y) on a camera specified in pixel coordinates. Let's redraw this figure by adding a reference frame that we position at the center of the projection as seen here:

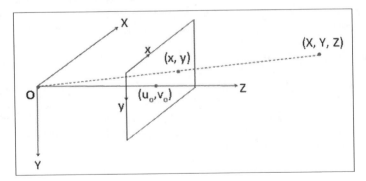

Note that the Y-axis is pointing downward to get a coordinate system compatible with the usual convention that places the image origin at the upper-left corner. We learned previously that the point (X,Y,Z) will be projected onto the image plane at (fX/Z,fY/Z). Now, if we want to translate this coordinate into pixels, we need to divide the 2D image position by, respectively, the pixel width (px) and height (py). We notice that by dividing the focal length f given in world units (most often meters or millimeters) by px, then we obtain the focal length expressed in (horizontal) pixels. Let's then define this term as fx. Similarly, fy =f/py is defined as the focal length expressed in vertical pixel unit. The complete projective equation is therefore:

$$x = \frac{f_x X}{Z} + u_0$$

$$y = \frac{f_y Y}{Z} + v_0$$

Recall that (u0,v0) is the principal point that is added to the result in order to move the origin to the upper-left corner of the image. These equations can be rewritten in matrix form through the introduction of **homogeneous coordinates** in which 2D points are represented by 3-vectors, and 3D points represented by 4-vectors (the extra coordinate is simply an arbitrary scale factor that need to be removed when a 2D coordinate needs to be extracted from a homogeneous 3-vector). Here is the projective equation rewritten:

$$s \begin{bmatrix} x \\ y \\ 1 \end{bmatrix} = \begin{bmatrix} f_x & 0 & u_0 \\ 0 & f_y & v_0 \\ 0 & 0 & 1 \end{bmatrix} \begin{bmatrix} 1 & 0 & 0 & 0 \\ 0 & 1 & 0 & 0 \\ 0 & 0 & 1 & 0 \end{bmatrix} \begin{bmatrix} X \\ Y \\ Z \\ 1 \end{bmatrix}$$

The second matrix is a simple projection matrix. The first matrix includes all of the camera parameters which are called the **intrinsic parameters** of the camera. This 3x3 matrix is one of the output matrices returned by the `cv::calibrateCamera` function. There is also a function called `cv::calibrationMatrixValues` that returns the value of the intrinsic parameters given a calibration matrix.

More generally, when the reference frame is not at the projection center of the camera, we will need to add a rotation (a *3x3* matrix) and a translation vector (*3x1* matrix). These two matrices describe the rigid transformation that must be applied to the 3D points in order to bring them back to the camera reference frame. Therefore, we can rewrite the projection equation in its most general form:

$$s\begin{bmatrix} x \\ y \\ 1 \end{bmatrix} = \begin{bmatrix} f_x & 0 & u_0 \\ 0 & f_y & v_0 \\ 0 & 0 & 1 \end{bmatrix} \begin{bmatrix} r1 & r2 & r3 & t1 \\ r4 & r5 & r6 & t2 \\ r7 & r8 & r9 & t3 \end{bmatrix} \begin{bmatrix} X \\ Y \\ Z \\ 1 \end{bmatrix}$$

Remember that in our calibration example, the reference frame was placed on the chessboard. Therefore, there is a rigid transformation (rotation and translation) that must be computed for each view. These are in the output parameter list of the `cv::calibrateCamera` function. The rotation and translation components are often called the **extrinsic parameters** of the calibration and they are different for each view. The intrinsic parameters remain constant for a given camera/lens system. The intrinsic parameters of our test camera obtained from a calibration based on 20 chessboard images are fx=167, fy=178, u0=156, v0=119. These results are obtained by `cv::calibrateCamera` through an optimization process aimed at finding the intrinsic and extrinsic parameters that will minimize the difference between the predicted image point position, as computed from the projection of the 3D scene points, and the actual image point position, as observed on the image. The sum of this difference for all points specified during the calibration is called the **re-projection error**.

To correct the distortion, OpenCV uses a polynomial function that is applied to the image point in order to move them at their undistorted position. By default, 5 coefficients are used; a model made of 8 coefficients is also available. Once these coefficients are obtained, it is possible to compute 2 mapping functions (one for the x coordinate and one for the y) that will give the new undistorted position of an image point on a distorted image. This is computed by the function `cv::initUndistortRectifyMap` and the function `cv::remap` remaps all of the points of an input image to a new image. Note that because of the non-linear transformation, some pixels of the input image now fall outside the boundary of the output image. You can expand the size of the output image to compensate for this loss of pixels, but you will now obtain output pixels that have no values in the input image (they will then be displayed as black pixels).

There's more...

When a good estimate of the camera intrinsic parameters are known, it could be advantageous to input them to the `cv::calibrateCamera` function. They will then be used as initial values in the optimization process. To do so, you just need to add the flag `CV_CALIB_USE_INTRINSIC_GUESS` and input these values in the calibration matrix parameter. It is also possible to impose a fixed value for the principal point (`CV_CALIB_FIX_PRINCIPAL_POINT`), which can often be assumed to be the central pixel. You can also impose a fixed ratio for the focal lengths fx and fy (`CV_CALIB_FIX_RATIO`) in which case you assume pixels of square shape.

Computing the fundamental matrix of an image pair

The previous recipe showed you how to recover the projective equation of a single camera. In this recipe, we will explore the projective relation that exists between two images viewing the same scene. These two images could have been obtained by moving a camera at two different locations taking pictures from two viewpoints, or by using two cameras, each of them taking a different picture of the scene. When these two cameras are separated by a rigid baseline, we use the term **stereovision**.

Getting ready

Let's now consider two cameras observing a given scene point as seen here:

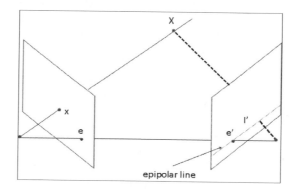

We learned that we can find the image x of a 3D point X by tracing a line joining this 3D point with the camera's center. Conversely, the image point that we observe at position x can be located anywhere on this line in 3D space. This implies that if we want to find the corresponding point of a given image point in another image, we need to search along the projection of this line onto the second image plane. This imaginary line is called the **epipolar line** of point x. It defines a fundamental constraint that must satisfy two corresponding points, that is, the match of a given point must lie on the epipolar line of this point in the other view. The exact orientation of this epipolar line depends on the respective position of the two cameras. In fact, the position of the epipolar lines characterizes the geometry of a two-view system.

Another observation that can be made from the geometry of this two-view system is that all of the epipolar lines pass through the same point. This point corresponds to the projection of one camera center onto the other camera. This special point is called an **epipole**.

Mathematically, it can be shown that the relation between an image point and its corresponding epipolar line can be expressed using a 3x3 matrix such as the following:

$$\begin{bmatrix} l_1' \\ l_2' \\ l_3' \end{bmatrix} = F \begin{bmatrix} x \\ y \\ 1 \end{bmatrix}$$

In projective geometry, a 2D line is also represented by a 3-vector. It corresponds to the set of 2D points (x',y') satisfying the equation l1'x'+ l2'y'+ l3'=0 (the prime superscript denotes that this line belongs to the second image). Consequently, the matrix F, called the **fundamental matrix**, maps a 2D image point in one view to an epipolar line in the other view.

How to do it...

Estimating the fundamental matrix of an image pair can be done by solving a set of equations which involve a certain number of known matched points between the two images. The minimum number of such matches is seven. Using the image pair from the previous chapter, we can manually selected seven good matches (seen in the following screenshot). These will be used to compute the fundamental matrix using the `cv::findFundementalMat` OpenCV function.

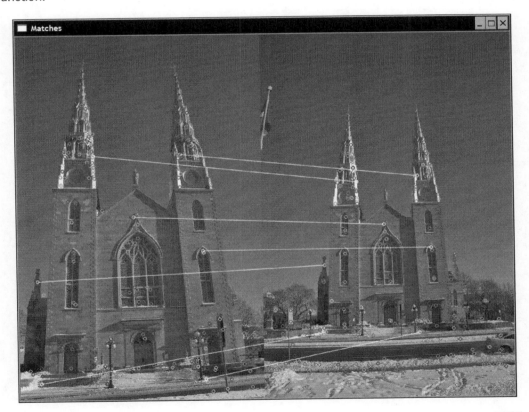

If we have the image points in each image as `cv::keypoint` instance, they first need to be converted into `cv::Point2f` in order to be used with `cv::findFundementalMat`. An OpenCV function can be used to this end:

```
// Convert keypoints into Point2f
std::vector<cv::Point2f> selPoints1, selPoints2;
cv::KeyPoint::convert(keypoints1,selPoints1,pointIndexes1);
cv::KeyPoint::convert(keypoints2,selPoints2,pointIndexes2);
```

The two vectors `selPoints1` and `selPoints2` contain the corresponding points in the two images. `keypoints1` and `keypoints2` are the selected `Keypoint` instances as detected in the previous chapter. The call to the `cv::findFundementalMat` function is then as follows:

```
// Compute F matrix from 7 matches
cv::Mat fundemental= cv::findFundamentalMat(
    cv::Mat(selPoints1), // points in first image
    cv::Mat(selPoints2), // points in second image
    CV_FM_7POINT);       // 7-point method
```

One way to visually verify the validity of the fundamental matrix is to draw the epipolar lines of some selected points. Another OpenCV function allows the epipolar lines of a given set of points to be computed. Once these are computed, they can be drawn using the `cv::line` function. The following lines of code accomplish these two steps (that is, computing and drawing epipolar lines in the right image from the points in the left):

```
// draw the left points corresponding epipolar
// lines in right image
std::vector<cv::Vec3f> lines1;
cv::computeCorrespondEpilines(
    cv::Mat(selPoints1), // image points
    1,                   // in image 1 (can also be 2)
    fundemental, // F matrix
    lines1);     // vector of epipolar lines
// for all epipolar lines
for (vector<cv::Vec3f>::const_iterator it= lines1.begin();
    it!=lines1.end(); ++it) {

        // draw the line between first and last column
        cv::line(image2,
          cv::Point(0,-(*it)[2]/(*it)[1]),
          cv::Point(image2.cols,-((*it)[2]+
                    (*it)[0]*image2.cols)/(*it)[1]),
                    cv::Scalar(255,255,255));
}
```

The result is then seen in the following screenshot:

Remember that the epipole is at the intersection point of all epipolar lines, and it is the projection of the other camera center. This epipole is visible on the preceding image. Often, the epipolar lines intersect outside the image boundaries. It is at the location where the first camera would be visible if the two images were taken at the same instant. Observe the image pair and take the time to convince yourself that this indeed makes sense.

How it works...

We explained previously that the fundamental matrix gives, for a point in one image, the equation of the line on which its corresponding point in the other view should be found. If the corresponding point of a point p (expressed in homogenous coordinates) is p', and if *F* is the fundamental matrix between the two views, then since p' lies on the epipolar line Fp, we have:

$$p'^T Fp = 0$$

This equation expresses the relation between two corresponding points and is known as the **epipolar constraint**. Using this equation it becomes possible to estimate the entries of the matrix using known matches. Since the entries of the *F* matrix are given up to a scale factor, there are only eight entries to estimate (the ninth can be arbitrarily set to 1). Each match contributes one equation. Therefore, with eight known matches, the matrix can be fully estimated by solving the resulting set of linear equations. This is what is done when you use the `CV_FM_8POINT` flag with the `cv::findFundamentalMat` function. Note that, in this case, it is possible (and preferable) to input more than eight matches. The obtained over-determined system of linear equations can then be solved in a mean-square sense.

To estimate the fundamental matrix, an additional constraint can also be exploited. Mathematically, the *F* matrix maps a 2D point into a 1D pencil of lines (that is, lines intersecting at a common point). The fact that all of these epipolar lines pass by this unique point (the epipole) imposes a constraint on the matrix. This constraint reduces, the number of matches required to estimate the fundamental matrix to seven. Unfortunately, in this case, the set of equations becomes non-linear with up to three possible solutions. The seven-match solution of the F matrix estimation can be invoked in OpenCV by using the `CV_FM_7POINT` flag. This is what we did in the example of the preceding section.

Lastly, we should mention that the choice of an appropriate set of matches in the image is important to obtain an accurate estimation of the fundamental matrix. In general, the matches should be well distributed across the image and include points at different depth in the scene. Otherwise, the solution will become unstable or degenerate configurations can result.

See also

The book by *R. Hartley and A. Zisserman, Multiple View Geometry in Computer Vision, Cambridge University Press, 2004* is the most complete reference on projective geometry in computer vision.

The next recipe which presents an additional flag that can be used with the OpenCV fundamental matrix estimation.

Matching images using random sample consensus

When two cameras observe the same scene, they see the same elements but under different viewpoints. We already studied the feature point matching problem in the previous chapter. In this recipe, we come back to this problem and we will learn how to exploit the epipolar constraint between two views to match image features more reliably.

The principle we will follow is simple: when we match feature points between two images, we only accept those matches that fall onto the corresponding epipolar lines. However, to be able to check this condition, the fundamental matrix must be known, and we need good matches to estimate this matrix. This seems to be a chicken-and-egg problem. We propose in this recipe a solution in which the fundamental matrix and a set of good matches will be jointly computed.

How to do it...

The objective is to be able to obtain a set of good matches between two views. Therefore, all found feature point correspondences will be validated using the epipolar constraint introduced in the previous recipe. We first define a class which will encapsulate the different elements of the solution that will be proposed:

```cpp
class RobustMatcher {

  private:

    // pointer to the feature point detector object
    cv::Ptr<cv::FeatureDetector> detector;
    // pointer to the feature descriptor extractor object
    cv::Ptr<cv::DescriptorExtractor> extractor;
    float ratio; // max ratio between 1st and 2nd NN
    bool refineF; // if true will refine the F matrix
    double distance; // min distance to epipolar
    double confidence; // confidence level (probability)

  public:

    RobustMatcher() : ratio(0.65f), refineF(true),
                      confidence(0.99), distance(3.0) {

      // SURF is the default feature
      detector= new cv::SurfFeatureDetector();
      extractor= new cv::SurfDescriptorExtractor();
    }
```

Note how we used the generic `cv::FeatureDetector` and `cv::DescriptorExtractor` interfaces so that a user can provide any specific implementation. The SURF features and descriptors are used here by default, but others can be specified using the appropriate setter methods:

```cpp
// Set the feature detector
void setFeatureDetector(
        cv::Ptr<cv::FeatureDetector>& detect) {

  detector= detect;

}

// Set the descriptor extractor
void setDescriptorExtractor(
        cv::Ptr<cv::DescriptorExtractor>& desc) {

  extractor= desc;

}
```

The main method is our `match` method that returns matches, detected keypoints, and the estimated fundamental matrix. The method proceeds in five distinct steps (explicitly identified in the comments of the following code) that we will now explore:

```cpp
// Match feature points using symmetry test and RANSAC
// returns fundemental matrix
cv::Mat match(cv::Mat& image1,
              cv::Mat& image2, // input images
  // output matches and keypoints
  std::vector<cv::DMatch>& matches,
  std::vector<cv::KeyPoint>& keypoints1,
  std::vector<cv::KeyPoint>& keypoints2) {

  // 1a. Detection of the SURF features
  detector->detect(image1,keypoints1);
  detector->detect(image2,keypoints2);

  // 1b. Extraction of the SURF descriptors
  cv::Mat descriptors1, descriptors2;
  extractor->compute(image1,keypoints1,descriptors1);
  extractor->compute(image2,keypoints2,descriptors2);

  // 2. Match the two image descriptors

  // Construction of the matcher
  cv::BruteForceMatcher<cv::L2<float>> matcher;

  // from image 1 to image 2
  // based on k nearest neighbours (with k=2)
  std::vector<std::vector<cv::DMatch>> matches1;
  matcher.knnMatch(descriptors1,descriptors2,
```

```
        matches1,  // vector of matches (up to 2 per entry)
        2);         // return 2 nearest neighbours

    // from image 2 to image 1
    // based on k nearest neighbours (with k=2)
    std::vector<std::vector<cv::DMatch>> matches2;
    matcher.knnMatch(descriptors2,descriptors1,
        matches2,  // vector of matches (up to 2 per entry)
        2);         // return 2 nearest neighbours

    // 3. Remove matches for which NN ratio is
    // > than threshold

    // clean image 1 -> image 2 matches
    int removed= ratioTest(matches1);
    // clean image 2 -> image 1 matches
    removed= ratioTest(matches2);

    // 4. Remove non-symmetrical matches
     std::vector<cv::DMatch> symMatches;
    symmetryTest(matches1,matches2,symMatches);

    // 5. Validate matches using RANSAC
    cv::Mat fundemental= ransacTest(symMatches,
                keypoints1, keypoints2, matches);

    // return the found fundemental matrix
    return fundemental;
}
```

The first step is simply detecting the feature point and computing their descriptors. Next, we proceed to feature matching using the `cv::BruteForceMatcher` class as we did in the previous chapter. However, this time we find the two best matching points for each feature (and not only the best one as we did in the previous recipe). This is accomplished by the `cv::BruteForceMatcher::knnMatch` method (with k=2). Moreover, we perform this matching in two directions, that is, for each point in the first image we find the two best matches in the second image, and then we do the same thing for the feature points of the second image, finding their two best matches in the first image.

Therefore, for each feature point, we have two candidate matches in the other view. These are the two best ones based on the distance between their descriptors. If this measured distance is very low for the best match, and much larger for the second best match, we can safely accept the first match as a good one since it is unambiguously the best choice. Reciprocally, if the two best matches are relatively close in distance, then there exists a possibility that we make an error if we select one or the other. In this case, we should reject both matches. Here, we perform this test in step 3 by verifying that the ratio of the distance of the best match over the distance of the second best match is not greater than a given threshold:

```
// Clear matches for which NN ratio is > than threshold
// return the number of removed points
// (corresponding entries being cleared,
// i.e. size will be 0)
int ratioTest(std::vector<std::vector<cv::DMatch>>
                                        &matches) {

  int removed=0;

    // for all matches
  for (std::vector<std::vector<cv::DMatch>>::iterator
        matchIterator= matches.begin();
      matchIterator!= matches.end(); ++matchIterator) {

      // if 2 NN has been identified
      if (matchIterator->size() > 1) {

        // check distance ratio
        if ((*matchIterator)[0].distance/
            (*matchIterator)[1].distance > ratio) {

          matchIterator->clear(); // remove match
          removed++;
        }

      } else { // does not have 2 neighbours

        matchIterator->clear(); // remove match
        removed++;
      }
  }

  return removed;
}
```

A large number of ambiguous matches will be eliminated by this procedure as it can be seen from the following example. Here, with a low SURF threshold (=10), we initially detected 1,600 feature points (black circles) out of which only 55 survive the ratio test (white circles):

The white lines linking the matched points show that even if we have a large number of good matches, a significant number of false matches have survived. Therefore, a second test will be performed in order to filter our more false matches. Note that the ratio test is also applied to the second match set.

We now have two relatively good match sets, one from the first image to second image and the other one from second image to the first one. From these sets, we will now extract the matches that are in agreement with both sets. This is the **symmetrical matching scheme** imposing that, for a match pair to be accepted, both points must be the best matching feature of the other:

```cpp
// Insert symmetrical matches in symMatches vector
void symmetryTest(
    const std::vector<std::vector<cv::DMatch>>& matches1,
    const std::vector<std::vector<cv::DMatch>>& matches2,
    std::vector<cv::DMatch>& symMatches) {
  // for all matches image 1 -> image 2
  for (std::vector<std::vector<cv::DMatch>>::
         const_iterator matchIterator1= matches1.begin();
       matchIterator1!= matches1.end(); ++matchIterator1) {
    // ignore deleted matches
    if (matchIterator1->size() < 2)
      continue;
    // for all matches image 2 -> image 1
    for (std::vector<std::vector<cv::DMatch>>::
         const_iterator matchIterator2= matches2.begin();
         matchIterator2!= matches2.end();
         ++matchIterator2) {
      // ignore deleted matches
      if (matchIterator2->size() < 2)
        continue;
      // Match symmetry test
      if ((*matchIterator1)[0].queryIdx ==
          (*matchIterator2)[0].trainIdx  &&
          (*matchIterator2)[0].queryIdx ==
          (*matchIterator1)[0].trainIdx) {
        // add symmetrical match
          symMatches.push_back(
            cv::DMatch((*matchIterator1)[0].queryIdx,
                       (*matchIterator1)[0].trainIdx,
                       (*matchIterator1)[0].distance));
          break; // next match in image 1 -> image 2
      }
    }
  }
}
```

In our test pair, 31 matches survived this symmetry test. The last test now consists of an additional filtering test that will this time use the fundamental matrix in order to reject matches that do not obey the epipolar constraint. This test is based on the RANSAC method that can compute the fundamental matrix even when outliers are still present in the match set (this method will be explained in the following section):

```cpp
// Identify good matches using RANSAC
// Return fundemental matrix
cv::Mat ransacTest(
    const std::vector<cv::DMatch>& matches,
    const std::vector<cv::KeyPoint>& keypoints1,
    const std::vector<cv::KeyPoint>& keypoints2,
    std::vector<cv::DMatch>& outMatches) {

 // Convert keypoints into Point2f
 std::vector<cv::Point2f> points1, points2;
 for (std::vector<cv::DMatch>::
         const_iterator it= matches.begin();
       it!= matches.end(); ++it) {

     // Get the position of left keypoints
     float x= keypoints1[it->queryIdx].pt.x;
     float y= keypoints1[it->queryIdx].pt.y;
     points1.push_back(cv::Point2f(x,y));
     // Get the position of right keypoints
     x= keypoints2[it->trainIdx].pt.x;
     y= keypoints2[it->trainIdx].pt.y;
     points2.push_back(cv::Point2f(x,y));
  }

 // Compute F matrix using RANSAC
 std::vector<uchar> inliers(points1.size(),0);
 cv::Mat fundemental= cv::findFundamentalMat(
    cv::Mat(points1),cv::Mat(points2), // matching points
     inliers,       // match status (inlier or outlier)
     CV_FM_RANSAC, // RANSAC method
     distance,      // distance to epipolar line
     confidence);   // confidence probability

 // extract the surviving (inliers) matches
 std::vector<uchar>::const_iterator
                   itIn= inliers.begin();
 std::vector<cv::DMatch>::const_iterator
                   itM= matches.begin();
 // for all matches
 for ( ;itIn!= inliers.end(); ++itIn, ++itM) {

    if (*itIn) { // it is a valid match
```

```
            outMatches.push_back(*itM);
        }
    }
    if (refineF) {
    // The F matrix will be recomputed with
    // all accepted matches
        // Convert keypoints into Point2f
        // for final F computation
        points1.clear();
        points2.clear();

        for (std::vector<cv::DMatch>::
                const_iterator it= outMatches.begin();
            it!= outMatches.end(); ++it) {
            // Get the position of left keypoints
            float x= keypoints1[it->queryIdx].pt.x;
            float y= keypoints1[it->queryIdx].pt.y;
            points1.push_back(cv::Point2f(x,y));
            // Get the position of right keypoints
            x= keypoints2[it->trainIdx].pt.x;
            y= keypoints2[it->trainIdx].pt.y;
            points2.push_back(cv::Point2f(x,y));
        }
        // Compute 8-point F from all accepted matches
        fundemental= cv::findFundamentalMat(
            cv::Mat(points1),cv::Mat(points2), // matches
            CV_FM_8POINT); // 8-point method
    }
    return fundemental;
}
```

This code is a bit long because the keypoints need to be converted into `cv::Point2f` before the F matrix computation.

The complete matching process using our `RobustMatcher` class is initiated by the following calls:

```
// Prepare the matcher
RobustMatcher rmatcher;
rmatcher.setConfidenceLevel(0.98);
rmatcher.setMinDistanceToEpipolar(1.0);
rmatcher.setRatio(0.65f);
cv::Ptr<cv::FeatureDetector> pfd=
        new cv::SurfFeatureDetector(10);
```

```
rmatcher.setFeatureDetector(pfd);

// Match the two images
std::vector<cv::DMatch> matches;
std::vector<cv::KeyPoint> keypoints1, keypoints2;
cv::Mat fundemental= rmatcher.match(image1,image2,
                    matches, keypoints1, keypoints2);
```

It results in 23 matches that are shown in the following screenshot with their corresponding epipolar lines:

How it works...

In the preceding recipe, we learned that it is possible to estimate the fundamental matrix associated with an image pair from a number of feature point matches. Obviously, to be exact, this match set must be made of only good matches. However, in a real context, it is not possible to guarantee that a match set obtained by comparing the descriptors of detected feature points will be perfectly exact. This is why a fundamental matrix estimation method based on the **RANSAC (RANdom SAmpling Consensus)** strategy has been introduced.

The RANSAC algorithm aims at estimating a given mathematical entity from a data set that may contain a number of outliers. The idea is to randomly select some data points from the set and perform the estimation only with these. The number of selected points should be the minimum number of points required to estimate the mathematical entity. In the case of the fundamental matrix, eight matched pairs is this minimum number (in fact, it could be seven matches, but the 8-point linear algorithm is faster to compute). Once the fundamental matrix is estimated from these random 8 matches, all of the other matches in the match set are tested against the epipolar constraint that derives from this matrix. All of the matches that fulfill this constraint (that is, matches for which the corresponding feature is at a short distance from its epipolar line) are identified. These matches form the *support set* of the computed fundamental matrix.

The central idea behind the RANSAC algorithm is that the larger the support set is, the higher the probability that the computed matrix is the right one. Obviously, if one (or more) of the randomly selected matches is a wrong match, then the computed fundamental matrix will also be wrong, and its support set is expected to be small. This process is repeated a number of times, and at the end, the matrix with the largest support will be retained as the most probable one.

Therefore, our objective is to pick eight random matches several times so that eventually we select eight good ones which should give us a large support set. Depending on the number of wrong matches in the entire data set, the probability of selecting a set of eight correct matches will differ. We however know that the more selections we make, the higher the confidence will be that we have, among those selections, at least one good match set. More precisely, if we assume that the match set is made of n% inliers (good matches), then the probability that we select eight good matches is $8n$. Consequently, the probability that a selection contains at least one wrong match is $(1-n8)$. If we make k selections, the probability of having one random set containing only good matches is $1-(1-8n)k$. This is the confidence probability c, and we want this probability to be as high as possible since we need at least one good set of matches in order to obtain the correct fundamental matrix. Therefore, when running the RANSAC algorithm, one needs to determine the number of selection k that needs to be made in order to obtain a given confidence level.

When using the cv::findFundamentalMat function with Ransacs, two extra parameters are provided. The first one is the confidence level that determines the number of iterations to be made. The second one is the maximum distance to the epipolar line for a point to be considered as an inlier. All matched pairs in which a point is at a distance from its epipolar line larger than the one specified will be reported as an outlier. Therefore, the function also returns a `std::vector` of `char` value indicating that the corresponding match has been identified as an outlier (0) or as an inlier (1).

The more good matches you have in your initial match set, the higher the probability that RANSAC will give you the correct fundamental matrix. This is why we applied several filters to the match set before calling the `cv::findFundamentalMat` function. Obviously, you can decide to skip one or the other of the steps that were proposed in this recipe. It is just a question of balancing the computational complexity, the final number of matches, and the required level of confidence that the obtained match set will contain only exact matches.

Computing a homography between two images

The second recipe of this chapter showed you how to compute the fundamental matrix of an image pair from a set of matches. Another mathematical entity exists that can be computed from match pairs: a homography. Like the fundamental matrix, the homography is a *3x3* matrix with special properties and, as we will see in this recipe, it applies to two-view images in specific situations.

Getting ready

Let's consider again the projective relation between a 3D point and its image on a camera that we introduced in the first recipe of this chapter. Basically, we learned that this relation is expressed by a *3x4* matrix. Now, if we consider the special case where two views of a scene are separated by a pure rotation, then it can be observed that the fourth column of the extrinsic matrix will be made of all 0s (that is, translation is null). As a result, the projective relation in this special case becomes a *3x3* matrix. This matrix is called a **homography** and it implies that, under special circumstances (here, a pure rotation), the image of a point in one view is related to the image of the same point in another by a linear relation:

$$\begin{bmatrix} sx' \\ sy' \\ s \end{bmatrix} = H \begin{bmatrix} x \\ y \\ 1 \end{bmatrix}$$

In homogeneous coordinates, this relation holds up to a scale factor represented here by the scalar value s. Once this matrix is estimated, all points in one view can be transferred to the second view using this relation. Note that as a side effect of the homography relation for pure rotation, the fundamental matrix becomes undefined in this case.

How to do it...

Suppose we have two images separated by a pure rotation. These two images can be matched using our RobustMatcher class, except that we skip the RANSAC validation step (identified as step 5 in our match method) since this one involves fundamental matrix estimation. Instead, we will apply a RANSAC step which will involve the estimation of a homography based on a match set (that obviously contains a good number of outliers). This is done by using the cv::findHomography function that is very similar to the cv::findFundementalMat function:

```
// Find the homography between image 1 and image 2
std::vector<uchar> inliers(points1.size(),0);
cv::Mat homography= cv::findHomography(
    cv::Mat(points1), // corresponding
    cv::Mat(points2), // points
    inliers,          // outputted inliers matches
    CV_RANSAC,        // RANSAC method
    1.);              // max distance to reprojection point
```

Recall that a homography will only exist if the two images are separated by a pure rotation, which is the case of the following two images:

The resulting inliers that comply with the found homography have been drawn on those images by the following loop:

```cpp
// Draw the inlier points
std::vector<cv::Point2f>::const_iterator itPts=
                                        points1.begin();
std::vector<uchar>::const_iterator itIn= inliers.begin();
while (itPts!=points1.end()) {

    // draw a circle at each inlier location
    if (*itIn)
        cv::circle(image1,*itPts,3,
                    cv::Scalar(255,255,255),2);
    ++itPts;
    ++itIn;
}

itPts= points2.begin();
itIn= inliers.begin();
while (itPts!=points2.end()) {

    // draw a circle at each inlier location
    if (*itIn)
        cv::circle(image2,*itPts,3,
                    cv::Scalar(255,255,255),2);
    ++itPts;
    ++itIn;
}
```

As explained in the preceding section, once the homography is computed, you can transfer image points from one image to the other. In fact, you can do this for all pixels of an image and the result will be to transform this image to the other view. There is an OpenCV function that does exactly this:

```
// Warp image 1 to image 2
cv::Mat result;
cv::warpPerspective(image1, // input image
    result,              // output image
    homography,          // homography
    cv::Size(2*image1.cols,
             image1.rows)); // size of output image
```

Once this new image is obtained, it can be appended to the other image in order to expand the view (since the two images are now from the same point of view):

```
// Copy image 1 on the first half of full image
cv::Mat half(result,cv::Rect(0,0,image2.cols,image2.rows));
image2.copyTo(half); // copy image2 to image1 roi
```

The result is the following image:

How it works...

When two views are related by a homography, it becomes possible to determine where a given scene point on one image is found on the other image. This property becomes particularly interesting for points that fall outside the image boundaries. Indeed, since the second view shows a portion of the scene that is not visible in the first image, you can use the homography in order to expand the image by reading in the other image the color value of additional pixels. That is how we were able to create a new image that is an expansion of our second image in which extra columns were added to the right.

The homography computed by `cv::findHomography` is the one that maps points in the first image to points in the second image. What we need in order to transfer the points of image 1 to image 2 is in fact the inverse homography. This is exactly what the function `cv::warpPerspective` is doing by default, that is, it uses the inverse of the homography provided as input to get the color value of each point of the output image. When an output pixel is transferred to a point outside the input image, a black value (0) is simply assigned to this pixel. Note that an optional flag `cv::WARP_INVERSE_MAP` can be specified as an optional fifth argument in `cv::warpPerspective` if one wants to use the direct homography instead of the inverted one during the pixel transfer process.

There's more...

A homography also exists between two views of a plane. This can be demonstrated by looking again at the camera projection equation as we did for the pure rotation case. When a plane is observed, we can, without loss of generality, set the reference frame of the plane such that all of its points have a Z coordinate which equals to 0. This will also cancel one of the columns of the *3x4* projection matrix resulting in a *3x3* matrix: a homography. This means that if, for example, you have several pictures from different points of view of the flat façade of a building, you can compute the homography between these images and build a large mosaic of the façade by wrapping the images and assembling them together as we did in this recipe.

A minimum of four matched points between two views are required to compute a homography. The function `cv::getPerspectiveTransform` allows such a transformation from four corresponding points to be computed.

10
Processing Video Sequences

In this chapter, we will cover:

- ▶ Reading video sequences
- ▶ Processing the video frames
- ▶ Writing video sequences
- ▶ Tracking feature points in video
- ▶ Extracting the foreground objects in video

Introduction

Video signals constitute a rich source of visual information. They are made of a sequence of images, called **frames**, taken at regular time intervals (specified as the **frame rate**) and showing a scene in motion. With the advent of powerful computers, it is now possible to perform advanced visual analysis on video sequences, and sometime at rates close to, or even faster than, the actual video frame rate. This chapter will show you how to read, process, and store video sequences.

We will see that once the individual frames of a video sequence have been extracted, the different image processing functions presented in this book can be applied to each of them. In addition, we will also look at a few algorithms that perform temporal analysis of the video sequence, compare adjacent frames to track objects, or cumulate image statistics over time in order to extract foreground objects.

Reading video sequences

To process a video sequence, we need to be able to read each of its frames. OpenCV has put in place an easy-to-use framework to perform frame extraction from video files, or even from a USB camera. This recipe shows you how to use it.

How to do it...

Basically, all you need to do in order to read the frames of a video sequence is to create an instance of the `cv::VideoCapture` class. You then create a loop that will extract and read each video frame. Here is a basic main function that simply displays the frames of a video sequence:

```cpp
int main()
{
   // Open the video file
   cv::VideoCapture capture("../bike.avi");
   // check if video successfully opened
   if (!capture.isOpened())
      return 1;

   // Get the frame rate
   double rate= capture.get(CV_CAP_PROP_FPS);

   bool stop(false);
   cv::Mat frame; // current video frame
   cv::namedWindow("Extracted Frame");

   // Delay between each frame in ms
   // corresponds to video frame rate
   int delay= 1000/rate;

   // for all frames in video
   while (!stop) {

      // read next frame if any
      if (!capture.read(frame))
         break;

      cv::imshow("Extracted Frame",frame);

      // introduce a delay
      // or press key to stop
      if (cv::waitKey(delay)>=0)
            stop= true;
   }
   // Close the video file.
   // Not required since called by destructor
   capture.release();
}
```

A window will appear on which the video will play as seen here:

How it works...

To open a video, you simply need to specify the video filename. This can be done by providing the name of the file in the constructor of the `cv::VideoCapture` object. It is also possible to use the `open` method if the `cv::VideoCapture` has already been created. Once the video has successfully opened (this can be verified through the `isOpened` method), it is possible to start frame extraction. It is also possible to query the `cv::VideoCapture` object for information associated with the video file by using its `get` method with the appropriate flag. In the preceding example, we obtained the frame rate using the `CV_CAP_PROP_FPS` flag. Since it is a generic function, it always returns a double even if in some cases another type would be expected. For example, the total number of frames in the video file would be obtained (as an integer) as follows:

```
long t= static_cast<long>(
            capture.get(CV_CAP_PROP_FRAME_COUNT));
```

Have a look at the different flags available in the OpenCV documentation in order to find out what information can be obtained from the video.

There is also a `set` method that allows you to input some parameter to the `cv::VideoCapture` instance. For example, you can request to move to a specific frame using the `CV_CAP_PROP_POS_FRAMES`:

```
// goto frame 100
double position= 100.0;
capture.set(CV_CAP_PROP_POS_FRAMES, position);
```

You can also specify the position in milliseconds using CV_CAP_PROP_POS_MSEC, or specify the relative position inside the video using CV_CAP_PROP_POS_AVI_RATIO (with 0.0 corresponding to the beginning of the video and 1.0 to the end). The method returns true if the requested parameter setting is successful. Note that the possibility to get or set a particular video parameter largely depends on the codec used to compress and store the video sequence. If you are unsuccessful with some parameters, that could be simply due to the specific codec you are using.

Once the video captured is successfully opened (this is verified by the isOpened method), the frames can be sequentially obtained by repetitively calling the read method as we did in the example of the previous section. One can equivalently call the overloaded reading operator:

```
capture >> frame;
```

It is also possible to call the two basic methods:

```
capture.grab();
capture.retrieve(frame);
```

Note also how, in our example, we introduced a delay in displaying each frame. This is done using the cv::waitKey function. Here, we set the delay at a value that corresponds to the input video frame rate (if *fps* is the number of frames per second, then 1000/fps is the delay between two frames in ms). You can obviously change this value to display the video at a slower or faster speed. However, if you are going to display the video frames, it is important to insert such a delay if you want to make sure that the window has sufficient time to refresh (since it is a process of low priority, it will never refresh if the CPU is too busy). The cv::waitKey function also allows us to interrupt the reading process by pressing any key. In such a case, the function returns the ASCII code of the key pressed. Note that if the delay specified to the cv::waitKey function is 0, then it will wait indefinitely for user to press a key. This is very useful when someone wants to trace a process by examining the results frame by frame.

The final statement calls the release method which will close the video file. However, this call is not required since release is also called by the cv::VideoCapture destructor.

It is important to note that in order to open the specified video file, your computer must have the corresponding codec installed, otherwise cv::VideoCapture will not be able to understand the input file. Normally, if you are able to open your video file with a video player on your machine (such as the Windows Media Player), then OpenCV should also be able to read this file.

There's more...

You can also read the video stream capture of a camera connected to your computer (a USB camera for example). In this case, you simply specify an ID number (an integer) instead of a filename to the open function. Specifying 0 for the ID will open the default camera installed. In this case, the role of the cv::waitKey function to stop the processing becomes essential since the video stream from the camera will be infinitely read.

See also

The recipe *Writing video sequences* in this chapter has more information on video codecs.

The `ffmpeg.org` website that presents a complete open source and cross platform solution for audio/video reading, recording, converting, and streaming. *The OpenCV classes to manipulate video files are built on top of this library.*

The `Xvid.org` website which offers an open source video codec library based on the MPEG-4 standard for video compression. Xvid also has a competitor called DivX which offers proprietary but free codec and software tools.

Processing the video frames

In this recipe, our objective is to apply some processing function to each of the frames of a video sequence. We will do this by encapsulating the OpenCV video capture framework into our own class. Among other things, this class will allow us to specify a function that will be called each time a new frame is extracted.

How to do it...

What we want is to be able to specify a processing function (a *callback* function) that will be called at each frame of a video sequence. This function can be defined as receiving a `cv::Mat` instance and outputting a processed frame. Therefore, we designed it to have the following signature:

```
void processFrame(cv::Mat& img, cv::Mat& out);
```

As an example of such processing function, consider the following simple function that computes the Canny edges of an input image:

```
void canny(cv::Mat& img, cv::Mat& out) {
    // Convert to gray
    if (img.channels()==3)
        cv::cvtColor(img,out,CV_BGR2GRAY);
    // Compute Canny edges
    cv::Canny(out,out,100,200);
    // Invert the image
    cv::threshold(out,out,128,255,cv::THRESH_BINARY_INV);
}
```

Let's then define a video processing class to which a callback function can be associated. Using this class, the procedure will be to create a class instance, specify an input video file, attach the callback function to it, and then start the process. Programmatically, these steps will be accomplished using our proposed class, as follows:

```
// Create instance
VideoProcessor processor;
// Open video file
processor.setInput("../bike.avi");
// Declare a window to display the video
processor.displayInput("Current Frame");
processor.displayOutput("Output Frame");
// Play the video at the original frame rate
processor.setDelay(1000./processor.getFrameRate());
// Set the frame processor callback function
processor.setFrameProcessor(canny);
// Start the process
processor.run();
```

Now that we have defined how this class will be used, let's describe its implementation. As one might expect, the class includes several member variables that control the different aspects of the video frame processing:

```
class VideoProcessor {

  private:

      // the OpenCV video capture object
      cv::VideoCapture capture;
      // the callback function to be called
      // for the processing of each frame
      void (*process)(cv::Mat&, cv::Mat&);
      // a bool to determine if the
      // process callback will be called
      bool callIt;
      // Input display window name
      std::string windowNameInput;
      // Output display window name
      std::string windowNameOutput;
      // delay between each frame processing
      int delay;
      // number of processed frames
      long fnumber;
      // stop at this frame number
      long frameToStop;
      // to stop the processing
      bool stop;
```

```
public:

    VideoProcessor() : callIt(true), delay(0),
            fnumber(0), stop(false), frameToStop(-1) {}
```

The first member variable is the `cv::VideoCapture` object, and the second one is the `process` function pointer that will point to the callback function. This can be specified using the corresponding setter method:

```
// set the callback function that
// will be called for each frame
void setFrameProcessor(
    void (*frameProcessingCallback)
                    (cv::Mat&, cv::Mat&)) {

    process= frameProcessingCallback;
}
```

And the following method is to open the video file:

```
// set the name of the video file
bool setInput(std::string filename) {

 fnumber= 0;
 // In case a resource was already
 // associated with the VideoCapture instance
 capture.release();
 images.clear();

 // Open the video file
 return capture.open(filename);
}
```

It is generally interesting to display the frames as they are processed. Two methods are therefore used to create the display windows:

```
// to display the processed frames
void displayInput(std::string wn) {

    windowNameInput= wn;
    cv::namedWindow(windowNameInput);
}
// to display the processed frames
void displayOutput(std::string wn) {

    windowNameOutput= wn;
    cv::namedWindow(windowNameOutput);
}
// do not display the processed frames
```

```
void dontDisplay() {

    cv::destroyWindow(windowNameInput);
    cv::destroyWindow(windowNameOutput);
    windowNameInput.clear();
    windowNameOutput.clear();
}
```

If either of these two methods are not called, then the corresponding frames will not be displayed. The main method, called `run`, is the one that contains the frame extraction loop:

```
// to grab (and process) the frames of the sequence
void run() {

    // current frame
    cv::Mat frame;
    // output frame
    cv::Mat output;

    // if no capture device has been set
    if (!isOpened())
        return;

    stop= false;

    while (!isStopped()) {

        // read next frame if any
        if (!readNextFrame(frame))
            break;

        // display input frame
        if (windowNameInput.length()!=0)
            cv::imshow(windowNameInput,frame);

        // calling the process function
        if (callIt) {

            // process the frame
            process(frame, output);
            // increment frame number
            fnumber++;

        } else {

            output= frame;
        }

        // display output frame
        if (windowNameOutput.length()!=0)
            cv::imshow(windowNameOutput,output);

        // introduce a delay
        if (delay>=0 && cv::waitKey(delay)>=0)
```

```
            stopIt();
          // check if we should stop
          if (frameToStop>=0 &&
                getFrameNumber()==frameToStop)
            stopIt();
       }
   }
   // Stop the processing
   void stopIt() {

      stop= true;
   }
   // Is the process stopped?
   bool isStopped() {

      return stop;
   }
   // Is a capture device opened?
   bool isOpened() {

      capture.isOpened();
   }
   // set a delay between each frame
   // 0 means wait at each frame
   // negative means no delay
   void setDelay(int d) {

      delay= d;
   }
```

This method uses a private method that reads the frames:

```
      // to get the next frame
      // could be: video file or camera
      bool readNextFrame(cv::Mat& frame) {

            return capture.read(frame);

      }
```

One might also wish to simply open and play the video file (without calling the callback function). We therefore have two methods to specify whether or not we want the callback function to be called:

```
      // process callback to be called
      void callProcess() {

         callIt= true;
      }
```

```
    // do not call process callback
    void dontCallProcess() {

        callIt= false;
    }
```

Finally, the class also offers the possibility to stop at a certain frame number:

```
    void stopAtFrameNo(long frame) {

        frameToStop= frame;
    }

    // return the frame number of the next frame
    long getFrameNumber() {

        // get info of from the capture device
          long fnumber= static_cast<long>(
                  capture.get(CV_CAP_PROP_POS_FRAMES));
          return fnumber;
    }
```

If this class is used to run the code snippet presented at the beginning of this section, then two windows will play the input video and the output result at the original frame rate (consequence of the delay introduced by the `setDelay` method) as seen in the following two samples. Here is one frame of the input video:

And the corresponding output frame will be as follows:

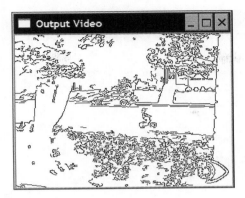

How it works...

As we did in other recipes, our objective was to create a class that encapsulates the common functionalities of a video processing algorithm. In this class, the video capture loop is implemented by the `run` method. It contains the frame extraction loop that first calls the `read` method of the `cv::VideoCapture` OpenCV class. There is a series of operations that are executed, but before each of them is invoked, a check is made to determine if it has been requested. The input window is displayed only if an input window name has been specified (using the `displayInput` method). The callback function is called only if one has been specified (using `setFrameProcessor`). The output window is displayed only if an output window name has been defined (using `displayOutput`). A delay is introduced only if one has been specified (using `setDelay` method). Finally, the current frame number is checked if a stop frame has been defined (using `stopAtFrameNo`).

The class also contains a number of getter and setter methods that are basically just a wrapper over the general `set` and `get` methods of the `cv::VideoCapture` framework.

There's more...

Our `VideoProcessor` class is there to facilitate the deployment of a video processing module. Few additional refinements can be made to it.

Processing a sequence of images

Sometimes, the input sequence is made of a series of images individually stored in distinct files. Our class can be easily modified to accommodate such input. You just need to add a member variable that will hold a vector of image filenames and its corresponding iterator:

```
// vector of image filename to be used as input
std::vector<std::string> images;
// image vector iterator
std::vector<std::string>::const_iterator itImg;
```

A new `setInput` method is used to specify the filenames to be read:

```
// set the vector of input images
bool setInput(const std::vector<std::string>& imgs) {

  fnumber= 0;
  // In case a resource was already
  // associated with the VideoCapture instance
  capture.release();

  // the input will be this vector of images
  images= imgs;
  itImg= images.begin();

  return true;
}
```

And the `isOpened` method becomes:

```
// Is a capture device opened?
bool isOpened() {

    return capture.isOpened() || !images.empty();
}
```

The last method that needs to be modified is the private `readNextFrame` method that will read from the video or from the vector of filenames depending which input has been specified. The test being if the vector of image filenames is not empty, then that is because the input is an image sequence. The call to `setInput` with a video filename clears this vector:

```
// to get the next frame
// could be: video file; camera; vector of images
bool readNextFrame(cv::Mat& frame) {

    if (images.size()==0)
        return capture.read(frame);

    else {

        if (itImg != images.end()) {

            frame= cv::imread(*itImg);
            itImg++;
            return frame.data != 0;

        } else {

            return false;

        }
    }
}
```

Using a frame processor class

In an object-oriented context, it may make more sense to use a frame processing class instead of a frame processing function. Indeed, a class would give the programmer much more flexibility in the definition of a video processing algorithm. We can therefore define an interface that any class that wishes to be used inside the `VideoProcessor` will need to implement:

```
// The frame processor interface
class FrameProcessor {

  public:
    // processing method
    virtual void process(cv:: Mat &input, cv:: Mat &output)= 0;
};
```

A setter method allows you to input a pointer to a `FrameProcessor` instance of the `VideoProcessor` framework:

```
// set the instance of the class that
// implements the FrameProcessor interface
void setFrameProcessor(FrameProcessor* frameProcessorPtr)
{
    // invalidate callback function
    process= 0;
    // this is the frame processor instance
    // that will be called
    frameProcessor= frameProcessorPtr;
    callProcess();
}
```

When a frame processor class instance is specified, it invalidates any frame processing function that could have been set before. The same now applies if a frame processing function is specified instead:

```
// set the callback function that will
// be called for each frame
void setFrameProcessor(
    void (*frameProcessingCallback)(cv::Mat&, cv::Mat&)) {

    // invalidate frame processor class instance
    frameProcessor= 0;
    // this is the frame processor function that
    // will be called
    process= frameProcessingCallback;
    callProcess();
}
```

And the `while` loop of the `run` method is modified to take into account this modification:

```
while (!isStopped()) {
    // read next frame if any
    if (!readNextFrame(frame))
       break;
    // display input frame
    if (windowNameInput.length()!=0)
       cv::imshow(windowNameInput,frame);
     // ** calling the process function or method **
    if (callIt) {
     // process the frame
     if (process) // if call back function
         process(frame, output);
     else if (frameProcessor)
         // if class interface instance
        frameProcessor->process(frame,output);
     // increment frame number
     fnumber++;
    } else {
     output= frame;
    }
    // display output frame
    if (windowNameOutput.length()!=0)
       cv::imshow(windowNameOutput,output);
    // introduce a delay
    if (delay>=0 && cv::waitKey(delay)>=0)
     stopIt();
    // check if we should stop
    if (frameToStop>=0 &&
        getFrameNumber()==frameToStop)
       stopIt();
}
```

See also

The recipe *Tracking feature points in video* in this chapter shows how to use the `FrameProcessor` class interface.

Writing video sequences

In the previous recipes, we learned how to read a video file and extract its frames. This recipe will show you how to write frames and therefore create a video file. This will allow us to complete the typical video processing chain: reading an input video stream, processing its frames, and then storing the results in a video file.

How to do it...

Let's expand our `VideoProcessor` class in order to give it the ability to write video files. This is done using the OpenCV `cv::VideoWriter` class. An instance of this is therefore added as a member of our class (plus few other member variables):

```
class VideoProcessor {

  private:

  ...

      // the OpenCV video writer object
      cv::VideoWriter writer;
      // output filename
      std::string outputFile;
      // current index for output images
      int currentIndex;
      // number of digits in output image filename
      int digits;
      // extension of output images
      std::string extension;
```

An extra method is used to specify (and open) the output video file:

```
      // set the output video file
      // by default the same parameters than
      // input video will be used
      bool setOutput(const std::string &filename,
                   int codec=0, double framerate=0.0,
                   bool isColor=true) {

        outputFile= filename;
        extension.clear();

        if (framerate==0.0)
           framerate= getFrameRate(); // same as input

        char c[4];
        // use same codec as input
        if (codec==0) {
           codec= getCodec(c);
```

```
        }

        // Open output video
        return writer.open(outputFile, // filename
            codec,          // codec to be used
            framerate,      // frame rate of the video
            getFrameSize(), // frame size
            isColor);       // color video?
}
```

Once the video file is opened, frames can be added to it by repetitively calling the `write` method of the `cv::VideoWriter` class. Proceeding as we did in the preceding recipe, we also want to give the user the possibility to write the frames as individual images. Therefore, the private `writeNextFrame` method handles these two possible cases:

```
        // to write the output frame
        // could be: video file or images
        void writeNextFrame(cv::Mat& frame) {

            if (extension.length()) { // then we write images

                std::stringstream ss;
                // compose the output filename
                ss << outputFile << std::setfill('0')
                    << std::setw(digits)
                    << currentIndex++ << extension;
                cv::imwrite(ss.str(),frame);

            } else { // then write to video file
                writer.write(frame);
            }
        }
```

For the case where the output is made of individual image files, we need an additional setter method:

```
        // set the output as a series of image files
        // extension must be ".jpg", ".bmp" ...
        bool setOutput(const std::string &filename, // prefix
            const std::string &ext, // image file extension
            int numberOfDigits=3,   // number of digits
            int startIndex=0) {     // start index

            // number of digits must be positive
            if (numberOfDigits<0)
                return false;

            // filenames and their common extension
            outputFile= filename;
            extension= ext;
```

```
        // number of digits in the file numbering scheme
        digits= numberOfDigits;
        // start numbering at this index
        currentIndex= startIndex;

        return true;
    }
```

A new step is then added to the video capture loop of the run method:

```
        while (!isStopped()) {
           // read next frame if any
           if (!readNextFrame(frame))
              break;
           // display input frame
           if (windowNameInput.length()!=0)
              cv::imshow(windowNameInput,frame);
            // calling the process function or method
           if (callIt) {
            // process the frame
            if (process)
                process(frame, output);
            else if (frameProcessor)
               frameProcessor->process(frame,output);
            // increment frame number
            fnumber++;

           } else {
            output= frame;
           }
           // ** write output sequence **
           if (outputFile.length()!=0)
              writeNextFrame(output);
           // display output frame
           if (windowNameOutput.length()!=0)
              cv::imshow(windowNameOutput,output);
           // introduce a delay
           if (delay>=0 && cv::waitKey(delay)>=0)
            stopIt();
           // check if we should stop
           if (frameToStop>=0 &&
                  getFrameNumber()==frameToStop)
```

```
                                      stopIt();
                }
        }
```

A simple program that will read a video, process it, and write the result to a video file would then be written as follows:

```
// Create instance
VideoProcessor processor;

// Open video file
processor.setInput("../bike.avi");
processor.setFrameProcessor(canny);
processor.setOutput("../bikeOut.avi");
// Start the process
processor.run();
```

If you want the result to be saved as a series of images, then you would change the preceding statement by this one:

```
processor.setOutput("../bikeOut",".jpg");
```

Using the default number of digits (3) and start index (0), this will create the files `bikeOut000.jpg`, `bikeOut001.jpg`, `bikeOut002.jpg`, and so on.

How it works...

When a video is written to a file, it is saved using a codec. A **codec** is a software module capable of encoding and decoding video streams. The codec defines both the format of the file and the compression scheme that is used to store the information. Obviously, a video that has been encoded using a given codec must be decoded with the same codec. For this reason, four-character codes have been introduced to uniquely identified codecs. This way, when a software tool needs to write a video file, it determines the codec to be used by reading the specified four-character code.

As the name suggests, the four-character code is made of four ASCII characters that can also be converted into an integer by appending them together. Using the CV_CAP_PROP_FOURCC flag of the get method of an opened cv::VideoCapture instance, you can obtain this code of an opened video file. We can define a method in our VideoProcessor class to return the four-character code of an input video:

```
// get the codec of input video
int getCodec(char codec[4]) {

    // undefined for vector of images
    if (images.size()!=0) return -1;

    union { // data structure for the 4-char code
        int value;
```

```
          char code[4]; } returned;
    // get the code
    returned.value= static_cast<int>(
                    capture.get(CV_CAP_PROP_FOURCC));

    // get the 4 characters
    codec[0]= returned.code[0];
    codec[1]= returned.code[1];
    codec[2]= returned.code[2];
    codec[3]= returned.code[3];

    // return the int value corresponding to the code
    return returned.value;
}
```

The `get` method always returns a `double` that is then casted into an integer. This integer represents the code from which the four characters can be extracted using a `union` data structure. If we open our test video sequence, then from the following statements:

```
char codec[4];
processor.getCodec(codec);
std::cout << "Codec: " << codec[0] << codec[1]
          << codec[2] << codec[3] << std::endl;
```

We obtain:

```
Codec : XVID
```

When a video file is written, the codec must be specified using its four-character code. This is the second parameter in the `open` method of the `cv::VideoWriter` class. You can use, for example, the same one as the input video (this is the default option in our `setOutput` method). You can also pass the value -1 and the method will pop up a window to ask you to select one from the list of available codec as seen here:

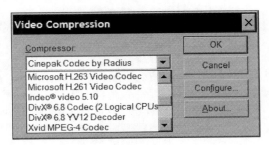

The list you will see on this window corresponds to the list of installed codecs on your machine. The code of the selected codec is then automatically sent to the open method.

Tracking feature points in video

This chapter is about reading, writing, and processing video sequences. The objective is to be able to analyze a complete video sequence. As an example, in this recipe, you will learn how to perform temporal analysis of the sequence in order to track feature points as they move from frame to frame.

How to do it...

To start the tracking process, the first thing to do is to detect feature points in an initial frame. You then try to track these points in the next frame. You must find where these points are now located in this new frame. Obviously, since we are dealing with a video sequence, there is a good chance that the object on which the feature points are found has moved (the motion can also be due to camera motion). Therefore, you must search around a point's previous location in order to find its new location in the next frame. This is what accomplishes the `cv::calcOpticalFlowPyrLK` function. You input two consecutive frames and a vector of feature points in the first image, the function returns a vector of new point locations. To track points over a complete sequence, you repeat this process from frame to frame. Note that as you follow the points across the sequence, you will unavoidably loose track of some of them such that the number of tracked feature points will gradually reduces. Therefore, it could be a good idea to detect new features from time to time.

We will now take benefit of the framework we defined in the previous recipes and we will define a class that implements the `FrameProcessor` interface introduced in the *Processing the video frames* recipe of this chapter. The data attributes of this class include the variables required to perform both the detection of feature points and their tracking:

```
class FeatureTracker : public FrameProcessor {

    cv::Mat gray;           // current gray-level image
    cv::Mat gray_prev;        // previous gray-level image
    // tracked features from 0->1
    std::vector<cv::Point2f> points[2];
    // initial position of tracked points
    std::vector<cv::Point2f> initial;
    std::vector<cv::Point2f> features;  // detected features
    int max_count;      // maximum number of features to detect
    double qlevel;      // quality level for feature detection
    double minDist;     // min distance between two points
    std::vector<uchar> status; // status of tracked features
    std::vector<float> err;     // error in tracking
  public:

    FeatureTracker() : max_count(500),
                    qlevel(0.01), minDist(10.) {}
```

Next, we define the `process` method that will be called for each frame of the sequence. Basically, we need to proceed as follows. First, feature points are detected if necessary. Next, these points are tracked. You reject points that you cannot track or you no longer want to track. You are now ready to handle the successfully tracked points. Finally, the current frame and its points become the previous frame and points for the next iteration. Here is how to do it:

```cpp
void process(cv:: Mat &frame, cv:: Mat &output) {
    // convert to gray-level image
    cv::cvtColor(frame, gray, CV_BGR2GRAY);
    frame.copyTo(output);

    // 1. if new feature points must be added
    if(addNewPoints())
    {
        // detect feature points
        detectFeaturePoints();
        // add the detected features to
        // the currently tracked features
        points[0].insert(points[0].end(),
                         features.begin(),features.end());
        initial.insert(initial.end(),
                       features.begin(),features.end());
    }

    // for first image of the sequence
    if(gray_prev.empty())
        gray.copyTo(gray_prev);

    // 2. track features
    cv::calcOpticalFlowPyrLK(
        gray_prev, gray, // 2 consecutive images
        points[0], // input point positions in first image
        points[1], // output point positions in the 2nd image
        status,    // tracking success
        err);      // tracking error

    // 2. loop over the tracked points to reject some
    int k=0;
    for( int i= 0; i < points[1].size(); i++ ) {
        // do we keep this point?
        if (acceptTrackedPoint(i)) {
            // keep this point in vector
            initial[k]= initial[i];
            points[1][k++] = points[1][i];
        }
    }
```

```
    // eliminate unsuccesful points
      points[1].resize(k);
    initial.resize(k);

    // 3. handle the accepted tracked points
    handleTrackedPoints(frame, output);

    // 4. current points and image become previous ones
    std::swap(points[1], points[0]);
    cv::swap(gray_prev, gray);
}
```

This method makes use of four other utility methods. It should be easy for you to change any of these methods in order to define a new behavior for your own tracker. The first of these methods detects the feature points. Note that we already discussed the `cv::goodFeatureToTrack` function in the first recipe of *Chapter 8*:

```
    // feature point detection
    void detectFeaturePoints() {

        // detect the features
        cv::goodFeaturesToTrack(gray,    // the image
            features,     // the output detected features
            max_count,    // the maximum number of features
            qlevel,       // quality level
            minDist);     // min distance between two features
    }
```

The second one determines if new feature points should be detected:

```
    // determine if new points should be added
    bool addNewPoints() {

        // if too few points
        return points[0].size()<=10;
    }
```

The third one rejects some of the tracked points based on some criteria defined by the application. Here, we decided to reject points that do not move (in addition to those that cannot be tracked by the `cv::calcOpticalFlowPyrLK` function):

```
    // determine which tracked point should be accepted
    bool acceptTrackedPoint(int i) {

        return status[i] &&
            // if point has moved
            (abs(points[0][i].x-points[1][i].x)+
            (abs(points[0][i].y-points[1][i].y))>2);
    }
```

Finally, the fourth method handles the tracked feature points by drawing on the current frame all of the tracked points with a line joining them to their initial position (that is, the position where they were detected the first time):

```
// handle the currently tracked points
void handleTrackedPoints(cv:: Mat &frame,
                         cv:: Mat &output) {

    // for all tracked points
    for(int i= 0; i < points[1].size(); i++ ) {

        // draw line and circle
        cv::line(output,
                 initial[i],  // initial position
                 points[1][i],// new position
                 cv::Scalar(255,255,255));
        cv::circle(output, points[1][i], 3,
                   cv::Scalar(255,255,255),-1);
    }
}
```

A simple main function to track feature points in a video sequence would then be written as follows:

```
int main()
{
    // Create video procesor instance
    VideoProcessor processor;

    // Create feature tracker instance
    FeatureTracker tracker;

    // Open video file
    processor.setInput("../bike.avi");

    // set frame processor
    processor.setFrameProcessor(&tracker);

    // Declare a window to display the video
    processor.displayOutput("Tracked Features");

    // Play the video at the original frame rate
    processor.etDelayetDelay(1000./processor.getFrameRate());

    // Start the process
    processor.run();
}
```

The resulting program will show the evolution of the tracked features over time. Here are, for example, two such frames at two different instants. In this video, the camera is fixed. The young cyclist is therefore the only moving object. Here is a frame at the beginning of the video:

And few seconds later, we obtain the following frame:

How it works...

To track feature points from frame to frame, we must locate the new position of a feature point in the subsequent frame. If we assume that the intensity of the feature point does not change from one frame to the next one, we are looking for a displacement (u,v) such that:

$$I_t(x,y) = I_{t+1}(x + u, y + v)$$

where It and It+1 are respectively the current frame and the one at the next instant. This constant intensity assumption generally holds for small displacement in images taken at two near by instants. We can then use the Taylor expansion in order to approximate this equation by an equation that involves the image derivatives:

$$I_{t+1}(x+u,y+v) \approx I_t(x,y) + \frac{\partial I}{\partial x}u + \frac{\partial I}{\partial y}v + \frac{\partial I}{\partial t}$$

This later equation leads us to another equation (as a consequence of the constant intensity assumption):

$$\frac{\partial I}{\partial x}u + \frac{\partial I}{\partial y}v = -\frac{\partial I}{\partial t}$$

This well-known constraint is the fundamental **optical flow** constraint equation. It is exploited by the so-called Lukas-Kanade feature tracking algorithm by making an additional assumption. The displacement of all points in the neighborhood of the feature point is the same. We can therefore impose the optical flow constraint for all of these point with a unique (u,v) unknown displacement. This gives us more equations than the number of unknowns (2), and we can therefore solve this system of equations in a mean-square sense. In practice, it is solved iteratively and the OpenCV implementation also offers the possibility to perform this estimation at different resolution to make the search more efficient and more tolerant to larger displacement. By default, the number of image levels is 3 and the window size is 15. These parameters can obviously be changed. You can also specify the termination criteria which define the conditions to stop the iterative search. The sixth parameter of the `cv::calcOpticalFlowPyrLK` contains the residual mean-square error that could be used to assess the quality of the tracking. The fifth parameter contains binary flags that tell us if tracking the corresponding point was considered successful or not.

The description above represents the basic principles behind the Lukas-Kanade tracker. The current implementation contains other optimizations and improvements to make the algorithm more efficient in the computation of the displacement of a large number of feature points.

See also

The *Chapter 8* of this book has a discussion on feature point detection.

The classic article by *B. Lucas and T. Kanade, An iterative image registration technique with an application to stereo vision in Int. Joint Conference in Artificial Intelligence, pp. 674-679, 1981*, that describes the original feature point tracking algorithm.

The article by *J. Shi and C. Tomasi, Good Features to Track in IEEE Conference on Computer Vision and Pattern Recognition, pp. 593-600, 1994*, that describes an improved version of the original feature point tracking algorithm.

Extracting the foreground objects in video

When a fixed camera observes a scene, the background remains mostly unchanged. In this case, the interesting elements are the moving objects that evolve inside this scene. In order to extract those foreground objects, we need to build a model of the background, and then compare this model with a current frame in order to detect any foreground objects. This is what we will do in this recipe. Foreground extraction is a fundamental step in intelligent surveillance applications.

How to do it...

If we had at our disposal an image of the background of the scene (that is, a frame containing no foreground objects), then it would be easy to extract the foreground of a current frame through a simple image difference:

```
// compute difference between current image and background
cv::absdiff(backgroundImage,currentImage,foreground);
```

Each pixel for which this difference is high enough would then be declared as a foreground pixel. However, most of the time, this background image is not readily available. Indeed, it could be difficult to guarantee that no foreground objects are present in a given image and in busy scenes, such situations might rarely occur. Moreover, the background scene often evolves over time because, for instance, the lighting condition might change (for example, from sunrise to sunset), or because new objects could be added or removed from the background.

Therefore, it is necessary to dynamically build a model of the background scene. This can be done by observing the scene for a period of time. If we assume that most often the background is visible at each pixel location, then it could be a good strategy to simply compute the average of all of the observations. But this is not feasible for a number of reasons. First, this would require a large number of images to be stored before computing the background. Second, while we are accumulating images to compute our average image, no foreground extraction would be done. This solution also raises the problem of when and how many images should be accumulated to compute an acceptable background model. In addition, the images where a given pixel is observing a foreground object would have an impact on the computation of the average background.

A better strategy is to dynamically build the background model by regularly updating it. This can be accomplished by computing what is called a **running average** (also called **moving average**). It is a way to compute the average value of a temporal signal which takes into account the latest values received. If pt is the pixel value at a given time t, and µt-1 is the current average value, then this average is updated using the following formula:

$$\mu_t = (1-\alpha)\mu_{t-1} + \alpha p_t$$

The parameter α is called the learning rate and it defines the influence of the current value over the currently estimated average. The larger this value is, the faster the running average will adapt to changes in the observed values. To build a background model, one has just to compute a running average for every pixel of the incoming frames. The decision to declare a foreground pixel is then simply based on the difference between the current image and the background model.

Let's then build a class that implements this idea:

```
class BGFGSegmentor : public FrameProcessor {

    cv::Mat gray;              // current gray-level image
    cv::Mat background;        // accumulated background
    cv::Mat backImage;         // background image
    cv::Mat foreground;        // foreground image
    // learning rate in background accumulation
    double learningRate;
    int threshold;             // threshold for foreground extraction

  public:

    BGFGSegmentor() : threshold(10), learningRate(0.01) {}
```

The main process consists then in comparing the current frame with the background model, and then updating this model:

```
    // processing method
    void process(cv:: Mat &frame, cv:: Mat &output) {

        // convert to gray-level image
        cv::cvtColor(frame, gray, CV_BGR2GRAY);

        // initialize background to 1st frame
        if (background.empty())
            gray.convertTo(background, CV_32F);

        // convert background to 8U
        background.convertTo(backImage, CV_8U);

        // compute difference between image and background
        cv::absdiff(backImage, gray, foreground);

        // apply threshold to foreground image
        cv::threshold(foreground, output,
                    threshold, 255, cv::THRESH_BINARY_INV);

        // accumulate background
        cv::accumulateWeighted(gray, background,
                                learningRate, output);

    }
```

Using our video processing framework, the foreground extraction program would be built as follows:

```
int main()
{
    // Create video procesor instance
    VideoProcessor processor;

    // Create background/foreground segmentor
    BGFGSegmentor segmentor;
    segmentor.setThreshold(25);

    // Open video file
    processor.setInput("../bike.avi");

    // set frame processor
    processor.setFrameProcessor(&segmentor);

    // Declare a window to display the video
    processor.displayOutput("Extracted Foreground");

    // Play the video at the original frame rate
    processor.setDelay(1000./processor.getFrameRate());

    // Start the process
    processor.run();
}
```

One of the resulting binary foreground images that will be displayed is:

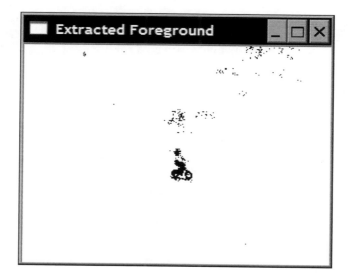

How it works...

Computing the running average of an image is easily accomplished through the `cv::accumulateWeighted` function that applies the running average formula to each pixel of the image. Note that the resulting image must be a floating point image. This is why we had to convert the background model into a background image before comparing it with the current frame. A simple thresholded absolute difference (computed by `cv::absdiff`, followed by `cv::threshold`) extracts the foreground image. Note that we then used the foreground image as a mask to `cv::accumulateWeighted` in order to avoid the updating of pixels declared as foreground. This works because our foreground image is defined as being false (that is, 0) at foreground pixels (which also explains why the foreground objects are displayed as black pixels in the resulting image).

Finally, it should be noted that, for simplicity, the background model that is built by our program is based on the gray-level version of the extracted frames. Maintaining a color background would require the computation of a running average for each channel of each pixel. In general, this extra computation does not significantly improve the results. Rather, the main difficulty is to determine the appropriate value for the threshold that would give good results for a given video.

There's more...

The preceding simple method to extract foreground objects in a scene works well for simple scenes showing a relatively stable background. However, in many situations, the background scene might fluctuate in certain areas between different values, thus causing frequent false foreground detections. These might be due to, for example, a moving background object (for example, tree leaves) or to glaring effect (for example, on the surface of water). In order to cope with this problem, more sophisticated background modeling methods have been introduced.

The Mixture of Gaussian method

One of these algorithms is the Mixture of Gaussian method. It proceeds in a way similar to the method presented in this recipe with the following additions:

First, the method maintains more than one model per pixel (that is, more than one running average). This way, if a background pixel fluctuates between, let's say, two values, two running average are then stored. A new pixel value will be declared as foreground only if it does not belong to any of the maintained models.

Second, not only is the running average maintained for each model, but also the running variance. This one is computed as follows:

$$\sigma_t^2 = (1 - \alpha)\sigma_{t-1}^2 + \alpha(p_t - \mu_t)^2$$

The computed average and variance form a Gaussian model from which the probability of a given pixel value to belong to this Gaussian model can be estimated. This makes it easier to determine an appropriate threshold since it is now expressed as a probability rather than an absolute difference. Also, in areas where the background values have larger fluctuations, a greater difference will be required to declare a foreground object.

Finally, when a given Gaussian model is not hit sufficiently often, it is excluded as being part of the background model. Reciprocally, when a pixel value is found to be outside the currently maintained background models (that is it is a foreground pixel), a new Gaussian model is created. If in the future, if this new model becomes frequently hit, then it becomes associated with the background.

This more sophisticated algorithm is obviously more complex to implement than our simple background/foreground segmentor. Fortunately, an OpenCV implementation exists called `cv::BackgroundSubtractorMOG` and is defined as a subclass of the more general `cv::BackgroundSubtractor` class. When used with its default parameter, this class is very easy to use:

```cpp
int main()
{
   // Open the video file
    cv::VideoCapture capture("../bike.avi");
   // check if video successfully opened
   if (!capture.isOpened())
      return 0;

   // current video frame
   cv::Mat frame;
   // foreground binary image
   cv::Mat foreground;

   cv::namedWindow("Extracted Foreground");

   // The Mixture of Gaussian object
   // used with all default parameters
   cv::BackgroundSubtractorMOG mog;

   bool stop(false);
   // for all frames in video
   while (!stop) {

      // read next frame if any
      if (!capture.read(frame))
         break;

      // update the background
      // and return the foreground
      mog(frame,foreground,0.01);

      // Complement the image
```

```
        cv::threshold(foreground,foreground,
                    128,255,cv::THRESH_BINARY_INV);

        // show foreground
        cv::imshow("Extracted Foreground",foreground);

        // introduce a delay
        // or press key to stop
        if (cv::waitKey(10)>=0)
            stop= true;
    }
}
```

As it can be seen, it is just a matter of creating the class instance and calling the method that simultaneously update the background and returns the foreground image (the extra parameter being the learning rate). One of the displayed segmentations would then be:

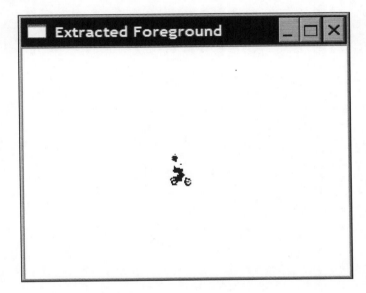

The number of possible Gaussian model per pixels constitutes one of the parameters of this class.

See also

The article by *C. Stauffer and W.E.L. Grimson, Adaptive background mixture models for real-time tracking, in Conf. on Computer Vision and Pattern Recognition, 1999,* for a more complete description of the Mixture of Gaussian algorithm.

Index

output image
  storing, on disk 26-29
overloaded image operators 62, 63

P

pass-by-reference mechanism 39
picture elements. *See* pixels
pin-hole camera model 218, 224
pixels 37, 89
pixel values
  about 89
  accessing 38-40
pkg-config utility package 25
pointers
  image, scanning with 41-44
policy-based class design 75
Prewitt operator 154
primary color channels 37
principal point 219
Probabilistic Hough transform 170
process function pointer 253
process method 79, 267
projection 217
projection matrix 226
projective geometry 217
ptr method 44

Q

QCoreApplication object 22
qmake 24
qmake project files
  features 25
qmake, variables
  CONFIG 24
  HEADERS 24
  INCLUDEPATH 25
  LIBS 25
  QT 25
  SOURCES 24
  TEMPLATE 24
QSlider widget 85
Qt
  about 19, 30
  benefits 19
  GUI application, creating with 30-35
  OpenCV project, creating with 20-25

URL, for downloading 20
Qt Console Application 20
QT variable 25

R

radial distortion 224
random sample consensus
  images, matching with 233-241
RANdom SAmpling Consensus. *See* RANSAC
  algorithm
range 66
ranges parameters 105
RANSAC algorithm
  about 241
  objective 241
RANSAC method 238
read method 250, 257
readNextFrame method 258
rect object 110
region of interest. *See* ROI
Release directory 19
release method 250
re-projection error 227
reshape method 47
RGB color space 86
rigid baseline 228
rigid transformation 227
Roberts operator 155
RobustMatcher class 239, 243
ROI
  about 64
  defining, for image 65, 66
rows variable 40, 44
run method 254, 257, 260
running average 272

S

salt-and-pepper noise 38
samples directory 8
Scale-Invariant Feature Transform. *See* SIFT
scale-invariant SURF features
  detecting 206-209
scene 217
Scharr operator 155
Select Color button 84
separable filter 145

Thank you for buying
OpenCV 2 Computer Vision Application Programming Cookbook

About Packt Publishing

Packt, pronounced 'packed', published its first book "*Mastering phpMyAdmin for Effective MySQL Management*" in April 2004 and subsequently continued to specialize in publishing highly focused books on specific technologies and solutions.

Our books and publications share the experiences of your fellow IT professionals in adapting and customizing today's systems, applications, and frameworks. Our solution based books give you the knowledge and power to customize the software and technologies you're using to get the job done. Packt books are more specific and less general than the IT books you have seen in the past. Our unique business model allows us to bring you more focused information, giving you more of what you need to know, and less of what you don't.

Packt is a modern, yet unique publishing company, which focuses on producing quality, cutting-edge books for communities of developers, administrators, and newbies alike. For more information, please visit our website: www.packtpub.com.

About Packt Open Source

In 2010, Packt launched two new brands, Packt Open Source and Packt Enterprise, in order to continue its focus on specialization. This book is part of the Packt Open Source brand, home to books published on software built around Open Source licences, and offering information to anybody from advanced developers to budding web designers. The Open Source brand also runs Packt's Open Source Royalty Scheme, by which Packt gives a royalty to each Open Source project about whose software a book is sold.

Writing for Packt

We welcome all inquiries from people who are interested in authoring. Book proposals should be sent to author@packtpub.com. If your book idea is still at an early stage and you would like to discuss it first before writing a formal book proposal, contact us; one of our commissioning editors will get in touch with you.

We're not just looking for published authors; if you have strong technical skills but no writing experience, our experienced editors can help you develop a writing career, or simply get some additional reward for your expertise.

Microsoft Visual C++ Windows Applications by Example

ISBN: 978-1-847195-56-2   Paperback: 440 pages

Code and explanation for real-world MFC C++ Applications

1.   Learn C++ Windows programming by studying realistic, interesting examples

2.   A quick primer in Visual C++ for programmers of other languages, followed by deep, thorough examples

3.   Example applications include a Tetris-style game, a spreadsheet application, a drawing application, and a word processor

OpenSceneGraph 3.0: Beginner's Guide

ISBN: 978-1-849512-82-4   Paperback: 412 pages

Create high-performance virtual reality applications with OpenSceneGraph, one of the best 3D graphics engines.

1.   Gain a comprehensive view of the structure and main functionalities of OpenSceneGraph

2.   An ideal introduction for developing applications using OpenSceneGraph

3.   Develop applications around the concepts of scene graphs and design patterns

Please check **www.PacktPub.com** for information on our titles

Python 2.6 Text Processing: Beginners Guide

ISBN: 978-1-849512-12-1   Paperback: 380 pages

The easiest way to learn how to manipulate text with Python

1. The easiest way to learn text processing with Python

2. Deals with the most important textual data formats you will encounter

3. Learn to use the most popular text processing libraries available for Python

4. Packed with examples to guide you through

Inkscape 0.48 Illustrator's Cookbook

ISBN: 978-1-849512-66-4   Paperback: 340 pages

109 recipes to create scalable vector graphics with Inkscape

1. Create interesting illustrations and common web design elements that can be used in real-life projects

2. Gain a thorough understanding of all common Inkscape tools and advanced features of Inkscape 0.48

3. Tips and tricks to speed up your drawing workflow

Please check **www.PacktPub.com** for information on our titles

5600879R00169

Printed in Great Britain
by Amazon.co.uk, Ltd.,
Marston Gate.